THIS IS VOLUME IV

IN

The Pioneer Heritage Series

# THE PIONEER HERITAGE SERIES

# MAN OF THE PLAINS

# MAN OF THE PLAINS

## RECOLLECTIONS

## OF LUTHER NORTH,

### 1856-1882

*Edited by*
DONALD F. DANKER

*With a foreword by George Bird Grinnell*

UNIVERSITY OF NEBRASKA PRESS · LINCOLN · 1961

# CONTENTS

# LIST OF MAPS

The map section begins on page 285, following the last page of the text.

The drawing of the mounted warrior used as a decoration on chapter-opening pages is copied from one of the figures on a Pawnee painted buffalo robe depicting battle scenes. The robe was photographed by W. H. Jackson at the Pawnee Agency in 1871.

# EDITOR'S PREFACE

*This book is about how*

The last serious opposition to white occupation of the North
American continent came from the nomadic tribes of the
Great Plains. Control of the prairie lands, the pastures of the
buffalo, was essential to the Indian way of life, and for nearly
two decades the red men fought to preserve their Great
Plains hunting grounds from the encroachment of white
hunters, emigrants, and settlers. *and how*

The Indian Wars of the '60's and '70's have left their mark
on American traditions and American literature as well as its
history. They were waged over a vast area comprising western Kansas and Nebraska, eastern Colorado, Wyoming,
Montana, and the Dakotas. From them there emerged a striking array of fighting men—both individual leaders and
troops—around whose names legends have clustered from
their day to our own. Not the least of this legendary company were the North brothers and the Pawnee Scouts. *hat*

White frontiersmen often were recruited to serve as scouts
with the United States Army, and the use of Indian aux-
iliaries also was not uncommon: from colonial times on, they
figured in campaigns against hostiles and in regions where

[ **xi** ]

their talents in wilderness warfare were invaluable. Thus, the service of Frank and Luther North and the Pawnee Scouts was in keeping with American frontier tradition. What was unique about it was the close relationship, the warm affection and respect, that developed between the brothers and their Indian troops.

To appreciate the role they played in the long battle for the control of the Great Plains, it must be remembered that the Plains Indian Wars were not massive, sustained hostilities between two armies; they were, rather, a series of skirmishes, punitive campaigns, scouting and patrolling expeditions, conducted by the United States Army against tribesmen who one month might be peaceably receiving annuities at their agency and the next raiding traffic and installations along the overland trails or hunting in areas to which they were prohibited entry by treaty agreement. In this type of warfare military operations often required highly mobile task forces which could be speedily deployed to strategic points. The Pawnee Scouts by instinct and training were skilled mounted warriors; moreover, from the beginning of their recorded history, the Sioux and Cheyenne—the hostiles they were most often called on to face—had been their hereditary foes. The extra impetus and efficiency deriving from these factors, combined with the rapid transport provided by the Union Pacific, made the Pawnee Scouts probably the most effective mobile unit on the Plains.

It was not until nearly a half century after the final muster out of the Scouts that Captain Luther North completed his recollections. Yet though his memory was occasionally faulty and he erred in giving names and other details, there appear to be no major discrepancies that can be established by reliable contemporary records. His narrative reflects the difference in viewpoint of independent scouts and frontiersmen and the regular army officers with whom they served. Friction between the two groups and disagreements as to methods characterized almost every American campaign from the French and Indian Wars to the end of the Plains Indian Wars. If North's work had failed to express this bias, which is in itself a part of frontier history, it would not have rung true.

North was persuaded to write his experiences by his friend George Bird Grinnell, the noted ethnologist and author, whom he first met in 1872. Grinnell became an authority on the Plains Indians, particularly the Cheyenne and the Pawnee, and drew upon his correspondence with North in preparing *The Fighting Cheyennes* (1915) and *The Cheyenne Indians* (1923). For years he urged North to get his recollections down on paper, and finally, in 1925, the work was completed. But Grinnell never did publish the manuscript as such; instead, he used extracts from it in conjunction with other sources—notably an unpublished memoir by Frank North and Alfred Sorenson—in *Two Great Scouts and Their Pawnee Battalion* (1928).

So far as is known, Luther North wrote no other extended account of his early youth on the Nebraska frontier, his experiences with the Pawnee Scouts, and his ranching partnership with Frank North and William F. Cody. All his life, however, he corresponded with historians, fellow frontiersmen, and others interested in the Plains Indian Wars. In 1932 a brochure of narratives and reminiscences culled mainly from his letters was compiled and edited by Mr. Robert Bruce, with whom North had been corresponding extensively since 1929. Titled *The Fighting Norths and Pawnee Scouts*, it was published with the cooperation and approval of the Nebraska State Historical Society.

North was proud of his brother Frank and of the Pawnee Scouts and he resented any attempt to belittle their achievements. He particularly resented publicity which credited William F. Cody with deeds performed by Major North, and he did what he could to set the record straight. Although

Frank probably would not have bothered to argue the point, Luther was especially incensed by Cody's claim to have killed the Cheyenne chief Tall Bull at the Battle of Summit Springs. (See pages 117 and 128.) Nonetheless, Luther remembered him as a "good fellow" and the best rifle shot from horseback he had ever known. He strongly deplored the fact that a Cody debunker, Herbert Cody Blake, published parts of Luther's letters out of context so that they painted a blacker picture of Buffalo Bill than he had intended. A 1929 letter to Dr. Richard Tanner makes his feelings very clear; it is given in full in Appendix A.

Luther North died in 1935 at the age of eighty-nine, having outlived his brother by fifty years and Cody by eighteen. Three years later, on the death of George Bird Grinnell, the Luther North manuscript and Grinnell's materials concerning the North brothers and the Pawnee Scouts were given to the Nebraska State Historical Society. Enclosed with the manuscript was a foreword by Grinnell bearing the date June 12, 1925. Except for passages which he later incorporated in the introductory matter of *Two Great Scouts*, it now appears as the foreword to MAN OF THE PLAINS.

DONALD F. DANKER

*Archivist,*
*Nebraska State Historical Society*

# *FOREWORD*

People of modern days and modern surroundings can hardly comprehend the conditions of life in the country and at the time of which this book tells.

The far west of early days was an unknown region of indefinite extent and without white inhabitants. Those who first traversed it were the trappers, the fur traders and the missionaries; and some of these learned the land and were able to journey through it with confidence. The new people who came were obliged to acquaint themselves with it by experience, or else to depend on those who already knew it— their guides. Later, when the wars began with Indians, a proportion of the men who knew the prairies and the ways of the Indians were termed scouts, for they were watchmen and outlookers for the fighting men. In early days almost every army post had its scout.

It was the scout who did the first work toward opening up the western country; who faced its unknown dangers and learned its secrets. He did what lay before him and did not look forward into the future. He did not think of the people and the events which were to follow him. His purpose was

[ xv ]

no more than to do his day's work, and this work he performed faithfully and bravely, troubling himself not at all
about what might happen to him tomorrow. He was the
leading figure in the evolution of the west from wilderness
to productiveness. The trapper, who penetrated the mountain valleys for beaver, the trader who followed him, the missionary who visited and preached to distant Indian tribes, the
soldier who sought out new roads and mapped them, the cat-
tleman who brought up his herds from the south, and,
finally, the first farmer, each in turn played his part toward
developing the country we know today; but most of them
followed the scout.

The old-time scout was a man of good intelligence, and,
above all, of keen observation and retentive memory. He had
courage. He was familiar with the ways of the wild things—
men, animals and birds—and his experience had taught him to
draw useful conclusions from the actions of these wild
things. He was skilled in the varied requirements of his pro-
fession; a tracker and trailer, a hunter and a fair shot with
the rifle. Incidentally, also, he was ready of wit, prompt in
making up his mind, and determined in carrying through the
course decided on. The number of men known as good
scouts is not great, because usually their achievements were
known to but few people, who often were not in a position
to tell what their helpers had done for them. The good scout
did not talk much about what he had done.

We read a little of the accomplishments of a few men
such as Bridger, Carson and Hamilton, and not long ago
much ink and many adjectives were devoted to praising the
late William F. Cody, who was sometimes spoken of as "the
last of the great scouts." Cody was a capital fellow and an
extremely good horseback shot, but he was scarcely to be
called a scout. He used his former position at Ft. McPherson,
his admirable physique, and the advertising given him by
E. C. Judson, to announce himself as scout and Indian fighter,

but this was merely to promote his show business. That the advertising was successful is shown by the newspaper descriptions of him.

Since the wars of the early west were against Indian enemies, some of the keenest scouts in those wars were Indians, and of the white scouts the best equipped were those who knew most about Indians. Such men understood how Indians would reason and react under certain conditions, and because of this knowledge they were peculiarly competent to form conclusions as to what the enemy would be likely to do. They could take his point of view about any set of conditions.

\*          \*          \*          \*

The achievements of many of these men, the dangers they faced, and the toils they underwent, are fit subjects for the pen of poet or historian. They were heroes whose greatness was never known and whose deeds are unsung. In their own view their daily life covered only the commonplace. They went on from day to day, doing what they had promised to do—fulfilling their agreements. The men of the present day cannot conceive—because they have not had the experience to make them understand—the risks and the labors involved in that old wild life. So the old wild life can never be written of, except in the simple straightforward narrative of one of the quiet, modest men who had a part in it.

\*          \*          \*          \*

The beginnings of the Pawnee Scouts are told of briefly by the officer responsible for their enlistment. General Grenville M. Dodge, who in 1864-65 commanded white troops which were fighting the hostile Sioux and Cheyennes, says that he knew Major [Frank] North "to be a brave level-headed leader," and that he asked for, and received from the Government, authority to enlist and muster into service two companies of Pawnee Indians under Major North's command, and then sent him on scout duty to the Sioux country to try to rescue white prisoners that the Indians had captured.

"In the campaign of the summer of 1865 and 1866 Major North with his two enlisted companies, to which I added two more, made some wonderful marches, scouts, battles and captures, and during that campaign we recaptured and had surrendered to us many of these women and children prisoners.

"After the war Major North became manager of the Indians in Buffalo Bill's Wild West Show, and died in that service. He was a noted man on the plains. My acquaintance with him commenced in 1856, and together we had seen and endured many hardships. It was seldom one met his equal in any of the different phases of plains life. Although he had led an eventful career, still I never heard him refer to what he had done or accomplished, or the part he had taken in battles, and probably no man was ever more worshipped than he was by the two tribes of Pawnee Indians, and his death was virtually their destruction, for during his life among them he held them under good discipline and kept them away from vice, disease and war."

★          ★          ★          ★

The experiences of Capt. L. H. North set forth in these pages cover more years than those of his brother, and so are wider. His journeyings have extended from the International Boundary south through Oklahoma (the old Indian territory), and he has spent much time in the Rocky Mountains. He is today the greatest, as he is almost the last, of the old-time scouts of America.

His knowledge of the Indian and of the Indian's ways of thought is profound.

As a hunter of wild game he was most expert and successful and the most certain and best rifle shot that I have seen. In the old days, while shooting at a target was not considered the final test of skill, nevertheless rifle matches constantly took place among the well-known shots, and in the contests in which Captain North had a part he was always the victor.

His knowledge of the way of animals—how they would act under all circumstances—was uncanny.

Many years ago in western Nebraska he and I were riding over a wide valley filled with grazing cattle, horses and antelope, when off to the left we saw a fine buck antelope walk out to the border of a range of high bluffs that rose above the valley a quarter of a mile away and stand there on the skyline. It seemed an opportunity to get some fresh meat, and we hastily dismounted and sat on the ground behind our horses to watch the animal and learn what he would do. The buck stood there for a few moments, seeming to look all over the valley, and then turned and walked back out of sight. I rose to my feet, intending to go over to the bluff to try to get a shot, but North checked me and said, "Better wait a little." I sat down and in a few moments the antelope reappeared in the same place and again seemed to give the valley a long scrutiny. When he went out of sight Captain North still advised me to wait, and the antelope appeared twice more—thus taking four long looks—and when after the fourth appearance he went out of sight, Captain North said: "Now go ahead." I walked over, climbed the bluff and saw the buck standing about 75 yards back from the edge sleepily chewing his cud.

I never understood, and doubt if even Captain North could have explained, why he held me back so many times. But in this case, as in others often seen, it appeared that he had some sense of the psychology of wild animals that most of us do not possess.

At this late day few men survive who were scouts in the Indian wars. Of these Captain North is probably the oldest, as he is certainly the most experienced and the most able—the greatest. Another survivor is Willis Rowland, a much younger man whose scouting, in fact, did not begin until about 1880. Captain North and his brother Frank North were in the class with Bridger and Carson, and the value of their services in the work of opening and developing the western country can hardly be overestimated.

The narrative told in these pages gives, better than any description could do, a sense of the feeling that his Pawnees had for Captain North. They followed him, as they followed his brother, wherever he might go, and with entire confidence that with him lay safety and success.

The recording in detail of all that can be set down as to the development of the early west is vital to its history. An important part of these events was the work of the Pawnee scouts. For many years I tried in vain to persuade Captain North to set down on paper his recollections of what he had seen and done during the eventful years of this Indian fighting. I am gratified that his reluctance to tell his story has been overcome. In writing down these memories he has made a real contribution to our country's history.

GEO. BIRD GRINNELL

June 12, 1925.

MAN OF THE PLAINS

The events here described cover nearly thirty years resi-dence in the region between the Missouri River and the Rocky Mountains—part of what was once the Far West.

The various incidents suggest details of the daily life of the settlers of those days. The country was without railroads, and the people were few. Danger to life and property from Indians was common.

Later, when the actual Indian wars began there was sys-tematic fighting, in which the Pawnee Scouts, commanded by my brother, had their part. The record of what they did has never been fully set down, but the services of these Pawnees contributed not a little to the building of the first railroads and to the work of opening up the western country. Those who commanded them and who worked with them know best what their services were.

LUTHER NORTH

# I

## *EDUCATION OF A FRONTIERSMAN*

*[Towns and localities mentioned in this chapter appear on Maps 1, 2, and 3 following page 285. The sign (\*), whether it occurs in the text or in a footnote, indicates that additional information may be found in the supplement at the end of this chapter, beginning on page 21.]*

I WAS BORN in Richland County, Ohio, March 6th, 1846, and came to Omaha in 1856. In the winter of 1857 in March my father [Thomas J. North], who was a surveyor, was frozen to death about ten miles west of Omaha. There were five children in the family, two brothers, older, and two sisters, both younger than myself.[1] My oldest brother, J. E. North, was 17 years old and my brother Frank 16 years old. I was 10 and my sisters [Elizabeth and Alphonsene] were 8 and 6 years old. J. E. North was a clerk in a store in

---

1. A note on the North family appears in Appendix C.

[ 3 ]

Florence, Nebr.[2] and Frank was living with the rest of the family in the woods near Omaha.

This timber belonged to a man named Pierce, who was having the trees cut into cordwood, and my father as his agent measured and kept account of the work of the choppers. Frank had a yoke of oxen and hauled wood to town (Omaha); after my father's death he acted in his place as timekeeper for Mr. Pierce. The house we lived in consisted of two rooms, a kitchen and bedroom, each ten by fourteen feet in size.

The winter of 1856-57 was the coldest and longest of any winter I have ever seen.* The snow was at least 6 feet deep on the level, and in many of the ravines it was twenty or thirty feet deep. My mother boarded several of the wood-choppers, and all the water that she used for cooking and washing was from snow that she melted in a washboiler on the stove. The weather was so cold that many wild animals were frozen to death. I remember that one day three deer came down through the woods. While they were walking they got along pretty well, but when they saw the men and attempted to run, they broke through the crust on the snow and went in so deep that the woodchoppers, who could run on the crust of the snow, overtook them and killed them with their axes.

Two or three families of Pawnee Indians lived in skin lodges not far from our house, and it was from their boys that I first began to learn the Pawnee language. One of the lodges belonged to the chief Spotted Horse, who was third

2. Florence was first surveyed in 1853, resurveyed and platted in 1854, and incorporated by an act of the legislature approved March 15, 1855. The town was on the site of the old Mormon Winter Quarters, from 1846 to 1848 a wintering place and staging area for the Salt Lake City-bound Mormon emigrant trains. After Florence was established, the Mormons again made this an outfitting point. The northern part of Omaha now extends over the site.

chief of the Skidi band. He was a very fine looking man and always a good friend of the whites. I never saw him after that winter. He was killed by the Sioux in the fall of 1859, I think, and buried near old Ft. Kearny.[3]

In the spring of 1857 my mother filed a preemption claim on eighty acres of land just north of where Hanscoms Park now is, and we went there to live.[4] When the time was up, six months I believe, she paid one dollar twenty-five cents ($1.25) an acre and got a patent from the Government. Later, I think she sold this land for three hundred dollars, took the man's note for it, and, I believe, never got a cent.

About this time my brother J. E., who was now head of the family, built a house in Florence, and we moved up there. I went to school that winter and the next spring my mother, my two sisters and myself went back to New York State. I went to school a little that summer. The next fall we came to our old home in Ohio, stayed there through the winter, and in the spring returned to Nebraska.

In the fall of 1858 my brothers had moved to Columbus, and when we reached Omaha Mother hired a man and team to take us to Columbus, and we drove to Fremont the first day. Fremont was a town of perhaps six or eight log houses, and aside from the stage stations, which were about fifteen miles apart, these were about the only houses we saw. The second day, or rather some time in the night, we reached Columbus,* and this is where my education as a scout began,

~~~~~~~~~~~

3. Although there was more than one Spotted Horse, North probably is referring to the Skidi chief who signed the treaty of 1833 ceding all the Pawnee lands south of the Platte to the United States. (See Appendix B.) In 1873 the chief's remains were removed from their original burial place to the cemetery at Fort McPherson.

4. In July 1857 Jane North purchased eighty acres of land—the W2 NW4 of Section 28, Township 15, Range 13 E, according to the Federal Land Office Tract Book, Vol. 154—near present-day Hanscom Park in Omaha. North apparently is in error in saying this was a preemption claim: the purchase was made with a land warrant. Military bounty land warrants were issued to veterans and were negotiable.

although it was some years after that before I did any real scouting.

My brother J. E. North had taken the contract to deliver the mail from Columbus to Monroe, a post office twelve miles to the west, and I carried it. I made the trip on horseback three times a week, Tuesdays, Thursdays and Saturdays. I had a good pony and enjoyed the ride. Perhaps seven miles of the distance was over open prairie, with only a few wagon tracks to follow and not a house to be seen, which made it a little lonely for a boy thirteen years old.

This was the summer of the so-called Pawnee War. So much has been written and said about this war by the whites that perhaps it will be well to tell what the Pawnees had to say about it. Pitalesharu, the head chief of the Pawnees and always a friend of the whites, talked to me about it several years afterwards.[5] He said that some of the young men had trouble with the settlers near Fremont over damage that their horses had done to the growing crops; then a cow was killed belonging to a settler, who claimed that the Pawnees killed it though really it was killed by a party of Ponca Indians.* When General Thayer[6] overtook the Pawnees at what is now known as Battle Creek, the Pawnees did not know what the trouble was, but Pitalesharu guessed that something was wrong and taking an American flag, that had been given him two years before when he was in Washington, he rode forward with his interpreter to meet the Gen-

5. Pitalesharu (1823?-1874) was a chief of the Grand or Chaui band of Pawnees. (See note on the Pawnee bands, Appendix B.) He was so highly regarded that he represented the entire band in treaty-making. Nonetheless he was unsuccessful in opposing the removal of the tribe from Nebraska to the Indian Territory (Oklahoma). Pitalesharu was accidentally shot while the tribe was en route there, and was buried at his old home near present-day Genoa, Nebraska.

6. John Milton Thayer (1820-1906), major general in charge of the Nebraska militia, commanded the First Nebraska Volunteer Infantry during the Civil War and saw action at Shiloh. He was one of the state's first two U.S. senators (1867-1871) and its governor (1885-1889).

eral, and found out that he was at war with the whites. After
holding a council with the rest of the chiefs, of which there
were sixteen in the tribe, they finally turned over to the
General a young man who had killed a pig belonging to one
of the settlers, and that was the end of the Pawnee War.

All accounts of it that I have ever read tell of the killing of
several of the Pawnees on the march up the Elkhorn, but my
brother J. E. North, who was one of the volunteers with the
expedition, said that if any Pawnees were killed he didn't
know it, and that he believed that if they had attacked the
Pawnees the whites would probably have been badly beaten,
because they were so poorly armed. Pitalesharu said that no
Pawnees were killed and that the Pawnees killed no white
people.

The following fall, 1859, the Pawnees moved from their
village near Fremont to their reservation,[7] where the town of
Genoa now stands. The day they passed through Columbus
I had gone to Monroe with the mail, but on the return trip
I met them about half way from Monroe to Columbus.
When I first saw them coming I didn't know what tribe it
was, and as there were three thousand of them you may
know I was a badly scared boy, but as I came near the leaders they said How, How, and I felt much better. As I knew
a few words of the Pawnee language I soon found out who
they were, but I was very glad when I reached the rear end
of the procession, and lost no time in getting home.

The next winter, while driving in the cows one evening,
my pony slipped on some ice and fell on my leg, spraining
my ankle so badly that I could not walk or bear any weight
on it for more than a month, but I never missed a trip with
the mail. My brother J. E. would carry me out and put me
on the pony, and I would ride to Monroe, where lived a fam-

7. A fifteen-by-thirty-mile tract of land on the Loup River in what
is now Nance County, Nebraska, assigned to the Pawnee by the
Treaty of Table Creek (September 24, 1857).

ily named Gerrard who kept the post office.[8] Some one would help me off my horse and into the house, and when it was time to start back would lift me on my pony. My mother used to cry every time I started out, and when I grew older I could understand how she felt about it, for the weather was very cold and if my horse had fallen with me I should very likely have frozen.

In the spring of 1860 the mail route was discontinued and I spent that summer herding cattle for two or three of our neighbors, and in the fall went with my brother Frank to Ft. Kearny with a load of freight, and while we were in Doby-town, three miles west of the Fort, we saw the pony express rider go through.[9] I went to the agent at the Fort and asked him for work, but as I was very small for my age he gave me nothing and I returned home with my brother.*

That winter we moved to Omaha and I went to school for a couple of months. In the spring I came back to Columbus and lived with my brother and helped him on the farm, and the next winter I got work at the Pawnee Agency.* We were hauling wood and logs to the mill that the Government had built for the Indians.

[*When the Pawnees agreed to go on the reservation and signed away the last of their lands in the 1857 Treaty of*

8. Leander Gerrard (1837-1913) emigrated from England, coming to Nebraska Territory from Iowa in 1856. He ran a trading post on the Pawnee Reservation (1860-1866), then moved to Columbus, where he practiced law, sold real estate, and became a state leader in the Republican party.

9. "Doby Town," or Kearney City, was on the western edge of the Fort Kearny military reservation. Its residents sold liquor, supplies, and entertainment to the emigrants and soldiers. Fort Kearny was established in 1847 to give protection to overland emigrants. Originally called Fort Childs, in 1848 it was renamed for General Stephen W. Kearny (1794-1848). For more than twenty years the fort was one of the best-known points on the Oregon Trail. The completion of the transcontinental railroad and the absence of Indian hostilities eventually made the maintenance of the post unnecessary, and it was abandoned in 1871. (Common usage added an *e* before the *y* to the names of the town and the county, both of which use the spelling *Kearney*.)

*Table Creek, the government had promised they would ac-
tively protect them from Sioux attacks. In 1860, the Sioux,
Cheyenne, and Arapahos made repeated raids on the Pawnee
villages, and though the military attempted to arrange a
peace council, the Sioux, strong and well-armed, were not
interested. The outbreak of the Civil War drew the regular
troops from Fort Kearny, and Sioux raids continued in 1861
and 1862.]*

After the grass had started the next spring, we used to turn
out our horses and mules at night to graze. One morning
[June 20, 1862] they were gone and I jumped on a little saddle mule, bareback, to hunt for them. I had no idea they
would be far so didn't take with me either a gun or revolver.
I rode along the foot of the hill looking up every ravine I
came to, till I had gone about a mile and had made up my
mind to turn back, when a band of Sioux Indians rode over
the hill.

They were between me and the agency buildings, and I
couldn't run in that direction, but south of me about a mile
lived Mr. H. J. Hudson, a trader,[10] and I started off for his
place.

The Sioux started after me, but after chasing me for perhaps half a mile, they turned toward a field where some Pawnee women were hoeing corn, all except one man who
followed me. He was armed with bow and arrows and a long
lance, and was riding a fast horse that was gaining on me at
every jump. I was surely riding that mule and he was doing
his best, but it was hardly good enough. We were about a
quarter of a mile from the trading post and the Indian was

10. Henry J. Hudson was a leader of a Loup River Mormon settle-
ment which had been dispossessed by the establishment of the Pawnee
Reservation. After running a store at the edge of the reservation for
several years, he moved to Columbus. (See Marguerette R. Burke, ed.,
"Henry James Hudson and the Genoa Settlement," *Nebraska History*,
XLI, 3 [September 1960], 201-235.)

just about ready to drive the lance into me, when his horse stepped into a prairie dog hole and fell down.

Before he could get up and get his bow and arrow out, I was safe, but the poor Pawnee women were not so lucky. Nine of them were killed and one of them that was running for the trading post was caught and scalped by the man that had chased me. He ran up to her, caught her by the hair with his left hand and cut a piece about four inches square off the top of her head. He didn't get off his horse. We were shooting at him but the guns we used were some old muskets that had been given the Pawnees and they were as likely to burst and kill the shooter as anyone who stood in front of them.

In the race I lost my straw hat, and about a month later Adam Smith [11] who was freighting to Cottonwood Springs saw a party of Sioux Indians at Fort Kearny and one of them was wearing my hat! They belonged to the Brule band of Sioux under Spotted Tail,* and at that time they were not at war with the whites, but that would not stop them from killing white men on the Pawnee Reservation. Adam Smith was killed by the same band of Sioux in 1864, while putting up hay for the Government near the Pawnee Reserve.

The winter of 1861-62 was very cold with lots of snow. The Pawnees did not kill many buffalo on their fall hunt, their corn crop was poor, and they were in a starving condition; in fact, some of them actually starved to death. Some time in January a party of young men, I believe about one hundred, started up the Loup River to hunt for elk. They were on foot. A few days after they had set out it began to snow and one storm followed another for about a month, and the hunting party was never heard from again, they just

11. Adam Smith (1838-1864) was a German immigrant.

vanished. When spring came several small parties started out to hunt for them but never found any trace of them.

About two weeks before this hunting party started Al Arnold, L. M. Cook and myself went hunting on the Cedar River.[12] We had camped on Timber Creek and I took one of the team horses and rode off to the northwest from camp. When about eight miles from camp I saw some elk, and leaving my horse in a ravine, I finally got near enough to shoot and to my surprise I killed one. This was my first elk and I was very proud.

I went back and got my horse and by the time I got back to the elk it was nearly dark and it was snowing and the wind was blowing. I knew I must get to camp before long, so I cut an ear off the elk to show the boys, put it in my overcoat pocket and started for camp. It was pretty dark and the storm had become a blizzard by the time I found our camp.

Al and Cook were eating supper. Neither of them had killed anything but prairie chickens. They asked if I had seen anything and I replied, "Yes, I killed an elk," just as though it was an every day occurrence. Of course they didn't believe it, and I said, "Well, I'll prove it. I cut off her ear," and I put my hand in my pocket for it and it was gone! I suppose that, in my excitement, I had dropped it on the ground instead of in my pocket.

Those two old hunters made life miserable for me the rest of that night, and I was afraid the snow would cover my elk so I couldn't find it. The storm moderated the next day and we took the wagon and I found my elk. A couple of days later I killed two deer and Al killed a couple. Cook didn't get

12. Albert Arnold (1831-1916) subsequently served with the North brothers in the Pawnee Scouts. The Arnold and North families were closely associated; they were neighbors both in Florence and in Platte County. Arnold was elected to the state legislature in 1873.

The other member of the hunting party, L. M. Cook, was a Columbus blacksmith.

[ 11 ]

any. From that time on I was always invited when any hunting parties started out.

[*On August 18, 1862, six years of Indian hostilities began with an uprising of the Santee Sioux on the reserve set aside for them along the Minnesota River. When troops were rushed to the scene many Santee fled across the Missouri, carrying the war into Dakota Territory. Alarmed by the uprising and by rumors that the Minnesota Sioux were drifting southward and would soon attack the Nebraska settlements, the territorial legislature on September 9 petitioned the War Department for authority to raise a regiment for home defense. Permission being granted, the Second Nebraska Cavalry was organized under the command of Robert W. Furnas.*]

In the fall of 1862 I enlisted in the 2nd Nebraska Cavalry. We went to Omaha, where we were mustered in, drew our arms and equipment, and were ordered to the Pawnee Reservation, where we spent the winter. In the spring 1863 we marched across the country to Sioux City, Iowa, where we joined the expedition against the Indians under General Alfred Sully.[13]

We had two regiments of Cavalry, the Iowa 6th and the Nebraska 2nd, and his transportation was one hundred eighty-six mule teams. About one thousand of the mules were unbroken when they came to Sioux City, and as we were in camp there for three or four weeks, the teamsters spent the time in breaking them, but they were still pretty wild when we started up the river.

One day a little dog belonging to our Colonel, Robert W.

---

13. Alfred Sully (1821-1879), after graduating from West Point in 1841, saw service in the Seminole and Mexican wars. As a Union officer in the Civil War, he won distinction at Fair Oaks and Malvern Hill. In 1862 he was appointed brigadier general of volunteers, and in 1863 was given the command of the Department of Dakota.*

Furniss,[14] ran up to one of the teams and began to bark. The mules got scared, the saddle mule began to buck and threw his rider and the team ran away. As they passed the team in front of them that also ran away, and in about five minutes pretty nearly every one of the 180 teams was running away, and before they were all caught they had scattered flour, sugar, coffee, bacon and beans over a large part of Dakota territory. The damage done was so serious that we went into camp and it took about two weeks to gather up the wreckage and repair the wagons and harnesses, so that we could again move.

Perhaps this would be as good a place as any to tell how we were armed. The guns were long-barrelled muzzle loading Springfield rifles, and our revolvers were colts, calibre .44, also muzzle loaders. Besides these firearms we wore the regulation sabre. It took a pretty expert horseman to load one of those long rifles; especially if his horse was not perfectly gentle. They tried drilling us on horseback, but the guns were so awkward that they gave us most of our drilling on foot.

We marched up the Missouri River as far as Old Fort Pierre, then across country to the head of the James River, and on the 3rd of September 1863, we overtook the Indians and fought them at White Stone Hills, which is now in North Dakota.[15]

The Indians discovered us before we got to the village and ran away, leaving their lodges standing, but after a chase of several miles we caught up with and surrounded them in a ravine; our regiment on one side of the ravine and the Iowa

14. Robert W. Furnas (1824-1905) was the editor of the *Nebraska Advertiser* at Brownville, agent to the Omahas, founder of the *Nebraska Farmer*, and governor of the state (1873-1875). A conservationist and proponent of irrigation, his name was associated with almost every agricultural advance in Nebraska from territorial times until his death.

15. White Stone Hill, the battle site, is in what is now Dickey County, in southeastern North Dakota.

[ 13 ]

6th on the other side. When we were perhaps a half mile away we were dismounted and, leaving the horses behind a hill, we marched down on foot till we were within two hundred yards of the Indians. The Iowa 6th Cavalry was on the opposite side of the canyon on horseback, so we had the Indians surrounded. Up to this time no shots had been fired by the troops or Indians.

Our regiment was drawn up in one long line and about the time we were halted an Indian that had been lying in the grass about a hundred yards in front of our line jumped up and started to run towards the canyon where the main body of Indians were, and some one shot at him. That seemed to be the signal and everybody commenced to shoot.

If there were any orders given I did not hear them, and after I fired one shot I found I had no more cartridges with me. I was suffering from a very painful boil on my hip and had taken off my belt on which I had my cartridge box and tied it on my saddle, and when we left our horses I forgot the cartridges. I still had my revolver and some cartridges for it in my pocket. I promptly emptied it in the general direction of the Indians, and then tried to reload it and got a bullet part way down the cylinder where it stuck and I could neither get it in or out. I had laid my gun on the ground and while I was wrestling with my six shooter we were ordered back to our horses, as it was now dark.

A few minutes before this a man by the name of Tucker who was next to me in the ranks was shot through the leg, and just at that time a German that stood next to Tucker asked him for a chew of tobacco.

Tucker dropped down on the ground, caught hold of his leg and said: "I'm shot through the leg."

"To h--l mit your leg; shoot me mit a chaw tobacker," returned the German.[16]

16. Tucker, the wounded man, probably was Joseph Tucker of De Soto, Nebraska, enrolled in Company K, Second Nebraska Cavalry.

When we started back to our horses I forgot my gun and left it lying on the ground. When we had gone about one hundred yards I thought of it and turned around and ran back to get it. It was now very dark and I was obliged to hunt for a little while before I found the gun, and about the time I straightened up and turned around our company faced back and fired a volley. I was between them and the Indians and when I saw the flash from their guns it looked as if they were all pointed straight at me. I knew it would take a little time for them to reload and made up my mind to get to them before they fired another volley. I think I broke all records for the distance and joined the company before they fired again. I had a couple of bullet holes through my overcoat, but was not touched by the bullets.

We moved back to our horses and mounted, and started to where the wagon train had gone into camp, but after wandering around for an hour or more found that we were lost, so the regiment was formed into a hollow square and dismounted, and we stood there and held our horses till daylight, when twenty of us were detailed as guards to look after the wounded men, and the regiment started off to find the camp.

One of the men had an arrow through his shoulder. It had struck him in front and gone through, so that the point stuck out about six or eight inches behind. I hadn't seen him until morning and don't know yet why it wasn't taken out, but he had it in there yet when the ambulance came out after them, and that was about three o'clock in the afternoon. This same man's horse was shot through the neck with an arrow, and it was still sticking in him when the ambulance came. The surgeon cut the spikes off the arrows and pulled them out. The man seemed much more concerned about his horse than about himself.

We finally got into camp about six o'clock and got something to eat for the first time in more than thirty-six hours, and the first time our horses had been unsaddled in the same length of time.

I don't remember how many men were killed in this battle, but we lost two men killed and several wounded from our company, though the two that were killed were not really killed in the battle but were out with a scouting party. I think in General Sully's report it was claimed something over one hundred Indians were killed and that we took one hundred and fifty-six prisoners.

Shortly after this battle the command returned to the Missouri River and went down it until we reached the Crow Creek Indian Agency, where our regiment was left to guard the Santee Sioux and the Winnebago Indians.[17] I think we were there about a month when we were ordered to Omaha, and about the first of December 1863 were mustered out, and I came home to Columbus.

My brothers, J. E. and Frank North, had taken adjoining claims about three miles from town and were living on these claims, Frank with my mother and two sisters. Both my brothers were doing some farming, and part of the time freighting between Omaha and Fort Kearny. About the time I came home Frank went to work as clerk for the trader at the Pawnee Agency, and I bought his team, four horses and the wagon, and started freighting.

The first load I hauled was corn, and it was to be delivered at Ft. Kearny. It was just a two-horse load (three thousand

17. The Santee, who had taken an active part in the Minnesota fighting, were kept at Fort Thompson in Dakota Territory, near Crow Creek. The Winnebago at the time of the uprising were living on a reservation at Blue Earth, Minnesota.* Although they had not joined in the hostilities, the people of the state demanded their expulsion. Many were moved to Crow Creek Agency, which had been established in 1863.

pounds) and they paid 3½¢ per pound from Columbus to Kearny. A neighbor, Adam Smith, went along with another load. The weather was pretty cold and the roads were good, so we made good time, and on the fourth day at noon we got to the bank of the river south of the Fort. By this time the weather was very cold and we debated as to whether we better wait there until the next morning or try to cross that afternoon, but finally decided to try it that afternoon.

It was perhaps two miles across the river at this point; there were about seven channels to cross, some of them perhaps a quarter of a mile wide, then an island, then another channel. The first channel was frozen over so it held up the wagons and we got over it all right, and the next two channels were partly open, so we had to double our teams and take one wagon over at a time. Then we came to the worse one called the ox channel—perhaps because so many oxen had perished there in the quicksands. This channel was about three feet deep and full of ice. By this time it was bitterly cold and almost sundown. We put the four horses on one wagon and started. We got across until we reached the ice on the south side, where there was a raise of about two feet. The horses jumped up all right, but when the wheels struck the ice they couldn't pull it. By this time we were both frozen more or less, so we left the wagons and started for the Fort with the horses.

We were still more than a mile from the Fort, it was now dark, and, as we found later, thirty degrees below zero. Our clothes had gotten wet and were frozen stiff. Adams' overalls had slipped down almost to his knees and frozen there, making it very hard for him to walk. There were three channels still to cross, but fortunately two of them were frozen over; the one that was open was about two feet deep and we had to wade that. When we finally got to the Fort we found a shed where we could put our horses, and a room with a stove in it, where we could sleep.

[ 17 ]

The horses legs were covered with ice and their tails were frozen so full of ice that they were as big around as a nail keg. The shed or stable that we put them in was full of horses, which made it warm for them, and we had a lot of bedding, so we put blankets on them and got what ice we could off their legs before we went to the house. We found we ourselves were pretty badly frozen. My hands and face were frozen and Adams' hands, face and feet were badly frozen. His feet were so bad that he lost the nails off his toes, and the next morning he couldn't wear his boots. I had a couple of pairs of mocassins made from buffalo skins and gave him one pair. They were made with the hair side in and were very warm. The pain as the frost came out of our faces and hands was very great and we did not sleep much that night.

In the morning we took our teams and went back to the wagons. We had to unload the one that was frozen fast in the ice, and then chop it loose. Our hands were so sore that we could hardly handle the ax, but we got it out at last, and after reloading it went back and got the other wagon. The river was frozen solid by that time and we had no further trouble in getting across, but it had taken us so long to chop the wagon out that it was nearly night when we got our corn unloaded at the Fort, and we worked until nine o'clock that night getting the ice out of our poor horses' tails. The next morning we started for home, where we arrived three days later.

I stayed at home for a couple of weeks until my hands and face got healed up, when I continued hauling freight until spring, when I began to farm.

About the middle of July I took a load of corn to Ft. Kearny and after I had unloaded and come back across the

Platte River to the north side, I met a man named Hunter, who was on the way to Virginia City, Idaho with several four mule teams.[18] He hired me to haul a load of grain for him as far as Pawnee Springs, which is a few miles from where Maxwell Station now is, on the Union Pacific. The morning I started back from there I drove down to Brady Island, where I stopped to feed my teams.

While they were eating a band of Indians came across the river from the south side. I was alone but didn't pay special regard to them, as there were small bands camped along the river at different points that were all supposed to be friendly. When they rode up out of the river about one hundred yards from me I saw they were all warriors and were well armed, some with guns but most of them with bows and arrows. There was about thirty of them, and as soon as they got out of the river they gave the war whoop and came for me on a run.

I still thought they were just bluffing and were trying to scare me, so sat still on the wagon tongue thinking that when they got near they would call out their how how and ask for something to eat, but instead they commenced to circle around my wagon and kept up their yelling. I saw that they were very much excited and, knowing Indians as I did, I felt I was in a pretty tight place and din't know just how I would get out of it. Finally a young warrior rode up in front of me, stopped his horse, fitted an arrow to his bow, pointed it straight at my breast and pulled it back almost to the point, and I surely thought my time had come.

While this man was doing all this—and I don't think it took him ten seconds—another man rode up to him shouting and gesticulating, and struck the arrow aside. Then they had quite an argument and I knew that some of them were in

18. Probably North meant Virginia City, Nevada, site of the Comstock silver lode. Settled in 1859, it was one of the richest mining towns of the West.

favor of killing me and others were in favor of letting me go. At last they turned and rode off toward the river, and as soon as they started across I hitched up my team and started on my journey home. As I left my camp I could see the Indian camp moving south on the other side of the river.

At this time there were some soldiers camped at or near Cottonwood Springs,[19] afterwards Ft. McPherson, and I believe that was the reason the Indians let me go. They had their women and children in camp on the Platte River opposite where I was camped, and wanted to move them to a safe place before commencing hostilities. When I saw them going south they were moving over to the head of Medicine Creek, where they made a permanent camp, from which they raided the emigrants on the Oregon Trail. The second night after I saw them they made a raid at Plum Creek, killing all of the people in the train, fourteen in number.[20]

I met a train of wagons on their way to California about ten miles from Brady Island, and as they had camped for the night I camped with them. The next day I drove down a little below Plum Creek, when one of my horses was taken sick, and I camped there until next morning. It was that morning that the Indians raided the train above Plum Creek stage station.[21] This was three or four miles above where I

19. McDonald's road ranch or trading post was located at Cottonwood Springs, which was a stage and Pony Express station on the Oregon Trail.

20. The train was made up of freighting wagons owned by Thomas Frank Morton of Sidney, Iowa, and Michael Kelly of St. Joseph, Missouri. Mrs. Morton and a boy, Danny Marble, were taken prisoner. Reports as to the number of persons killed vary from eleven to fourteen. The raid occurred on August 7, 1864 in the northwest corner of what is now Phelps County. (See Leroy W. Hagerty, "Indian Raids Along the Platte and Little Blue Rivers, 1864-1865," *Nebraska History*, XXVIII, 4 [October-December 1947], 241.)

21. Plum Creek stage station was on the Oregon Trail on the south side of the Platte, about ten miles southeast of the site of the town named Plum Creek, which was established in 1866 on the

was camped and across the river, and I knew nothing of it until I got to the river opposite Ft. Kearny that evening.

Three days later I got home.

## SUPPLEMENT

"The Hard Winter of 1856-1857" (page 4)

The previous winter had been a mild one, and few pioneer Nebraskans had any idea of the extremes of which weather in the Great Plains was capable. Perhaps because they were unprepared for its violence, "The Hard Winter of 1856-1857" was ranked by early settlers in the same category with "The April Blizzard" (April 14-16, 1873) and "The School Children's Storm" (January 12-13, 1888). A blizzard struck early in December 1856, and storms continued until early spring with temperatures at times said to reach forty degrees below zero. According to the only official meteorological records at the time, which were kept at Fort Kearny, the mean temperature for January 1857 was nine degrees as compared with an average mean temperature (1921-1950) of twenty-five degrees for that month. (Clark Irwin, "Early Settlers Enroute," *Transactions and Reports of the Nebraska State Historical Society*, First Series, Vol. III [Lincoln: 1892], 195-196; Climate of Nebraska, United States [Signal Office] 51st Congress, 1st Session, Senate Executive Document No. 115

north (or Union Pacific Railroad) side of the river. The town was renamed Lexington in 1889.

[ 21 ]

[Washington, D. C.: Government Printing Office, 1890], 51.)

COLUMBUS (page 5)

"Columbus was laid out in 1856 by a few Germans impressed by the favorable location for a town. J. E. and Frank North came in '58; that year there was a ferry across the Loup Fork. . . . The first bridge was a pontoon built by the Government—a Platte Co. history says in 1863; but I was away all that year, and remember very well when soldiers were doing the work. It was washed out soon after, while I was here—so would say more likely in '64. Contract for the first bridge was probably let in the summer of '69.

"I have seen hundreds of emigrant trains ford the Loup; also trains of 100 or 200 wagons waiting their turn to cross on the one boat, carrying only two of them with one team to each at a time. . . . In '59 two hand-cart trains of Mormons passed through Columbus, traveling toward Utah at the rate of about 15 miles a day. Men, women and children pulled or pushed those two-wheeled vehicles (some fitted with good-sized boxes holding loads probably up to a thousand pounds) from the Missouri River to Great Salt Lake. I remember two women with a sort of harness over their shoulders, walking ahead and pulling their cart while the men pushed from behind" (Letter of Luther North quoted in Robert Bruce, *The Fighting Norths and Pawnee Scouts* [Brooklyn: Brooklyn Eagle Press, 1932], 13).

The founders of Columbus came from Columbus, Ohio; and among the early settlers were a number of German, Swiss, and Polish birth.

THE PONCA (page 6)

A Siouan tribe belonging to the Dhegiha group, in the

time of Lewis and Clark they were settled on the Missouri at the mouth of the Niobrara. Since their hunting grounds stretched west along the Niobrara, they often met with Sioux bands, particularly Oglala and Brûlé. They were friendly with them for a time and fought the Pawnee together. In 1858 the Ponca were removed to land farther west, but were allowed to return to their former home in 1865. In 1877 most of the tribe was forced to move to Indian Territory.

### North and the Pony Express (page 8)

Although it is not clear from the text, the job North applied for apparently was that of Pony Express rider. He later wrote that he and his brother "went to the manager's office, and I tried to get a job from him, but he told me that they could not hire anyone under 20 years of age. William F. Cody, later known as 'Buffalo Bill,' less than two weeks older than I, claimed to have ridden the Pony Express that year—or at least the claim was put forward by others for him. I had ridden on the Columbus-Monroe mail route several months before, when I was only 13 years old" (Bruce, *The Fighting Norths*, 13).

### The Pawnee Agency (page 8)

By the Treaty of 1857, the government had agreed to build an agency, with sawmill, gristmill, blacksmith, and other shops; and to provide a farmer, blacksmith, teachers, and other employees. The agent was charged with putting into effect the treaty arrangements with the Pawnee, distributing allotments, protecting their interests from whites and other Indians, and teaching them the ways of the white men both in school and by demonstration from the farmer and blacksmith.

Under the first agent, Judge J. L. Gillis of Pennsylvania, appointed in August 1859, the saw- and gristmill was completed: it was steam operated and its whistle enchanted the Indians. He also built a large granary and a bridge across Beaver Creek to the Pawnee villages, but no school had been put up by the spring of 1861, at which time Gillis and many others in the Indian Service were removed by President Lincoln to make way for political appointees. Of the five agents who followed—H. W. DuPuy, Benjamin F. Lushbaugh, Daniel H. Wheeler, John P. Becker (q.v.), and Charles H. Whaley—they were "perhaps no worse than the other Indian agents of the day, but that is not saying much in their favor. There were six Pawnee agents during the first ten years. . . . three of the six were dismissed after being caught in peculations; the other three were only suspected of shady dealings. Old Judge Gillis seems to have been the best of the six" (George Hyde, *Pawnee Indians* [Denver: University of Denver Press, 1951], 217).

After ten years during which the government had expended at least $400,000 for education, building, and agriculture, there had been little progress in any direction. There had been no school at all until 1862, and until 1867 it was housed in a dilapidated log shanty. A two-story brick building, 45 x 125 feet, finally had been put up, but Pawnee House, as it was called, had been badly planned and despite its large cost was hardly fit for use. The other agency buildings—log houses bought from Genoa settlers and some cheap frame houses—were falling apart; the grist- and sawmill would not run, and although money had been lavished on "agricultural improvements," they existed almost entirely in the agents' reports (Hyde, *Pawnee Indians*, 227-228).

In 1869 a new policy, initiated by the Grant administration, was to bring a measure of improvement in some respects. (See text and supplement, Chapter 6.)

SPOTTED TAIL AND THE SIOUX (page 10)

The Sioux—in their own language they called themselves Dakota or Lakota—belonged to the Siouan linguistic group. There were seven major divisions, four of which (the Wahpeton, Sisseton, Mdewakanton, and Wakpekute) were known collectively as the Santee. The other three divisions were the Yankton, the Yanktonnais, and the Teton. There were seven sub-tribes of Teton Sioux: Oglala, Brûlé, Two Kettle, Sans Arc, Hunkpapa, Minneconjou, and Blackfoot. The Santee divisions, which occupied lands east of the Mississippi, sometimes were designated as the Sioux of the East, and the divisions on the other side of the river were known as the Sioux of the West (Herbert S. Schell, *History of South Dakota* [Lincoln: University of Nebraska Press, 1961], 18-19).

Spotted Tail (1833?-1881) belonged to the Brûlé sub-tribe of the Teton Sioux. He was not a hereditary chief. "When a boy nineteen years old he is said to have accepted a challenge to a duel with a sub-chief of the band, and a long and bloody encounter with knives occurred, in which the chief was killed. This affair, with other deeds of prowess, brought Spotted Tail into general prominence in the band, and upon the death of the hereditary chief, he was made his successor" (D. W. Robinson, "Editorial Notes on Historical Sketch of North Dakota and South Dakota," *South Dakota Department of History Collections* [Pierre: 1902], I, 85-121). Spotted Tail participated in the Grattan fight in 1854, and signed the Treaty of 1868 which established the Spotted Tail Agency in northwest Nebraska. He was killed on the Rosebud Agency by an Oglala sub-chief, Crow Dog, who claimed that he fired in self-defense. Spotted Tail was an uncle of Crazy Horse.

MILITARY DEPARTMENTS OF THE WEST (page 12, footnote 13)

The U.S. Army during the time of the North brothers' service was organized into administrative areas designated as divisions and departments. The boundaries and headquarters of these sectors were changed when the conditions warranted. In the fall of 1865 the Military Division of the Mississippi included the Department of Missouri (the states of Minnesota, Iowa, Missouri, and Kansas; the territories of Colorado, Utah, Nebraska, Dakota, New Mexico, and Montana) with headquarters at St. Louis. In 1867 the Department of the Platte was organized with headquarters in Omaha; it embraced Iowa and Nebraska, the territory of Utah, and parts of Dakota and Montana. The Department of Dakota took in the remainder of Dakota and Montana in addition to Minnesota (William A. Ganoe, *The History of the United States Army* [New York: D. Appleton and Co., 1924], 524-528).

THE WINNEBAGO (page 16, footnote 17)

The Winnebago tribe was a division of the Siouan family. When they were forcibly removed from their reservation at Blue Earth, Minnesota, to the Crow Creek Agency, they were placed in close proximity to their ancient foe, the Sioux. Moreover, conditions at the agency were very bad. The Winnebago began abandoning it in 1863-1864, even in the face of the severe winter weather, and "visited" the friendly Omahas in Thurston County, Nebraska, in increasing numbers. "Agent Robert W. Furnas, with the consent of the tribe, did what he could to assist the destitute Winnebagoes, but their presence posed a serious problem. In 1865 Furnas took a delegation of Omaha chiefs to Washington, where they agreed to cede part of their reservation to the

Winnebagoes. The Omaha-Winnebago reservation still remains in Nebraska, although most of the land has been allotted to individual members of the tribes" (James C. Olson, *History of Nebraska* [Lincoln: University of Nebraska Press, 1955], 136).

# II

## THE PAWNEE SCOUTS

[*See Maps 2 and 3; chapter supplement begins on page 40.*]

[*It was in the blood-stained summer of 1864 that the Indians offered their fiercest resistance to white occupation
of Nebraska. Already chafing under the constant pres-
sure of expanding settlement, made apprehensive by the
increasing activity on the overland trails, and newly ex-
acerbated by the military's punitive measures after the
Minnesota uprising, the Cheyenne, Arapaho, and Brûlé no
longer could be appeased by isolated raids such as that on
June 28, 1864, in which the Norths' neighbor, Adam
Smith, lost his life.*

*On August 7 they "launched a concerted attack upon
stagecoaches, emigrant trains, stations, and ranches all
along the central and western stretches of the Platte Valley. That day and the next they struck every stage station
and ranch between Julesburg and Fort Kearny. . . . The
attack spread to the valley of the Little Blue; here there
was no telegraph to warn the settlers and station keepers,*

[ 28 ]

*and the loss of life was considerably greater. The entire Nebraska frontier was thrown into a state of panic. Almost all the settlers in the Platte and the Little Blue valleys fled eastward. . . . Stage coaches and freight wagons ceased operating altogether"* (James C. Olson, History of Nebraska [Lincoln: University of Nebraska Press, 1955], 141-142).]

ABOUT THAT TIME, or perhaps a little later, General Sam   *Aug. 20,*
Curtis, who was in command of this Department   *1864*
with headquarters in St. Louis, came through Columbus on his way to Ft. Kearny to organize an expedition against the hostile Indians. He was the originator of the idea of using as scouts the Indians that were friendly to the whites.[1]

Knowing that the Pawnees were always at war with the Sioux and Cheyennes he decided to try and get some of them to go with the expedition as scouts, and he took my brother Frank and a man named McFayden as interpreters.[2] About seventy of the Pawnees agreed to go. They furnished their own horses and were to receive the pay of enlisted men, besides getting pay for their horses. They were never enlisted or mustered into the service, and although they joined the expedition at Ft. Kearny and campaigned with it until the troops went into winter quarters, they never were paid one cent for their services.

When the expedition left Ft. Kearny they marched to

1. Samuel Ryan Curtis (1805-1866), a New York Stater and West Point graduate, served in the Mexican War as colonel of the Third Ohio Infantry. He resigned from the army to practice law in Iowa, was twice elected to Congress, and became colonel of the Second Iowa Infantry at the outbreak of the Civil War. Advanced to major general in 1862, he commanded the Department of Missouri and in 1864 took over the command of the Department of Kansas.

2. Joseph McFadden clerked in the trader's store at the Pawnee Agency; his wife was an Indian woman. Because of McFadden's previous military experience Curtis gave him the temporary rank of captain, while Frank North was made a lieutenant.

[ 29 ]

Plum Creek, then south to the Republican and Soloman [Solomon] Rivers, where General Curtis turned over the command to General Mitchell.[3] McFayden, with all of the Pawnees except two, accompanied the command, and Frank went with the command under General Curtis to Ft. Riley in Kansas. It was on this trip that General Curtis gave Frank authority to enlist a command of 100 Pawnee Indians, and he was to have the rank of Captain. The organization was to be known as the Pawnee Scouts.*

*Oct.-Nov., 1864*    On Frank's return home from Ft. Riley he went to the Pawnee Reservation, and soon had the names of the men, but there was some hitch about mustering them in, and Frank went to Omaha. He was gone a couple of weeks, and when he got back the Pawnees had gone on their annual fall hunt and the men that he enlisted had gone with them, except perhaps ten or fifteen young fellows that had no horses. Frank was going back again to Omaha and before going he asked me to take one of the Indian boys that was still here and follow the tribe, and get the men that he had enlisted to come back.

I took a young fellow about my own age, eighteen years, and we followed the trail to where Grand Island is now, where they had crossed the Platte River and gone south. We followed till we got to the Little Blue, where we were

---

3. Robert Byington Mitchell (1823-1882) moved in 1855 from Ohio to Kansas where he held various state political offices. When the Civil War began he served as colonel of the Second Kansas Volunteer Infantry, was promoted to brigadier general, and assigned to the Nebraska District of the Department of Kansas early in 1864. Shortly after being transferred to the District of North Kansas in 1865 he was appointed governor of New Mexico territory by President Andrew Johnson.

caught in a terrific blizzard that lasted for three days. All of the shelter we had we made out of some willow brush, and when the storm was over the snow was so deep that we couldn't follow the trail, and we were out of provisions, so we started for home.

We were four days in reaching home, and din't have a bite to eat and the weather was very cold, twenty degrees or more below zero all the time. We got to Eagle Island—Silver Creek—on the third day, but we were on the south side of the river and our horses were barefooted, so we camped there that night and the next morning went down the river a couple of miles below the stage station, where we started across. The ice was partly covered with snow, and by picking our way we got to within about a hundred yards of the north bank of the river. From there on the ice was as smooth as glass and I was wondering how we would ever make it, but the Indian boy chopped a hole in the ice where he could reach the bottom and would scoop up a handfull of wet sand and throw it on the ice.

It was surprising how little it took to roughen the ice so the ponies could walk on it. Of course it was slow work, but at last we got over, and just at sundown we got to the Loup River opposite our house. We left our horses there and walked across on the ice, and when we got to the house my mother was just getting supper. She had some honey and was baking biscuits, and we kept her busy baking them for about two hours, I guess. I think that was the best meal I ever ate.

After we got filled up we took a spade and an axe and went to the river and built a sand path across for our horses, and brought them over. I think they were as glad to get their corn and hay and a warm place to sleep as we were. I have often wondered how our horses stood it on some of those trips. They had nothing to eat but dead grass, and we were traveling about thirty miles a day through deep snow.

In some way they made the journey and after a few days rest were as good as ever.

About a month after we got home we learned that the Pawnees were returning from their hunt and were camping at different places on the Platte River. Frank went from the Pawnee Agency up the Loup and crossed over to Grand Island, and a few miles above there found a camp, and enlisted about fifty men. I went up the Platte from Columbus and at a camp near Lone Tree—now Central City [4]—I got thirty-five young men. These with the fifty my brother got and those still at the Agency, made up the hundred men, and they *Jan. 13, 1865* were mustered in at Columbus as Company A Pawnee Scouts, with my brother as Captain, Charley Small as first lieutenant and Jimmy Murie as second lieutenant.[5]

My brother chose his officers and I wanted him to take me, but that would have left mother and my two sisters alone on the farm, and so we gave it up and I stayed at home. That winter I did some freighting and farmed the next summer, 1865.

That summer [1865] the Indians were committing depredations all along the Platte River from Grand Island west, and many of the settlers were leaving their claims and going back to their old homes in the east.* Many rumors were heard of the coming of Indians to clean out all of the people who were living in the Platte Valley, and in one expedition

4. Lone Tree, a giant cottonwood, was a landmark for travelers on the Mormon Trail. Lone Tree Ranch, established nearby in 1858, was a "20-mile-stopping-place" for the Overland stage and, after the railroad was built, a Union Pacific station. The name Lone Tree later was changed to Central City.
5. Charles G. Small had been the private secretary of Benjamin Lushbaugh, agent to the Pawnees (June 1862-July 1865). James Murie, who was married to a Pawnee woman, had emigrated from Scotland.

under Colonel Cole, which passed through Columbus on the *July 7,* way to Powder River, Wyoming Territory, to meet the *1865* command under General P. E. Connor that was starting from Fort Laramie . . . there were sixteen hundred men and several pieces of artillery. The men were all splendidly mounted, and it seemed to me they could whip all the Indians on the plains, but, as it turned out, they came near being annihilated themselves. They failed to make junction with Connor's command, ran out of rations, abandoned their artillery, and seven hundred of their horses died from exposure in one night. The Indians harassed them continually, and when they were finally found by my brother and his Pawnee scouts, they were almost starved.[6]

In my brother's account of his life [7] he tells of the finding of the Cole command, and their coming into Fort Reno on Powder River, so I will go back to what we were doing here. [*At this point North apparently has confused the summers of 1864 and 1865. Cole's command passed through Columbus in the summer of 1865, but the events which he describes occurred in the summer of 1864.*] Shortly after Cole's com-

~~~~~~~~~~~~~~~

6. Colonel Nelson Cole's command was organized in Omaha in June 1865. As it passed through Columbus, July 7, 1865, it consisted of about 1,400 men and a supply train of 140 six-mule wagons. By early September the supplies had been exhausted and the men were reduced to eating the mules. Colonel Cole condemned his superiors for poor planning and lack of foresight. Although General Connor had a measure of success, destroying an Arapaho village on Tongue River, he was relieved of his command ("Report of Col. Nelson Cole," *War of the Rebellion*, XLVIII, Pt. 1, 366-383; Fred B. Rogers, *Soldiers of the Overland* [San Francisco: The Grabhorn Press, 1938] Chapter XXI).

7. "A Quarter of a Century on the Frontier or the Adventures of Major Frank North the 'White Chief of the Pawnees,' The story of his Life as told by himself and written by Alfred Sorenson," typewritten manuscript at the Nebraska State Historical Society. George Bird Grinnell incorporated much of the information in *Two Great Scouts and Their Pawnee Battalion* (Cleveland: Arthur H. Clark Co., 1928). A serialized biography of Major North based on this manuscript was written by Sorenson and appeared in the Omaha *Weekly Bee*, December 8, 1886.

mand had passed through here we had another report that the Indians were coming, and all of the settlers in the vicinity of Columbus [8] moved into town and built a stockade around the town, for protection from the Indians and as a corral for the stock, as they brought all of their live stock with them. Their horses, cattle and a few sheep and hogs, all of which were turned outside of the stockade and herded along the river through the day, and brought inside at night.

Two companies of militia were organized, one of cavalry and one of infantry. I think there was about fifty men in each company. Every night a guard of infantry men patrolled inside the stockade, and three or four of the cavalry were sent outside as pickets.

The officers seemed rather hazy as to the duties of the picket guard. I belonged to the cavalry and one night when I was assigned to picket duty with a couple of other boys about my age, I asked the Captain what we were supposed to do and where we were to be posted. He said, "Oh, just sort of scout around up the road and if you see any Indians just come to the stockade to beat hell." We told him we would sure do that.

One of the farmers named Needham, whose home was about six miles west of town, had driven out to his farm the day we were sent out on picket duty and he was late in getting to town. We had ridden out about a mile and a half when we saw him coming. He was in a lumber wagon. It was nearly dark and we thought we would have some fun with him. We rode down out of sight under the bank beside the road, wrapped our red blankets around us and, when he had passed us, and was two or three hundred yards away, we rode up the bank, gave the war whoop and started after him. He whipped his horses into a run and we chased him to within a quarter of a mile of the stockade, when we turned

8. In the original typescript North wrote "Oklahoma" instead of Columbus; this was unquestionably a slip of the pen.

back and rode out to where we knew there was a water-mellon patch, where we filled up on mellons and went peacefully to sleep until morning.

In the morning when we rode in we intended to tell what we had done, but we found the people all so excited that we began to realize what we had done. Needham had told them that he had been chased by a big band of Indians and, of course, our people were wondering what had become of us. My mother was very anxious and I guess didn't sleep much that night. I told my family what we had done, but none of us told anybody else.

Our farm was only about three miles from town, so what [when] we moved in I just took my horses and left the rest of the stock at home. Every morning I went out to milk my cows, and my youngest sister, who was fourteen years old and could ride as well as I could, would ride out with me and keep watch while I did the chores. Then we would turn out the cattle and drive them down the river towards town, where we left them until evening, when we went out and took them home.

One evening while I was in the shed milking, my sister called me. I ran out and she pointed toward the hills to the north and said, "There is something there that looks like men on horseback."

I could see them against the skyline, and they did look like horsemen, and there were quite a lot of them. It was nearly night, and as they seemed to be standing still or moving slowly, I finished milking and we went to town. I never did find out what it was we saw that night.

After three or four weeks the excitement in town died down. A company of cavalry was sent to Columbus to protect the settlers; they began moving back on their farms, and everything was quiet again.

Shortly after the coming of the troops to Columbus, it

was reported that another company of cavalry was to come across from the Missouri River at Dakota City, to be stationed here while the company at Columbus was to go somewhere else. The quartermaster here could not get word from the company that was expected, and he wanted to get someone to go across country and guide them here. He asked me to go, and this was my first work as scout for the government.

I rode over to Dakota City alone, making the trip in three days, found the company had taken an old trail that went across to Genoa, and as they had been gone four days when I got there, I came back to Columbus on my own trail, which again took me three days. When I got home I found the troops had not put in an appearance. I went to Lieut. Robley and explained to him why I had not followed their trail, as it was so much longer than the way I went, and that they would be in the next day about noon. Of course I was guessing at it, but it proved a good guess, and the next day at noon they came in.

A short time after this I was sent with despatches to North Bend, and as I rode out of town I overtook a Pawnee boy who was on foot. He asked me where I was going and I told him. We were just at the edge of town and it was just noon. I was riding at a good jogtrot and the boy trotted along with me. I asked where he had come from and he said from the village of Genoa, which was twenty-two miles from Columbus. He ran along with me all the way to North Bend, which was thirty-five miles from Columbus, and we got there at five o'clock, having made seven miles an hour for the whole distance.

When I stopped at the stage station he asked, "Are you going to stay here all night?", and when I said, "Yes," he said, "My father is camped on the river at Fremont. I am going there tonight," and as far as I could see him he was still running. Fremont was still sixteen miles further on. That would be seventy-three miles from the Pawnee village and he had eaten nothing, and although the day was very hot he had taken only one drink of water. At the crossing of Shell Creek, where I stopped to water my pony, he dipped up a couple of handfuls of water and put them on his head, and then drank a very little, certainly not a glass full. This shows the endurance of the Pawnees.

This boy was not one of their noted runners, but just an average runner. One of their great runners, Koot-tah-we-coots-oo lel-le-hoo-La Shar (Big Hawk Chief) once ran from the Pawnee Agency in Oklahoma to the Wichita Agency, one hundred and twenty miles, in 24 hours, and came back in 24 hours or less—this over a rough, hilly and stony country.* This Indian was one of my scouts and I will have more to say about him later.

In the fall of 1865 my brother returned from the Powder River Expedition and his company of scouts were quartered at the Pawnee Agency. He was married on the 24th of December 1865,[9] and in January 1866 he received orders to send fifty of his men to Ft. Kearny to join a scouting party that was to start from there and scout west along the Republican River.

He sent Lieut. Jimmy Murie with the men, and I asked to go along, and Frank said, "all right." This was my first trip out with the Pawnee scouts and I had no command.

We marched to Fort Kearney where we joined the scouting party. It was composed of two troops of cavalry besides the fifty Pawnee scouts, and we had quite a wagon train.

9. Mary Louise Smith (1845-1883) was married to Frank North on Christmas Day, 1865, in Columbus, Nebraska. She was born in Hartford, Connecticut, and came to Nebraska with the family of her uncle, Samuel C. Smith (q.v.).

We went southwest from Kearney and we got to the Republican, followed it up until we crossed the Frenchmans Fork,[10] and perhaps twenty miles further we made a permanent camp from which the commanding officer sent out scouting parties. Murie usually went with the scouts that were sent out, and sometimes I went with him, but as I did not belong to the scouts I did as I pleased and put in a good deal of the time hunting. The country was full of elk, deer and wild turkeys, and there were some buffalo, but not as many as I saw in the country a year or two later.

One morning the commanding officer sent word to Murie to send ten men south fifteen or twenty miles to see what they could find, and I proposed to Murie to let me go with them, and he said, "All right." We rode south until the middle of the afternoon, and I had just said to one of the boys that we would go to the top of the hill that we were going up, when we would turn back to a dry creek bed we had crossed and go into camp, when off to the southwest we saw a band of Indians. They had seen us and were coming on a run. I think there must have been 150 of them.

I told the boys we would run back to the creek where we could get under the bank, and we would fight them there. The Pawnees were armed with spencer carbines and I had a ballard rifle.* The carbines were seven shooters, and as the Indians were mostly armed with bows and arrows, and the weather was very cold, I did not think they would fight very long. We were well mounted and started back on a gallop, but did not hurry our horses much. The Indians gained on us, and when we were within perhaps half a mile of the creek my horse slipped on some ice and fell. I went down and str[u]ck my head so hard on the frozen ground that I was knocked unconscious.

10. During the time of the Indian Wars the Frenchman's Fork also was known as Whiteman's Fork. It is now called Frenchman Creek.

When I came to, one of the boys had my head in his lap and was rubbing snow in my face; the rest of them with their horses had formed a circle around me and were fighting the Indians off. They had charged up pretty close at first, but the repeating guns were new to them and they broke and circled around us. Five of our horses were wounded with arrows, and that made them hard to handle. The boys had all dismounted when my horse fell. I think that showed a great deal of bravery on their part, as there were at least one hundred Indians in the band that was after us. The scouts were well mounted and could easily have outrun them if they had left me, but I believe they never thought of that.

When I came to enough to sit up, the boy that was taking care of me helped me on my horse, and we started for the creek. The Indians charged us, but when we stopped and faced them, they also stopped. When we started on again, of course some of them were between us and the creek, but they scattered and got out of the way as we got near them. A few of them got into the creek bed, but we drove them out and took possession ourselves.

I was pretty well shaken up and had to lie down for a while, but in a half hour or so I felt better. The Indians made two or three charges but never came very close, and about sundown they rode off toward the south. We found that three of our horses were so badly wounded that they could not live, so we put them out of their misery and started for the camp. We got to camp some time after midnight and reported what had taken place.

The next morning, about the time the command was ready to start in pursuit of the Indians, a courier came out from Fort Kearney ordering the whole command back to the fort, and this ended that campaign. Soon after reaching Fort Kearney the scouts were ordered back to the Pawnee Agency, where they were mustered out the following April —1866.

# SUPPLEMENT

THE FIRST COMPANY OF PAWNEE SCOUTS (page 30)

According to an account by Luther North in Bruce, *The Fighting Norths and Pawnee Scouts*, in 1864 the hostile Southern Cheyenne and their allies in frequent raids on the Kansas frontier had "practically sealed up the important Smoky Hill route west to Denver, were interfering with travel and emigration along the Arkansas River, and harassing the fringe of settlements in eastern Colorado. . . . When the hostile Indians broke out in the early summer of [1864], Gen. Curtis . . . planned an expedition against them from Fort Kearny, Nebraska." After the recruitment as related in the text: "Of that first company, Joseph McFadden was captain and my elder brother Frank North lieutenant." McFadden's commission, signed by Curtis, was dated August 25, 1864, and began on the twentieth of that month. Although Curtis soon left the expedition "somewhere on that trip, [he] gave my brother a verbal commission to enlist the first regular company of Pawnee scouts" (22).

Luther North in the same source also states that "except for that short time in 1864, my brother was at the head of his Pawnees, Capt. McFadden not appearing again in the records connected with them. My acquaintance with [McFadden] was very slight, but he had been in the military service under Gen. W. S. Harney, participating in the battle of Ash Hollow (or the Blue Water), Neb., September 3,

1855, which probably led to his being selected as Captain the first time the Pawnees were called out. . . . Of course, his experience at that time was greater than my brother's; but from what I have been told, he had little aptitude for command . . . McFadden returned to Columbus and married here, but died soon after—probably in 1866" (23).

Frank North's commission as captain, Company A, Pawnee Scouts, signed by the territorial governor, Alvin Saunders, was dated October 24, 1864.

THE CHIVINGTON RAID (page 32)

After the Curtis-Mitchell expedition, and with troops again stationed at Fort Kearny, the Indians were temporarily checked; they "made no further concerted attacks, but confined themselves to small, sporadic hit-and-run raids against isolated points." However, on November 29, 1864, "Colonel J. M. Chivington, formerly presiding elder in the Nebraska Methodist Conference but then commanding the Third Colorado Cavalry, fell without warning on Black Kettle's band of Cheyennes encamped on Sand Creek in Colorado to await peace negotiations. This bloody massacre of a group who had voluntarily surrendered brought to an end any hope for early peace on the plains" (Olson, *History of Nebraska*, 142).

Early in January 1865, Julesburg was attacked and plundered by the hostiles (Sioux, Cheyenne, Arapaho), who then attacked all along the Overland Trail above the forks of the Platte. Before moving north to Powder River, they burned ranches and stage stations and destroyed miles of telegraph wire. In May the Sioux returned: after attacks on a wagon train and a station, they "swung from the road west of Fort Kearney to points east, massacring a force of the Third U. S. Volunteers (Confederate prisoners who had enlisted to fight Indians and had been sent out unarmed, the road being considered perfectly safe), and destroying every stage station and ranch on the Blue from Buffalo to Elm Creek" (Hyde, *Pawnee Indians*, 207).

BLACK HAWK CHIEF'S RUN (page 37)

In *The Fighting Norths*, previously cited, Luther North wrote that "Black Hawk Chief was the fastest runner in the tribe and I believe in the world. One time in 1876 or '77 ..., he ran from Pawnee Agency to the Wichitas, a distance of about 120 miles, inside of 24 hours. The Wichita chief wouldn't believe it, and when the Hawk was ready to start home, asked if he could run back in the same time. When he said he could, the skeptical chief sent a relay horse ahead about 60 miles and told the Pawnee that he would go along. They left at sunrise, the Wichita chief mounted and Big Hawk afoot. Before reaching the relay horse, the old chief's first one gave out. Big Hawk went right on, and the Wichita chief saw no more of him on that trip. Reaching the Pawnee village before sunrise, less than 24 hours after their start from the Wichitas, he found the great runner asleep in his own lodge" (35).

THE SPENCER CARBINE AND THE BALLARD RIFLE (page 38)

The Spencer carbine was a seven-shot .50 caliber weapon proved effective in the last days of the Civil War and was used in the Indian campaigns. It took a rim-fire copper cartridge containing black powder. The Spencer also was produced in .52 and .56 calibers. Because of its use in the Indian Wars, a .50 caliber Spencer 37 inches long and weighing 8.75 pounds was known as the Indian Model (Charles Edward Chapel, *The Gun Collector's Handbook of Values* [New York: Coward-McCann, Inc., 1951], 272).

The Ballard was a single-shot breech-loader with a lever

action. It took a .56 caliber rim-fire cartridge. There also were .45, .46, and .54 caliber Ballards. The weapon was known for its accuracy and dependability (Arcadi Gluckman, *United States Muskets, Rifles and Carbines* [Buffalo: Otto Ulbrich Co., 1948], 301-302).

# III

## GUARDING THE U. P.

[*See Map 4; supplement for this chapter begins on page 69.*]

[*The construction of the Union Pacific Railroad across Nebraska, once it really got under way, proceeded with incredible speed. The official ground-breaking was held in Omaha on December 2, 1863, but during the next two years only forty miles of track were laid. Then in 1866, with the war over, money available from increased government land subsidies, and a large labor force of veterans and Irish immigrants, the rails began to leap westward through the Platte Valley. General Grenville Dodge* was the chief engineer, and the Casement brothers, Jack and Dan, were in charge of construction. Under their vigorous direction by October 1867 the railroad spanned the state.*]

I N THE SPRING of 1866 my brother, James E. North, had a contract to get out piling for a bridge that the Union Pacific Railroad was building across the Loup River, and I worked for him, hauling piles for about a month, and then took a load of freight to North Platte, where Mr. J. P. Becker [1] of Columbus had started a store.

On my way back from North Platte, I stopped at the grading camp of Joe Boyd and Harper. They had contracted to do a mile of grading near Brady Island, and were to have it completed at a specified time. The end of track was within about twenty miles of their work, and they were hiring every team they could get to work for them. I hired out to them and worked there until they had finished their contract, and, as I remember it now, the rails were laid over that mile the next day after it was finished. [2]

When I got home my brother Frank and I commenced putting up our hay, and while we were working in the hay-field something occurred that I think will show about how the Pawnees regarded my brother Frank.

That summer while the Pawnees were on their buffalo hunt the Skee-dee band for some reason got separated from the other three bands, and had no luck in killing buffalo. The Chaw-we, Pete-tah-how-u-rat and Kit-kah-hawk * had very good luck and killed so many buffalo that they cached a lot of dried meat on the Little Blue River. The Skee-dees found the cache and broke it open, taking some of the meat. Later they found buffalo and made a good killing before they came home. The other three bands got home from their hunt first, and when the Skee-dee band came they camped on the south side of the Loup River.

La-tah-cots La-shar, Eagle Chief, head chief of the Skee-

---

1. John Peter Becker (1833-1892) came to America from Germany. One of the group which founded Columbus, he built the first grist-mill and was a pioneer merchant and grain dealer. He was the Pawnee Indian agent from September 1866 until June 1867 (*Past and Present of Platte County, Nebraska* [Chicago: S. J. Clarke Publishing Co., 1915], 267).
2. The end-of-track reached Cozad, Nebraska, on October 5, 1866, and North Platte on December 11. Brady Island is about midway between.

[ 45 ]

dee band, crossed the river and going to the lodge of Pete-ah-La-shar-oo, Chief Man, head chief of the Pawnees,[3] told him about the taking of the meat, and asked him to call a council of all of the chiefs to decide what the Skee-dee band should pay for the meat. The council was called, but they could not agree, and after some pretty fiery speeches had been made, and they were about to declare war, Sha-tah-lah-La-shar, Lone Chief, a Skee-dee, proposed that they all go down to see my brother Frank, Pawnee La-shar, chief of the Pawnees.[4]

There were sixteen chiefs in the Pawnee tribe, four for each band; so one day while we were lying under the wagon in the shade at noon time these sixteen chiefs came riding into our camp, and they were a mighty fine looking lot of men. After shaking hands with both of us they sat down in a circle, filled the pipe, and after smoking told their story. Then Tee-rah-wat-La-shar, Spirit Chief, who was the greatest orator in the Pawnee tribe, made a speech praising my brother as a great warrior, and a man of wisdom, and wound up by telling the trouble they had, and asking my brother to decide how much the Skee-dee should pay. They had all agreed that his decision should be final.

My brother then answered his speech and appointed a committee of four of the chiefs, one from each band, to find out how much meat the Skee-dee had taken, and they were to return the same amount to the families owning the cache.

3. This Pitalesharu is not to be confused with the chief of the same name who was famed for his rescue, in 1816, of a captive Comanche girl about to be sacrificed in the Morning Star spring-planting ceremony. The Skidi alone of the Pawnee bands practiced human sacrifice. See Appendix B.

4. "Major Frank North received the name Pawnee La Shar, meaning Pawnee Chief, after his first fight on the Powder River Expedition of 1865. . . . Though often written White Chief of the Pawnees, the word 'white' was not used as part of the name" (Luther North quoted in Bruce, *The Fighting Norths and Pawnee Scouts*, 35).

The chiefs he chose were Kurux-ta-puk, Fighting Bear, Tee-rah-wat-La-shar, Spirit Chief, Ska-lah-tah-La-shar, Lone Chief, and the other, I believe, was Pete-ah-la-shar, Chief Man. No one questioned his decision. They all said, "How, how," and went home satisfied.

Ska-dick, Crooked Hand, the greatest warrior in the tribe and a Skee-dee, who had been against paying anything for the meat that was taken, said, "Well if our father says that is right it is right, and we will pay."

This man, Crooked Hand, was, as I say, the greatest warrior in the Pawnee tribe. It was said that he had killed more than one hundred of the enemies of the Pawnees. He was a good friend of the whites. In one of the Pawnee battles with the Sioux near Genoa he killed six Sioux warriors, and at the scalp dance after the fight he wore a robe made from the hide of a black and white steer, and fastened around the border of the robe were seventy-one scalps that he had taken. He was a medium size man, quick in action and speech, and also quick tempered, but good natured and always full of fun.*

He told me a story about one of his adventures. The Pawnees and the Yankton Sioux had made a treaty and had visited back and forth, and Crooked Hand had gone to visit the chief of the Yanktons. While he was there a Yankton who had been out with a hunting party came home with a report that while hunting on the Cedar River, they were attacked by a Pawnee war party and all were killed but himself. The Yanktons were very much excited over the news and a lot of the young warriors went to the lodge of the chief where Crooked Hand was visiting, and crowding into the lodge said they were going to kill Crooked Hand. The chief got in front of Crooked Hand and tried to reason with them, but they insisted on killing him. He could not understand the Sioux language, but knew they were after him. So, he stepped out from behind the chief and com-

[ 47 ]

menced talking in the sign language. He told them he had come as a friend and had done nothing to make them angry, but that he was not afraid; he had fought the Yanktons many times; that he was full of Yankton blood up to his neck, and that if they wanted him now to come and get him.

When he got this far with his story, he laughed and said, "Oh, my father, I talked very brave, but down here (and he pointed with his finger to his heart) I was jumping up and down."

Well, the young Yanktons did not get him and that night the chief took him across the Missouri River, gave him two good horses and told him to ride, and three or four days later he came home.

A few days after a war party of Yanktons came down to the Pawnee village and, surprising a lot of Pawnee women in the cornfield, killed a number of them. In the fight that followed the Pawnees killed a great warrior and medicine man of the Yankton tribe. He was killed by the government interpreter, Baptiste Behale, and the Pawnees had a great scalp dance over it.

In the fall of 1866 my brother Frank was appointed government trader of the Pawnees, and in December I went to Michigan to take a course in a business college.

In March 1867 my brother got orders to enlist two hundred Pawnees.[5] They were to be divided into four companies of fifty men each, with two white men, a captain and first lieutenant, to each company, and my brother Frank as major of the battalion, and he was to choose his own officers.

5. The Pawnee Scouts were reactivated upon the authorization of Major General C. C. Augur (q.v.), Commander of the Department of the Platte, to escort Union Pacific engineers and commissioners and to protect grading and working parties from the hostiles.

He telegraphed me offering me a captaincy of one of the companies, and I started at once for home.

The Chicago and Northwestern was the only railroad running into Council Bluffs at that time, and when the train that I was on got as far as Marshalltown, Iowa, the track was so blocked with snow that we were there for eight days before we could get through to Council Bluffs. This made me late in getting home and my brother had gone to Fort Kearney with the scouts before I got there.

My brother J. E. North had bought the goods from Frank and succeeded him as trader. My mother was matron and one of my sisters was teacher at the Indian school at the Pawnee Agency. I rode up from Columbus on horseback to see them, and after spending one day with them came back to Columbus and took the train for Fort Kearney, where I joined my brother Frank and the scouts.

There was one company from each of the four bands of Pawnees, and they were divided and designated as follows: Chow-we (Grand) Pawnees Co. A, E. W. Arnold Captain, Commissioner Lee Lieutenant; Pe-tah-haw-ee-kat (Living Above) Co. B, James Murie Captain, Isaac Davis Lieutenant; Skee-dee (Wolf) Co. C., C. E. Morse Captain, Fred Mathews Lieutenant; Kit-kah-hawk (Republican) Co. D, L. H. North Captain, G. G. Beecher [Becher] Lieutenant.[6]

~~~~~~~~~~

6. Enlisted Indian scouts were in every respect soldiers of the regular army,* but the officers of the Pawnee Scouts were hired by the Quartermaster's Department. Although not in the regular army, they were by courtesy known and referred to as lieutenant, captain, or major (Bruce, *The Fighting Norths and Pawnee Scouts*, 24). Of the men mentioned here, Arnold and Murie have been identified previously (I, footnote 10; II, footnote 5).

Captain Charles E. Morse (1840?-1908), who married Alphonsene North in 1868, was born in New York State. His family moved to Illinois in the '40's. About 1859 he went to California, but returned and settled in Columbus.

Lieutenant Fred Mathews (1831-1890), a Canadian, drove a stage-coach west from Columbus during the years 1864-1866. After serving with the Pawnee Scouts he joined Buffalo Bill Cody's Wild West

The Platte River was still frozen over and we crossed on the ice to the camp, which was on the south bank of the river. We were in camp there for some time, as the government was buying ponies to mount the scouts. The horses came in April, and then we drew rations, arms and equipment, and started for Fort McPherson. The men were armed with Springfield muzzle loading guns and Colts paper cartridge revolvers.

The weather was cold and rainy; the roads were bad, but we made good time by putting in long days, and got to McPherson in three days. After one day's rest, we moved on up the river to above where North Platte now is, and camped over night. The South Platte was bank full, and we were all of one day getting across.

At this time the Sioux chief Spotted Tail with about two thousand Brule Sioux was camped above five or six miles above the town of North Platte on the North Platte River; we were on the South Platte, about five miles from him, and our men were very anxious to make a raid on his camp. My brother explained to them that Spotted Tail's band was not at war with the whites and we must let them alone. Our men did not believe the Sioux were very friendly with the whites, but of course, they would do as my brother said and gave up the idea. At this time the government was furnishing Spotted Tail with rations.

The next day after we crossed the River we moved on west and a day later we camped at the end of the Union Pacific Railroad, which was about where the town of Ogallala

Show, and was the driver in the popular act depicting an Indian attack on the Overland coach.

Lieutenant Gustavus G. Becher (1844-1913) was born in Pilsen, Bohemia. In 1847 his parents emigrated to America, coming to Columbus in 1856. Becher became a prominent Columbus real estate dealer; he was elected to the state legislature in 1895. (North spells his name *Beecher* throughout. This error has been emended to avoid confusion with another Lieutenant Beecher.)

now is. My company and that of Capt. Morse were to act as guards for the track layers, and as they were laying from two to three miles every day, we moved camp about that distance each day. The other two companies were sent to Fort Sedgwick,[7] now Julesburgh, where they were to exchange their muzzle loading rifles for breech-loading Spencer carbines, seven shooters, and then return to relieve us, while we went to make the exchange.

The Indians had been raiding the track layers and grading camps near the end of the track about every day, and they would nearly always kill some of the men and run off a lot of mules and horses. A couple of days after we got there, they made a raid at daylight in the morning, on a grading camp about three miles from our camp, and ran off fifty or sixty mules. My brother, Capt. Morse and myself, with twenty of our best mounted men, started after them, and about ten miles north of Ogallala we overtook them. They left the mules and ran, and we chased them over to the North Platte River. They were well mounted and all got away except one, whom we overtook and killed. This Indian had a package of food in which were several biscuits, or hard tack, bacon and coffee, which was pretty good evidence that he belonged to Spotted Tail's band, as they were getting soldiers rations.

Here I must tell about the killing of this man. One of our scouts that year was a half breed Pawnee whose father was a Spaniard. He was government interpreter at the Pawnee Agency. His name was Baptiste Behale, and when he enlisted he took with him his bow and a quiver full of arrows. When starting after the Indians that morning he took his bow and arrows and left his gun in camp. The Sioux we got was armed with bow and arrows, and after his horse had been

7. Fort Sedgwick, at the junction of Lodge Pole Creek and the South Platte River, was established in August 1864 and abandoned in 1871.

shot he started to run on foot, shooting his arrows at us until they were all gone, when Baptiste, who was close to him, shot him with an arrow. It struck him under the right shoulder, went clear through his body and came out low down on the left side. He stopped, took hold of the spike end of the arrow, pulled it through himself, fitted it on to his bow, shot it back at Baptiste and fell over dead. Baptiste threw himself flat down over his horse's neck and the arrow whizzed over his neck about two inches too high.*

This put a stop to the raiding of the graders camps and nothing was too good for the scouts when we brought the mules back to the owners.

When Captains Arnold and Murie got back from Fort Sedgewick, Capt. Morse and I started to go there. On the second day, when we were within ten miles of Sedgewick but on the north side of the river, which was very high, we saw some horsemen across the river. We halted and got out our field glasses to look, and found it was part of a company of cavalry from Fort Sedgewick, and while we were looking, about a hundred warriors dashed over the hills from the south and attacked them. The soldiers ran for the fort and we started for the river, to go to their assistance. We plunged off the bank into swimming water and were swept down stream for some distance and on to a sand bar on the same side of the river as we started from. Three of our horses were drowned and all of our ammunition was wet, and as we had paper cartridges we were pretty nearly helpless. The Indians chased the soldiers to the fort killing nine of them.

We went on up the river on the north side and camped opposite the fort. The next morning we got a flat boat that belonged to the government, tied several lariat ropes to it, and Capt. Morse loaded his guns in it, and he and I got into the boat. His men grabbed the ropes, gave the war whoop and plunged in. The water was swimming deep in some places, but most of the way they could wade, and we got across all right.

The carbines that we got in exchange for the muzzle loaders were old guns, and a good many of them were defective, so we had to examine each one to see that all were right. The ordinance sergeant would hand me a carbine, I would put a cartridge in the breech, then throw down the lever of the breechblock, and if the shell slipped through all right I would pull the lever up and the shell would be forced into the barrel of the gun. Many of the guns would not work and the shells would not go in. When I found one of those, I would hand it back and try another.

General Emory [8] was in command at Fort Sedgewick at this time, and he came over to the stock house where we were getting the carbines. When I got one of the guns that the cartridge stuck in and handed it back to the sergeant, he said: "What is the matter with that gun." I told him the shell stuck. He said: "Let me see it," and I handed it to him. The shell was about half way into the chamber. He took hold of the lever and gave a quick jerk and the breechblock struck the cartridge—they were rim fire—with so much force that it exploded and the whole charge of powder blew out into his face.

Fortunately he was wearing glasses and they saved his eyes, but the blood spurted from his face in streams. He did not have anything further to say, and left us to select our own guns. It took us two days to get the guns, ammunition, rations and forage and haul it across the river in the boat.

We went into camp on the north side of the river, and

8. William Hensley Emory (1811-1877), a Marylander and a West Point graduate, served in the Mexican and Civil wars and played an important part in securing Missouri for the Union. In 1876 he retired with the rank of brigadier general.

that evening General W. T. Sherman [9] and General Augur [10] came from the end of the track with several troops of cavalry. My brother was with them. They were going out to inspect the frontier forts, and we were to accompany them. We marched up the Platte River as far as Fort Morgan.[11] Many of the soldiers were deserting, and one night the man who was on guard over the tent of General Sherman deserted and took one of the horses belonging to an officer. The next day General Sherman ordered my brother to furnish the guard for headquarters, and for the remainder of the time that we were with them, there was a Pawnee Indian scout on guard over the tent of the head of the United States Army, and there were no more horses stolen from the staff officers.

In telling of the organizing of the Pawnee scouts I said there were two white men to each company. I should have said three, as there were two commissioned officers and one non-commissioned officer, a commissary sergeant. The sergeant of my company in 1867 we knew as Billy Harvey, and as I will have more to say of him later, we will call him by that name now. He was a quiet, low spoken and very pleasant fellow, and somewhat eccentric. He was a crack

9. William Tecumseh Sherman (1820-1891) was born in Ohio and graduated from West Point in 1841. After eleven years in the service he retired to enter private business, but re-enlisted at the outbreak of the Civil War. One of the most famous of the Union leaders, in 1866 he was promoted to lieutenant general and commanded the Military Division of the Missouri. He succeeded Grant as general and commander of the army in 1869.

10. Christopher Columbus Augur (1821-1898), also a West Point graduate, served in the Mexican War and became commander of cadets at West Point in 1861. He won promotion to major general of Volunteers and brevet colonel in the regular army for gallantry in action in 1862. After the Civil War, Augur commanded various military departments, including the Department of the Platte.

11. Fort Morgan, near the South Platte River in present-day Morgan County, Colorado, was known successively as Camp Tyler and Camp Wardell before it was named for Colonel C. C. Morgan in 1866.

rifle shot and at that time he carried a Ballard 44 caliber rifle.

One day, while going up the Platte, Billy and I rode off into the hills to get an antelope. We soon saw some and managed to get within shooting distance. I held the horses and Billy crept up to the top of the hill and shot. He seldom missed a shot, and I was about to ride up to him, when he reloaded his gun and shot again. He looked for a moment, put in another shell, and fired the third shot. Then he stood up, swung his gun around and threw it as far as he could in the direction of the antelope and came down towards me.

I said: "What's the matter?", and he replied, "They weren't more than seventy yards away!", and got on his horse and started off.

"Aren't you going after your gun?" I asked.

He answered, "No, I don't want it."

"Well," I said, "I do," and I rode over and picked it up. As soon as I looked at it, I saw what was the matter; the front sight had been knocked over to one side about an eighth of an inch. When I called his attention to it he grinned and said, "Well, you can have it," and although he carried the gun afterward, he always said it was mine, and three years later I had it for good.

On leaving Fort Morgan we went north until we came to Crow Creek, then crossed the divide to Lodge Pole Creek, then up the Lodge Pole one day, where we ran into a small war party of Arapahoes, and after a running fight that took us ten miles, we overtook and killed two of them and captured two mules and one pony.*

A few days later, when near Fort Laramie,[12] we were

12. Fort Laramie was established as a fur-trading post in June 1834. After its purchase by the government from the American Fur Company in 1849, it was converted into a military post and became an

ordered back to the line of the Union Pacific Railroad to guard a camp at Granite Canyon, 18 miles west of where Cheyenne City was afterward built. After resting for a couple of days at Granite Canyon, my brother and I, with ten men and four wagons, started for Fort Sanders [13] for rations and forage. On the second day, when we were within three or four miles of Sanders, he and I rode on ahead, and just as we were riding up to the officers quarters we saw perhaps eight or ten Indians riding away to the south as fast as they could go.

The officer in command who knew my brother, came out to meet us. He was laughing and said, pointing toward the fleeing Indians, "There goes Little Crow and his warriors. He is an Arapahoe. He came up here to make a complaint against the Pawnee scouts for killing a couple of his warriors over at Cheyenne Pass. I told him that his warriors had some mules that had been taken from emigrants over on the Laramie River. Then he said that he would like to meet the white chief of the Pawnees; he would fix him." It was about that time Frank and I came in sight, and the officer pointed to us and said, "There comes Major North now, you can talk to him." Little Crow seemed to have pressing business at home, for he certainly got away from there in a hurry.

After drawing rations and forage at Fort Sanders we returned to Granite Canyon, and a few days later I was ordered to Crow Creek, where there was a graders camp, and while at this camp someone built a log house on the west side of the creek opposite my camp, and that was the first house that was built in Cheyenne, Wyoming.*

important stopping place on the Overland Trail. It was abandoned on April 20, 1890.

13. Fort Sanders was a few miles south of the present town of Laramie, Wyoming.

Not long after, I was ordered to the end of the track to guard the track layers. The Company A. of the scouts was at the end of the track and I was to relieve them, and they were to go farther west to a grader camp. The end of the track was about where Sidney is now. When I got there they were laying three miles per day, so we were soon up to Potter Station. I had to go to Fort Sedgewick every ten days for rations and forage. I usually went to Julesburgh on the train and got a saddle horse there to ride over to the fort. I would be in Julesburgh for a couple of nights, and they were pretty wild nights too.

There were about two thousand people in Julesburgh at that time, made up mostly of gamblers, saloon men, dance hall people and freighters; everyone went armed and there were killings almost every day. One evening I was sitting outside the hotel with perhaps half a dozen other men, when a man came walking down the middle of the street with a big Colts 45 in his hand. One of the men in our crowd said, "That is Slim Jim, he runs the dance hall up on the corner, and Swede Charley got one of his girls from him and he is going over to kill him."

Another man said, "Charley is a bad man; Jim better let him alone."

Jim crossed the street to Charley's restaurant. There were a couple of steps up to the door, and he stepped up, opened the door, and went inside, closing the door behind him. We heard two shots and Jim opened the door and walked out. He crossed the street and when he was just in front of us, he stopped, stooped down and pulled up his trouser's leg and looked at his ankle, then pushed it down again, straightened up and walked up the middle of the street to his dance hall, a full block from there. Several of the girls were watching him from the back door, and when he got within about twenty feet of them he stumbled, dropped his gun and fell forward on his face, dead.

[ 57 ]

I was told afterward that he was shot through the heart. Swede Charley, I believe, was never arrested for the killing; everyone said it was a case of selfdefense.

About the first of August 1867 the Cheyenne Indians* under Chief Turkey Leg derailed a freight train on the Union Pacific Railroad near Plum Creek Station, Nebraska.[14] They killed all of the train crew and also a party of men who were repairing telegraph lines near Plum Creek Station. One of the line men was scalped and left for dead, but recovered. This man, whose name was Wilson, after being scalped, lay still until the Indians rode away. The Indian that scalped him dropped the scalp when he jumped on his horse, and when Wilson got up after they had gone, he found his scalp and took it along with him. He was three days getting to Omaha, where he could have medical attention. A Dr. Moore attended him, and after Wilson got well he had the scalp framed and took it with him back to England. About twenty-five years later he sent the scalp back to Dr. Moore, who gave it to the Public Library in Omaha, where it is now, kept under a glass case.*

Immediately after the derailing of the train at Plum Creek a company of the scouts was ordered there. My brother went with them, and a few days after their arrival there the Cheyennes came back to make another raid. I had asked and obtained a leave of absence to go home, and when the train reached Plum Creek, my brother was waiting for me at the depot with an extra saddle horse.

He said there was a report that the Cheyennes were com-

14. A Cheyenne named Spotted Wolf was the actual leader of the party that wrecked the train, according to George Bird Grinnell in *The Fighting Cheyennes* (New York: Charles Scribner's Sons, 1915), 245 n.

ing back, that he had started Capt. Murie with the Company, that if I wanted to go along it was all right, but that he would advise me to go on home, as he thought it very doubtful that there were now any Indians in that part of the country. I decided to go on home, and so missed out on the battle with Turkey Leg. Before the train I was on got out of sight I saw my brother overtake his command and start to ford the river.

I got home that evening and the next morning got a telegram from my brother saying he had defeated Turkey Leg, killing seventeen of his warriors and capturing a woman and a boy, besides taking thirty-five head of stock and recovering a lot of the plunder that they had taken when they raided the train, and this without the loss of a single man, though a couple of horses were killed and one man wounded.

When he crossed the river and saw the Indians they were on the south side of Plum Creek. My brother had forty men and there were one hundred fifty of the Cheyennes. There was an old bridge across Plum Creek near the old stage station, and that was where they met. My brother and ten or twelve of his men crossed the bridge, but the rest of the Pawnees tried to ford the creek, and their horses stuck in the mud. The men jumped off their horses and ran up the bank on foot. The Cheyennes were close to them, and at the first volley they killed seven of them. The Cheyennes turned and ran back to where their women were on the hills, and as soon as the men could get their horses out of the mud they followed them.

When the Cheyennes got to their women and children, they stopped and fought, while the women and children threw off the packs and mounted the horses and ran away. After that it was a running fight all the afternoon, and at night, when the Pawnees turned back, they had three prisoners, a woman, a boy and a little girl, but in crossing the Platte River in the dark, the little girl, who was perhaps ten years old, got away, and in some manner found her way back to her people and was still living the last I heard of her.[15]

A short time after this fight Generals Sherman, Harney, Terry, Auger, and Sanborn, of the Army, and N. G. Taylor, Colonel Tappan and Senator Henderson, came to the North Platte to hold a council with the Brules Sioux under Spotted Tail, Man Afraid of his Horses, Man that Walks under the Ground, Pawnee Killer, Standing Elk and other chiefs of the Brules, and Turkey Leg and other chiefs of the Cheyennes.[16]

My brother went to North Platte on the train with the Commissioners, and in the council tent met Turkey Leg, who knew him from having seen him in the fight at Plum Creek. He asked my brother through an interpreter about the prisoners he had, and said he had some white prisoners he would change for them. My brother agreed and Turkey Leg sent a messenger to his camp on Medicine Creek and brought in three girls, two boys and a baby, and a few days after my brother took his two prisoners to North Platte and the ex-

15. In the original manuscript, the following note appears: *The Cheyennes named her Island Woman because she escaped while they were crossing an Island in the Platte River. The boy, from the circumstances of his capture, was called Pawnee.* In all probability, this note was supplied by George Bird Grinnell.

16. This was the Peace Commission created by an Act of Congress, June 30, 1867, with the objectives of removing the causes of the Indian wars and of persuading the Indians to accept reservation status.* The Commission was led by Colonel J. B. Sanborn. Its members, in addition to the four regular army generals mentioned in the text, were N. G. Taylor, the Commissioner of Indian Affairs and a former Methodist minister with philanthropic leanings; Senator John Henderson of Missouri, Chairman of the Senate Committee on Indian Affairs; and Colonel S. F. Tappan of Colorado, a friend of the Indians. The meeting at North Platte was held about September 21, 1867 ("Report to the President by the Indian Peace Commission, January 7, 1868," *Report of the Commissioner of Indian Affairs 1868* [Washington: Government Printing Office, 1868], 26-27; Stanley Vestal, *Warpath and Council Fire* [New York: Random House, 1948], 115-116; Omaha *Weekly Herald*, September 19, 1867).

change was made in the railroad eating house. Two of the girls were named Martin [17] and had been captured several months before, a few miles south of Grand Island, the other girl and the two boys, I believe, were captured somewhere on the Solomon River.*

When I got back to my camp from my visit home I was ordered to Cheyenne. My brother came up from Plum Creek and went along; we there joined a couple of troops of cavalry and went to Fort Laramie. After camping there for a day or two we were ordered back to Pine Bluffs.

On the way to Pine Bluffs we met a band of about 100 Sioux in charge of Nick Janise.[18] Most of them were warriors, but there were some women and children. When we first came in sight of them we thought they were a war party and started to charge them, but Janise came toward us on a gallop waving a white flag, and we stopped. When he got to us he said that he was taking the Sioux to Laramie, where they were to meet some representative of the government to make a treaty. Our boys were anxious for a fight, but Frank told them no, so we stood there and Janise went back to his

17. The sisters were the daughters of Peter Campbell, who had a farm near the present town of Doniphan, Hall County, Nebraska. They were captured along with their twin brothers on July 24, 1867. The Martin family living near Grand Island had been raided in 1864, and North probably confused the names (Plattsmouth, Nebraska, *Nebraska Herald,* August 7, 1867; John R. Campbell, "The Indian Raid of 1867," *Nebraska State Historical Society Collections* [Lincoln: 1913], Vol. XVII, 259-262).

18. Nick Janis served as interpreter and scout for the government and was with the Powder River Expedition of 1865. A French trader born in St. Louis, he had been employed by the American Fur Company, by James Bordeaux, and others. He married a Brûlé Sioux, and in later life was known for his knowledge of Indian genealogy (Interview with Mrs. Nichols Janis, Eli S. Ricker Interviews, Tablet 8; Interview with William Garnett, Tablet 22, Ricker Collection, Nebraska State Historical Society).

party and turned them off the trail and passed by us about fifty yards away. I guess that was the first time that the Pawnees and Sioux ever got so close together without exchanging shots.

Three days later we reached Pine Bluffs in a snowstorm. The end of the track had just reached there, and as soon as Frank reported by wire to General Augur at Omaha, we got orders to march to Fort Kearney, Nebraska. Frank telegraphed again, telling of the weakened condition of our horses and the deep snow, and Augur told him to ship to Kearney. Early the next morning the cars were there ready for us, and we loaded up and started and got to Kearney some time that night.

The rest of the Battalion had been ordered to Kearney and had arrived there the night before, and we went into camp on the south side of the river near the fort, where we stayed until we were mustered out. I was sent out several times with scouting parties both north and south of the Union Pacific Railroad, going as far north as the North Loup, where we found and killed many elk and deer, but saw no sign of hostile Indians. On our trips to the south we went as far as the Solomon River, and saw great herds of buffalo, but no Indians.

While we were at Kearney a party of Union Pacific Railroad officials came out from the East, and we took them out on a buffalo hunt. In the party was Sidney Dillon, President of the railroad, Oakes Ames, Thomas A. Durant, George Francis Train, and several others, whose names I have forgotten.[19] My brother's wife and our younger sister, who were

~~~~~~~~~~

19. The Union Pacific sponsored this excursion of newspaper men and railroad officials to end-of-track. Thomas Clark Durant, the vice president of the railroad, organized the Crédit Mobilier, the construction company which built it. Oakes Ames, Congressman from Massachusetts (1863-1873), was also an organizer of the Crédit Mobilier and a director of the U.P. He was censured by the Forty-second Congress for his part in the financial manipulations involved

visiting in our camp, were also on this hunt. We had an ambulance for officials to ride in until we found buffalo, when they were given saddle horses that we had taken along for them to ride in the chase.

Fifteen miles from the fort we found a band of about one hundred, and Mr. Dillon, Mr. Durant and George Francis Train mounted their horses to join in the chase. The rest of the party stayed in the ambulance and watched the fun. I had picked out a good reliable buffalo horse for Mr. Dillon, and explained to him as well as I could what he should do, and had given him my revolver, for I always used a rifle. When we got as near to the herd as we could without frightening them, my brother gave the word and the chase was on.

The ground was dry and by the time we overtook the buffalo the air was filled with such clouds of dust that it was hard to see a buffalo until you were within a few feet of it. I had a very fast horse and overtook them before anyone else, and thought I would cut one out and get it away from the dust where the people in the ambulance would get a good sight of it, but just as I had succeeded in getting a fine three year old heifer out to the edge of the herd, my horse stepped in a hole and fell, and that finished my hunt. The horse jumped up and ran away after the herd and I was left on foot.

About this time Mr. Dillon went past me. He was not a very good horseman and had perhaps lost his stirrups the

---

in the building of the Union Pacific. Ames and his associates brought about Durant's removal from the management shortly after the railroad had been completed.

George Francis Train (1829-1904) was a noted promoter, author, and eccentric. He was chief of publicity for the new railroad, boomed townsites, and built many a paper city. The ebullient Train reported on the progress of the excursion in telegraphic despatches and often referred to it afterward in speeches. By his count, the excursionists killed eighteen buffalo (Omaha *Weekly Herald*, October 17, 24, 1867).

[ 63 ]

first jump, and when he went by me he was holding on to the pommel with one hand and in the other was the revolver sticking straight out to the right, the bridle reins were flapping on the pony's neck, and he was doing his best to overtake the buffalo, but, like my horse, he found a hole and went down, and Mr. Dillon was badly bruised but no bones were broken. Our men caught the horses after a long chase.

In the meantime the herd had scattered and the Indians succeeded in getting a couple of old bulls back near the ambulance, where one of the men killed one with bow and arrow. He shot him with two arrows; the first one was driven in up to the feathers, and the second was driven clear through and dropped out on the opposite side. Mr. Durant killed one buffalo, and our men killed quite a number. My brother's wife and our sister, who was sixteen years old, were in the thick of the chase and had as much fun as anyone. I think this was the only buffalo hunt that either of them ever took part in.

In December we were mustered out and returned to the Pawnee Agency, where I went to work for my brother J. E. North, as clerk in the trading post.

The Pawnees had a very successful hunt that fall, and we got about five hundred robes from them that winter, besides a lot of beaver skins and other furs, and I bought a good many ponies from them. When on their winter hunt they had to ride their best horses pretty hard, and they always came home very thin. As the Indians never made any provisions for wintering their horses, they sold those that were so thin that they thought them likely to die before spring. There was much hay put up by the settlers near the reservation, and we could buy it cheaply, and if the ponies lived through until spring, the Indians would buy them back. The thinnest ones were usually the fastest and best buffalo horses, and as the Indians got an annual money payment of forty thousand dollars from the Government, they had something to buy with.

In the spring of 1868 my brother Frank got orders to enlist two companies of scouts and came to the reserve after them. He offered me the captaincy of one of the companies and, of course, I said I would go, but J. E. said, "What shall I do without you?", for he could not talk the language very well.

Frank said to me, "Well, General Augur thinks he will want one or two more companies in a couple of weeks, so you had better wait until I get them, and in the meantime J. E. can look for someone to take your place."

I agreed to that and so missed being with the scouts that year, as no others were enlisted after the first two companies.

Captain C. E. Morse had command of A Company, with Billy Harvey as Lieutenant, and Capt. Fred Mathews of B Company, with G. G. Becher as his Lieutenant. They were divided into squads of twenty men and stationed at different points along the Union Pacific Railroad, from Wood River Station to Julesburgh, and I believe there were only two raids made between those points that summer. A small war party ran off some stock belonging to some settlers near Wood River, but Billy Harvey got out after them, and after following them north of the Loup River about forty miles, he overtook them and in the fight that ensued he killed two of them and recovered all the stock they had stolen.

The other raid was near Ogallala, where the Indians piled some ties on the track and attacked a train containing a carload of workmen. My brother got there with part of a company of the scouts and drove them off before they had done much harm, though I believe that some of the workmen were wounded. He followed the Indians to the North Platte near

Ash Hollow, where they had a camp which they abandoned, and then crossed the North Platte River. He captured thirty head of horses and all the camp equipage, and killed three of the Indians.

In July of that year, he took twenty-five men from each of the companies and with Capt. Morse and Capt. Mathews went south from Plum Creek to the Republican River on a scout. A party of gentlemen from Chicago, I believe, accompanied him to hunt buffalo.* The Pawnees from the reservation with the Omaha and Ponca Indians, numbering altogether about five thousand, were on their summer hunt in the Republican country, and my brother joined them. There were plenty of buffalo in the country, and my brother's guests killed quite a number of buffalo.

After traveling with the Pawnees for a few days, he decided to return to the railroad. They were camped on Mud Creek at this time, and the Pawnees had gone off to the East to make a surround of a large herd of buffalo. My brother with his scouts was in camp when one of his men came to his tent and said there was a small herd of buffalo three or four miles off to the west of the camp. As my brother intended to start for his camp at Willow Island the next day, he thought it would be a good plan to kill some buffalo and take the meat with them. Leaving Capt. Mathews in camp with twenty-five men, he and Capt. Morse went after the buffalo.

They had killed a number of buffalo and were pretty well scattered, when my brother noticed that there seemed to be quite a number of Indians in sight besides his scouts, but they were Pawnees. Just then one of his men rode up to him and said, "We are surrounded by Sioux."

My brother asked, "Where are the rest of our men?"

The Indian answered, "They are scattered everywhere, but Capt. Morse is over that hill," pointing.

They rode over the hill, where they found Morse with

four more of the scouts, and just then two more joined them, making nine in all, seven Pawnees and my brother and Capt. Morse. By this time the Sioux had gotten together to make a charge; there were about one hundred of them.

My brother, who had a fast running horse, asked Capt. Morse how his horse was, and he answered that he was exhausted, and could go no further.

"Then," said my brother, "we will fight here."

They dismounted and led their horses into a ravine, where they were somewhat sheltered by the bank. They were armed with Spenser carbines, and when the Indians charged they waited until they were pretty close before firing, then pumped their guns as fast as they could. The Indians split and went on either side of them, but done such good shooting that they killed six of the nine horses and wounded two of the men. They themselves left five dead men and several horses.

They rode off about a mile, where they got ready for another charge, and soon came again, but broke before they got very near and did no damage. Then they got together on a hill about a half mile away, where they made ready for another charge.

There was one man who appeared to be the leader or chief and who carried a small American flag that they had probably captured in some fight with the United States soldiers; perhaps from a party of ten soldiers and a lieutenant, all of whom had been killed some distance west of there not long before. My brother made up his mind if this man was killed, the others would not be so anxious to tackle them, so leaving his men and Capt. Morse where they were he crept up the ravine for some distance, and got within about two hundred yards of this man and shot him off his horse. After this the others seemed to lose heart, and rode back over the hill out of sight, and my brother ran back to his men.

The Indians soon returned, however, and surrounded

[ 67 ]

them and kept them penned up there all afternoon. In the meantime, a large party of Sioux warriors, perhaps a thousand men, had attacked the Pawnee camp, and as the Pawnees were scattered out killing buffalo, it was some time before enough of them could get together to put up much of a fight.

When they did begin to fight they began to drive the Sioux, and with the help of the twenty-five scouts under Capt. Mathews they slowly drove them back past the ravine where my brother and his men were. They were just in time, as their ammunition was about all gone, and as it was a very hot day they suffered from thirst, but they got out with only the two men wounded, though two of the scouts were killed farther out, and quite a number of the Pawnees were killed in the camp.

My brother's guests had every day been expressing the wish that they might see a battle between the Pawnees and the Sioux, and they certainly had their wish gratified and were ready and anxious to get back to the railroad.

The next day my brother with his scouts left the Pawnees and returned to the camp at Willow Island, and in the fall they were mustered out and sent home to the Pawnee Reservation.

# SUPPLEMENT

GENERAL DODGE (page 44, headnote)

As George Bird Grinnell mentions in the foreword, Grenville Mellen Dodge (1831-1916) began to figure at a very early date in the life of Major Frank North. Born in Massachusetts, as a young man Dodge was associated with Peter Dey in conducting Iowa railroad surveys and lived in Council Bluffs. He first met Frank North in 1856 shortly after the Norths had moved from Iowa to Nebraska. During his service in the Civil War Dodge won commendation from General Grant and rose to the rank of major general of Volunteers. In 1865 he commanded the Department of the Missouri. In May 1866 he resigned from the army to become chief engineer of the Union Pacific. Dodge was active in railroad work for a half century, and at one time (1892) was president of the Union Pacific, Denver and Gulf Railroad.

INDIAN NAMES (page 45)

Although North's spellings of Indian names, including those of the bands, are inconsistent, e.g., *Chaw-we = Chaui; Kit-kah-hawk = Kitkehaki; Pete-ah-how-u-rat = Pitahaue-rat; Skee-dee = Skidi*, they are reasonably consistent as to sound, when pronounced aloud. His translations of Indian names are sometimes inconsistent, too, though conceptually similar, e.g., in this book he refers to "the greatest orator in the Pawnee tribe" as Spirit Chief (*Tee-rah-wat-La-shar*) and

[ 69 ]

elsewhere uses the spelling *Tira Wahut La Shar*, which he translates as Sky Chief (Bruce, *The Fighting Norths and Pawnee Scouts*, 20).

In regard to the translation of Indian names, George H. Roberts, son of Pawnee Scout Rush Roberts (*Latakuts Kalahar*), wrote: "There is much imperfection in the translation of Indian names, due to mistakes by interpreters many years ago . . . but after prominent characters have become well known by names even incorrectly interpreted, it is impracticable, or at least difficult to change them" (Bruce, *The Fighting Norths and Pawnee Scouts*, 18).

CROOKED HAND (page 47)

"I not only knew him well," wrote Luther North, "but considered him one of my best friends. . . . I was at the Pawnee Reservation the day when Crooked Hand killed six Sioux with his own hand and three horses were shot under him; and personally saw him on his return to the village that evening. He was covered with blood, and a Sioux arrow had been driven through his neck from the front as he was facing one or more of his antagonists. It had gone into his throat on one side of the windpipe, and about half the length of the arrow protruded from the back of his neck. The old Indian doctor at the Reservation had to cut off the iron head before he could pull it out. Crooked Hand was laid up for some time and his throat probably never healed; but he lived 10 to 11 years after that fight and killed some more enemies of his people." North believed that Crooked Hand died about 1873, aged somewhere between forty and forty-five. "At one time when he had plenty of scalps, some white man said, 'I suppose you are not afraid any more, as you have been so lucky in battle?' Crooked Hand answered, 'Every enemy I kill brings me so much nearer my own death. Who knows but that I have killed enough, and will be the next?'" (Bruce, *The Fighting Norths and Pawnee Scouts*, 18).

According to the same source, George H. Roberts said that the name Ska-dick or Crooked Hand probably came from the word *Skah-dece:* paralyzed hand (18).

REGULAR ARMY STATUS OF PAWNEE SCOUTS (page 49, footnote 6)

Thirty-ninth Congress, 1st Session, Chapter 299—An Act to increase and fix the Military Peace Establishment of the United States (approved July 28, 1866); Section 6.— . . . ; and the President is hereby authorized to enlist and employ in the Territories and Indian country a force of Indians, not to exceed One Thousand, to act as scouts, who shall receive the pay and allowances of cavalry soldiers, and be discharged whenever the necessity for their further employment is abated, or at the discretion of the department commander.

"COUNTING COUP": POSTSCRIPT TO THE BEHALE INCIDENT (page 52)

Baptiste Behale not only narrowly missed being winged by his own arrow, he also was deprived of credit for the kill. According to an account by Luther North in Bruce, *The Fighting Norths and Pawnee Scouts*:

> As soon as the Sioux fell, Behale rode down on him and leaned over to strike the fallen foe with his bow—that was what was called "counting coup." But the horse shied off and Baptiste failed to touch him, whereupon a Pawnee warrior rushed in and struck the dead Sioux with his bow, afterward claiming the honor of having been the first to count coup on him. Behale also claimed that honor, because he was the first to reach the enemy, and would have struck him if the horse had not shied. They held a council

in camp that night, and the wise men were unanimous in awarding the honor to the Pawnee.

His name, I believe, had been Fox; and as that brave act gave him the privilege of changing his name, according to the custom of the Plains tribes, it was done that night by the medicine men. Thus he became Luk-tuts-oo-ri-ee-Coots (*Brave Shield*).

I asked them how they figured the Pawnee as deserving the honor, as Baptiste had actually killed the Sioux. They said—anybody might shoot a person at a distance, but a warrior had to be brave to ride up and strike a man he didn't know was dead or not. It was their rule to award the honor to the first man that struck the body of the foe— and Behale had missed him! That shows the curious way the Pawnees had of giving credit to the warriors for bravery in a fight (27).

RUNNING FIGHT WITH THE ARAPAHO (page 55)

This may have been the occasion which ended in North's being given an Indian name. In Bruce, *The Fighting Norths and Pawnee Scouts*, he wrote: "After that running fight with the Arapahos near Cheyenne Pass in 1867, the Pawnees called me *Kit-E-Butts* (Little Chief)" (56).

The Arapaho was an important Plains tribe closely associated with the Cheyenne. According to tribal tradition, they had migrated west and south from the Minnesota region. The Northern Arapaho centered about the Upper North Platte River, while the southern branch settled on the Arkansas. In 1867 the Southern Arapaho and the Southern Cheyenne were placed on a reservation in Oklahoma. When it was opened to white settlement in 1892, the Indians were given allotments in severalty. The Northern Arapaho were placed on the Wind River Reservation in Wyoming in 1876 (F. W. Hodge, *Handbook of American Indians North of Mexico*, Smithsonian Institution, Bur. of Ethnology Bul. 30 [Washington: Government Printing Office, 1912], 72-73).

CHEYENNE, WYOMING (page 56)

On July 4, 1867, General Grenville Dodge designated a point on Crow Creek as a future railroad terminal, and there were several buildings up before the official survey was completed on July 19. General Dodge recalled that "While we camped there, the Indians swooped down out of the ravine of Crow Creek and attacked a Mormon grading train and outfit that had followed our trail and killed two of its men; . . . but we saved their stock and started the grave-yard of the future city" (Grenville M. Dodge, *How We Built the Union Pacific Railway and Other Papers and Addresses* [Council Bluffs: The Monarch Printing Co., 1910], 23).

THE CHEYENNE (page 58)

The Cheyenne, like the Arapaho, were an important Plains people of the Algonquian family who had migrated from Minnesota along the Cheyenne River and on past the Black Hills to the Upper Platte. The Northern Cheyenne stayed in this area and now live in Montana; the Southern Cheyenne ranged along the Arkansas. Like other Plains tribes, the Cheyenne were primarily nomadic buffalo hunters. They are tall, handsome people and were brave warriors. Their heroic and hopeless resistance to white domination is perhaps the most striking chapter in the history of the Plains Indian Wars (Hodge, *Handbook of American Indians*, 250-257).

THE SURVIVOR AND THE SCALP (page 58)

The name of the scalped man was not Wilson, but Thompson. According to a contemporary newspaper story:

One of the victims reaches Omaha alive—He brings his own scalp along with him! Mr. William Thompson ar-

[ 73 ]

rived from the west yesterday evening. He is one of the victims of the late massacre and is being provided for at the Hamilton House under good care under the professional charge of Drs. Peck and Moore. Mr. Thompson brings his own scalp with him—a painful object to look at —while he is a great sufferer for the loss of it and from a flesh wound in the arm from an Indian bullet and a severe cut in the neck from a knife (Omaha *Weekly Herald*, August 22, 1867).

Henry M. Stanley, the noted English explorer and journalist, who was in Omaha at the time, described Thompson's arrival in *My Early Travels and Adventures in America and Asia* (New York: Charles Scribner's Sons, 1895). He noted that "In a pail of water by his side was his scalp about nine inches in length and four in width, somewhat resembling a drowned rat as it floated, curled up, on the water" (I, pp. 155-156). Dr. Richard C. Moore related that Thompson was placed under his care thirty-six hours after the scalping. The scalp was nine inches by seven. After Thompson's return to Walburn, England, he sent the scalp back; it is still on display at the Omaha Public Library. (Letter from Dr. R. C. Moore to Clarence Paine, January 28, 1914; letter from Frank Gibson, Librarian, Omaha Public Library, to Donald F. Danker, August 31, 1960.)

THE PEACE COMMISSION AND THE TREATY OF 1868 (page 60, footnote 16)

This commission was an attempt to implement the peace advocates' theory that "it is cheaper to feed than to fight the Indians." In October 1867, the commissioner negotiated treaties with the Kiowa, Comanche, Apache, and a part of the Arapaho and Cheyenne at the Medicine Creek Council near the Arkansas River. The Comanche and Kiowa relinquished their claims to the Texas Panhandle; and they and the other participating tribes accepted removal to new reservations. However, the hostiles under Red Cloud (q.v.) refused to come to Fort Laramie for negotiations while the new forts along the Bozeman Trail were occupied by the whites. In April 1868, the commissioners returned and acceded to the Indian demands.

The Treaty of Fort Laramie provided that Fort C. F. Smith, Fort Phil Kearny, and Fort Reno be abandoned. The area north of the North Platte and east of the Big Horns was to be regarded as unceded Indian territory, and the portion of present-day South Dakota west of the Missouri was to be a Sioux reservation. The United States agreed to build an agency on the Missouri River and furnish food for four years and clothing for thirty. The treaty was signed by Red Cloud on November 6, 1868, and ratified by the U. S. Senate on February 16, 1869. (*Dictionary of American History,* III [New York: Charles Scribner's Sons, 1942], 246, 270.)

TURKEY LEG'S CAPTIVES (page 61)

The Omaha *Weekly Herald* (September 26, 1867) printed a report of the exchange and of the captivity which read in part:

> Of course these poor girls were subject to great suffering. They have been in captivity two long months playing the part of squaws to the Indians to whom they were assigned by lot. They complained of no harder work than carrying water and say they were generally well treated. . . . He [the reporter] says indeed sun burnt and in squaw costume they look like Indians . . . the two boys were fat and happy and rode their ponies in true Ogallala style. They seem to think the Indian business was not such a bad thing to take after all. . . . We understand the captives were set free in exchange for Indian prisoners taken by the Pawnee Scouts.

[ 75 ]

Gentlemen buffalo hunters (page 66)

An account of the hunt by J. J. Aldrich appeared in the Omaha *Weekly Herald*, August 19 and 26, under the heading "Diary of Twenty Days Sport Buffalo Hunting on the Plains with the Pawnees Accompanied by Major North USA and an escort of forty US Pawnee Soldiers, Captain Morris and Mathews and four Private Gentlemen." Besides Aldrich, the "private gentlemen" were F. W. Dunn, editor of the Chicago *Freeman;* G. W. Magee, a Chicago merchant; and Sumner Oaks, the son of the proprietor of Omaha's St. Charles Hotel.

# IV

## ON THE TRAIL OF SIOUX
## HORSE THIEVES

[See Map 5; supplement for this chapter begins on page 92.]

IN JULY 1868 a war party of Sioux from Spotted Tail's camp made a raid near the Pawnee Village * and ran off a bunch of horses from the Gerrard ranche. Alan Gerrard [1] followed them on horseback for a mile or two, when they turned on him, and as there were seven of them and he was armed only with a muzzle loading rifle, he took one shot at them and ran for the house. He was mounted on a very fast horse and easily outrun them. He immediately notified the

1. Edward Allen Gerrard (1834-1925) emigrated from England. In 1853, at the age of nineteen, he crossed the Plains to California. He came to Nebraska in 1858, and at the time of this raid was a government guide for cattle herds being driven to Fort Randall. His brother, Frederick Henry Gerrard (b. 1848), became his partner in the general merchandising business in Monroe, Nebraska.

neighbors and as soon as he could get eleven men besides himself he started on the trail after the Indians.

First, however, he sent his brother to the reservation to notify the people there, as well as the settlers between his house and the agency. Henry came to the store where I was and in a little while we got seven men together and started north to meet Allan Gerrard and his party.

By this time it was late in the afternoon and when we reached Shell Creek it was dark. Here we found the trail of the Indians, but a terrific thunder and wind storm came up which lasted nearly all night, and it was so dark that we could not see a thing, so we waited until daylight, when we started on. The rain had washed out the trail, so it was pretty slow work to follow it, but after about five miles we came to where Allan Gerrard and his party had stayed over night, and after that it was easy to follow the trail.

We soon came to where the Indians had camped the night before, and a few miles farther on found where the trail divided, part of the tracks leading off to the north toward the Elkhorn River, and the rest turning west toward Beaver Creek.

We had no way of knowing which trail Allan and his party had followed, but as the lefthand trail toward Beaver Creek semed to be much larger, we took that. We were somewhat puzzled because Allan Gerrard had said there were only seven Indians that ran off the horses, while the trail we were now following looked as though there must be at least a hundred horses in the bunch. Finally we came to the head of a dry branch of Beaver Creek and the tracks turned down that toward the creek. It was about noon and we had been travelling since daylight. We had had little rest the night before, and our horses were pretty nearly worn out. The pony I was riding was no good, as my best saddle horses were with Gerrards bunch, and the Indians had gotten them.

I had been walking and leading my horse for several miles,

[ 78 ]

and now I turned off the trail and went down the bank of the dry creek, to see if I could find a waterhole where the horses could drink. Presently one of the boys called to me, saying he could see Indians. I climbed up the bank and as soon as we all got together we moved away from the creek about half a mile and went up the side of a hill high enough so that we could look up the valley of the Beaver, where we could see a band of fifty or sixty horses, but we had not yet seen any Indians.

I proposed that as there were only seven Indians the best thing to do would be to charge across Dry Creek and try to round up the loose horses before the Indians saw us, but before we had decided what to do a bunch of ten or twelve Indians rode over the hill to our right and across the dry creek, and came down into the creek bottom out of sight. They had hardly disappeared when more of them came in sight, and in less than five minutes we had counted thirty-five well armed warriors that came over the hill and into the timber along the dry creek. Then it struck me what a lot of idiots we were. Of the seven men in our party three were armed with muzzle loading shotguns, three with muskets, and I was armed with a Spencer carbine and a Colts revolver. The Indians were armed most[ly] with guns, several of which were Henry rifles, sixteen shooters.*

I had a field glass with me and had been taking particular notice of the arms that the Indians were carrying, and when I saw how well they were armed, I knew we were up against it, and if they intended to fight that we stood a very poor show. Finally I proposed that we move away towards the top of the hill and see what the Indians would do, but I warned the boys not to get excited, and told them that if the Indians started to charge us we must stop and dismount and face them.

We started up the hill on a walk, and before we had gone fifty yards the Indians rode up in sight, and giving their war whoop came for us as fast as their horses could run. We immediately dismounted and faced them, and they stopped about a quarter of a mile away, and after talking together for a few minutes one of them rode out from the rest, held his gun up so we could all see it, then handed it to another Indian and rode out toward us, at the same time holding one hand up in the air, then pointed to us and motioned for one of us to come and meet him.

After telling the boys that they must stick together no matter what happened to me, I went out to meet him. He could talk a few words of English, and with that and by making signs we could understand.*

I told him we were after horses that they had stolen and I pointed to loose horses that we could see up the creek about a mile. He said they were not our horses, but were some they had taken from the Omahas. I told him to go and drive them over so I could look at them, and he told me to ride over to where the horses were.

The Indians kept slowly moving toward us and were now within a hundred yards. I told him if they came any nearer I would have my men fire on them. He called to them and they stopped. Then he said he wanted to trade for something to eat, and he pointed to one of our boys (Bob McCray) who had part of a sack of flour behind his saddle. I told him we did not want to trade and motioned him back to his men, and I rode back to our boys.

We again mounted and started slowly away. They watched us until we were about half a mile away, when they again charged. We again stopped and dismounted, and they also stopped and motioned for a parley. This time Bob Mc-Cray and I both went out to meet him, and he repeated that they wanted to trade. I told him we had nothing to trade, to go back to his men, and if they followed us again we would fight them. He rode back and we again started away toward home.

The Indians watched us until we were perhaps a mile away, when they started off up the creek, and that was the last we saw of them.

We got back to the Pawnee Agency about dark that night and found that Allan Gerrard and his party had also returned without getting any of their horses back. They had followed the trail that led off to the north, but had not overtaken the Indians, and had finally given it up. I think he was on the trail of our horses and that the war party we found was another party, and that probably the Indian that talked to me told the truth when he said the horses they had were taken from the Omahas.* The two parties met accidentally, and after travelling together for a few miles separated again, the party I followed heading for North Platte where a part of Spotted Tail's band of Brule Sioux were still camped, the other party going to the Whetstone Reservation [2] on the Missouri River where Spotted Tail himself was located.

In October 1868 the Indians made another raid and took several head of horses from the settlers, and again a mob of us started after them. I think I am right in calling it a mob, as there was no discipline or organization, no leaders; we just went, every fellow for himself. There were about thirty in the Party, and I had said that if we did not overtake the Indians before night that I was coming back.

We followed the trail up Beaver Creek until night, then camped. The next morning sixteen of the party turned back.

2. The Whetstone Agency was set up in 1868 at the mouth of Whetstone Creek on the Missouri's west bank, eighteen miles above Fort Randall. The only Indians who frequented it were the "Loafers"—a group of about a thousand who broke away from the Sioux and Cheyenne bands. Since the Brûlé under Spotted Tail refused to come in to the agency, it was moved in 1871 to the White River in Nebraska (Wesley R. Hurt and William E. Lass, *Frontier Photographer* [Lincoln: University of Nebraska Press, 1956], 57).

I had intended to go back with them, but Allan Gerrard asked me to go on for another day, and I did. We followed the trail nearly to the head of Beaver Creek, where it turned to the north through the sand hills. We followed on until dark, when we camped. A bad thunderstorm came up in the night and the horses broke loose and ran away. In the morning I was the only one who had a horse. The other horses had gone only a short distance and I soon found and drove them to camp.

We then followed on after the Indians, and before noon we reached the Elkhorn River. Our horses were pretty tired and we had nothing to eat. Gerrard had brought some flour along, but no salt or baking powder, and we had eaten up everything that we had when we started except the coffee, and mixed some dough, which we wrapped around the ends of sticks and baked by holding it over the fire. After resting for a couple of hours someone proposed that we turn back for home. I think everyone was in favor of going back except Gerrard. He wanted to go on. I told him I was in favor of going back, but if he was going on I would go with him. Finally the crowd all decided to go back except Allan Gerrard, Samuel Smith[3] and myself. We went on with the intention of going to Fort Randall and reporting our loss to the commanding officer there.

The Whetstone Agency, where Spotted Tail was located, was twenty-five miles up the river from Fort Randall, and an army officer had charge of the Indians. The second day after leaving Elkhorn River we got to the town of Niobrara at the mouth of the Niobrara River. We were pretty hungry by this time, and we did enjoy the chicken dinner that we got there.

The next day we went to Fort Randall.[4] A Colonel Cham-

3. The uncle of Mrs. Frank North.
4. Fort Randall, named for Colonel Daniel Randall, was established in 1856 on the Missouri's west bank 110 miles above Yankton. While

bers was in command then, but could tell us nothing and suggested that we had better go to the Whetstone Agency and see if the officer who was acting agent there could help us find the horses. Mr. Smith was not very well and concluded he would stay at Randall, while Gerrard and I went to the agency.

The road was on the east side of the Missouri River, and thus we were obliged to cross. There was no ferry, and we hired a man with a skiff to take us over. We put our saddles, guns and blankets in the skiff and we got in. Allan sat in the bow and I sat in the stern and led the horses, and I had a difficult job, for the horses kept trying to climb into the boat, and came pretty nearly swamping it before we got across.

The next day we rode up the river until we were opposite the Whetstone Agency, when we left our horses at the house of a Frenchman that was living there and crossed over to the agency. The officer in charge sent for the interpreter, Nick Janice, who told us the horses were up at the Crow Creek Agency—one hundred miles further up the river—and that the Indians that took them did not belong to Spotted Tail's band. I was in favor of giving it up and going home, but Allan was a good sticker and wanted to go on.

We crossed back that night to the other side of the river, and the next morning started for Crow Creek, where we arrived in due time to find that the Indians had gone on their annual buffalo hunt. The agent said that we could not have gotten the horses anyway; that the Indians had stolen his saddle horse when they started on the hunt. I think he was from the East and did not know much about the Indians and was somewhat disgusted with his job.

The next morning we started back to Fort Randall, and that night stopped with a man that had married a Sioux

it was important during the years 1862-1866, thereafter it was not closely connected with active operations and was abandoned in 1892.

woman. He told us there was a small band of the Indians from Crow Creek Agency camped across the river from his house; that they had quite a bunch of horses and he had heard them talking of a wonderful running horse among them. One of my horses that they had stolen was a fast race horse, and we made up our minds to go over and take a look at their horses.

This man had a skiff and after supper we borrowed it from him and crossed the river. It was a bright moonlight night. The camp was in the timber and there were twenty or twenty-five lodges. We walked through the camp, and although the dogs made a good deal of noise no one came out, and we went out on the prairie where their horses were grazing. There were, perhaps, a hundred of them, but none of ours were with them. Allan proposed that we run off the whole bunch, but, of course, he was joking, so we left them and went back across the river. I have often wondered what we would have done if we had found our horses there, and have thought what fools we were to go poking around that camp in the night.

We got back across the river about midnight and the next day we got to the house of a Frenchman whose wife was a negro woman. By this time we were out of money, but we had a little bread and meat. The Frenchman had a double log house in one end of which he lived, and the other end he said we could sleep in. We had given him what money we had for some hay for our horses, and had spread our blankets on the floor to sleep on, when he came in and said supper was ready. Allan told him we had no money, but that we would be all right. The Frenchman went out and had a talk with his wife, and came back and invited us again to supper. When we got to their end of the house, Allan told the woman that we had no money.

She said, "Oh that's all right, it seems too bad to see poor white folks starving to death in a civilized country."

We had fried chicken for supper and it tasted mighty good to us.

The next day we got to the river opposite the Whetstone Agency, and I stayed there with the horses while Allan went over to see the agent. There was a rope ferry across the Missouri at this point, and the ferryman who took Allan across the river went with him to the agency, leaving his boat until they were ready to come back.

While I was waiting a team of horses hitched to a spring wagon and driven by an Indian boy came up from Fort Randall. In the wagon were two very pretty girls sixteen and eighteen years of age. They were the daughters of a Frenchman named Beauvais, and their mother was a Sioux woman that Beauvais had married. He had taken the girls to St. Louis when they were four and six years and put them in a convent, where they had been for twelve years and had now come home. They could neither of them talk the Sioux language. The older girl had asked me if I knew where the ferryman was, and when I told her she told me who they were. She seemed to be very much excited and was very glad to get home to her people.

In an hour or so the ferryman and Allan put in their appearance, and Allan and I started for Fort Randall.

About eighteen months later I was at the Whetstone Agency and while in the store of the trader a Sioux woman came in. She was dressed as a squaw, wearing a black calico shirt, buckskin leggins and skirt, with a blanket wrapped around her. She walked past me and up to the counter, where she bought some things, after which she went out. I asked the clerk if she was one of the Beauvais girls, and he said she was.

"But she can talk English," I said.

"Yes," he replied, "but she won't. She is married to a big buck Indian and lives in a teepee."

This was the older girl. The younger girl, I was told, had

married a white man and followed the white man's ways.

When we got to the river opposite Fort Randall we left our horses and crossed in a skiff, and after various adventures set out for the Pawnee Agency, which we reached nearly four weeks after we had left it.

Between Christmas and New Years the Indians made another raid and took two horses from me and two from the man that carried the mail between Columbus and Genoa. These horses were taken out of the agency stable. I wrote to Colonel Chambers at Fort Randall giving him a description of the horses and asking him to look out for them, as I was sure they had gone to the Whetstone Agency. In about two weeks I got an answer saying that he had two of the horses, one of mine and one belonging to Mr. Regan, the mail carrier. Colonel Chambers said that he liked my horse and that if I didn't care to come after him he would send me two hundred and fifty dollars for him. The horse had been presented to me, and, of course, I did not want to part with him, and decided that I would go after him, and Mr. Regan said he would go along.

We started on the eighteenth of January 1869. We went to Sioux City by railroad, and from there to Fort Randall by stage. I went at once to Colonel Chambers. He said that the horses were there, but that it would be necessary for me to get an order from the acting agent at Whetstone Agency before he could let me have them. I told him that I had no way of getting to the agency, and he said that I could take my horse and ride up there and get the order for the two horses, and he would turn them over to me.

Leaving Mr. Regan at the fort I went on up to the agency. The weather was very cold. I crossed the river on the ice and went up on the east side, and when I got opposite the agency I left my horse with a man who lived there and walked across the river.

It was about noon, and I went to the office and found the lieutenant who was acting agent, introduced myself, and stated my business. He said he was very busy and asked me to come around later. I was hungry and started out to find some place to eat. I hadn't gone far when I met Nick Janice, who asked me to have dinner with him, which I did.

After waiting at his house for about an hour Nick and I went back to the agent. He again put me off and asked me to come back at six o'clock. As Nick and I started back for his house I said, "What is the matter with that fellow, he does not act as though he wants to give me an order for the horses?"

Nick laughed and said, "I guess they don't want you to take that horse away. Didn't they make you an offer for him?"

This made me pretty angry, and I told Nick I was going back. He went with me, and when we got to the office I told the lieutenant that I was in a hurry and wanted the order for the horses.

He said, "I have been looking over your letter and in it you say that the bay horse has both hind feet white. Now, the horse I got from the Indians has only one white foot. He is down to Fort Randall."

When he got that far I interrupted him. I said, "The horse you got from the Indians has two white feet. He is not at Fort Randall, but is in my possession, and I am going to take him home and I don't give a d--n whether you give me an order for him or not."

He hesitated for a minute, then turned to his clerk and told him to write me an order for the two horses.

I took the order and I am very much afraid that I forgot to thank him for it.

That evening after supper Nick and I went over to the

trading post. The store was full of Indians. In the back end of the room there was a big stove, which stood out from the wall about four feet. I walked back and sat down in a chair behind the stove.

Some of the Indians asked Nick who I was. He told them what I had come for, and instead of letting it go at that, he said, "He is from the Pawnees and was with the Pawnee scouts that killed Spotted Tail's brother at Ogallala."

This certainly started something. The Indians crowded up toward the stove. I didn't understand what Nick had told them, but knew that something was up. They were growing more excited every minute, and tomahawks and knives were brandished, and they were crowding up close to me. I was trying to pretend that I did not know what was wrong, and was wondering what was best to do.

There was a window in back of the stove, and I made up my mind that if any one of them made a pass at me, I would start the old six-shooter and jump through the window. I noticed one big fellow pushing through the crowd. He had a tomahawk that he had been smoking.[5] He was talking very excitedly, and I had about made up my mind that he was the man I would take the first shot at, when he pushed the Indians nearest to me to one side, and put out his hand to shake with me. I shook hands with him. Then he held out toward me the tomahawk he was smoking, and I smoked with him. He was talking all the time and the others quieted down and soon began to leave the store.

All of this time Nick was standing there as white as a sheet. I guess he was as badly scared as I was. I asked him how this man kept them from killing me, and he replied that he told them that it would be foolish to kill me; that the troops that were there and the soldiers from Fort Randall would attack their camp and kill their women and children.

5. A combination tomahawk and pipe was a popular item of Indian trade goods.

After they had gone the Indian bade me goodbye and followed them.

I stayed with Nick over night, and the next morning started back to Fort Randall. Nick thought that some of the young fellows might follow or waylay me, but I reached the fort all right. The next morning Mr. Regan and I started home. We went down the east side of the Missouri River, as the snow was deep and there was no road on the west side.

We got to the Yankton Indian Agency at noon the first day, and stopped there to get dinner and feed our horses. They had no grain but had some wheat. I was afraid to give my horse much of it, and warned Regan not to feed his horse too much, but he gave her a big feed. When we had ridden about two hours that afternoon she was taken sick, and before we could get to a house she died.

Regan looked down at her and said, "Two hundred dollars for the mare, two hundred dollars for the horse they stole, two hundred for expenses; I'll have a bill of six hundred dollars against the government. It's singular how we can figure these things out ain't it Mr. North." He then walked on with me until we came to a stage station.

I left him there and went on alone, and when I got to Sioux City there was not much snow, so I cut across country from there. I crossed the river and stayed over night in Dakota City.

The next morning I started across country for the Elkhorn River, where I knew there were a few settlers and thought I might find a place to stay over night. I followed a wagon trail—just a few tracks. The weather was very cold, but there was no snow on the ground here, as there had been farther up the Missouri. When I had ridden about ten or fifteen miles it began to snow and the wind commenced to blow. I met a man with a team going to Dakota City, and he told me it was thirty miles to the first house, and the road was hard to follow. That did not sound good to me, and I had not gone far after meeting him when the storm developed into a blizzard and I could not see the road at all.

The horse I had at this time was perhaps the best that I ever owned, and I knew that I must trust to his instinct and intelligence to reach a house somewhere. I gave him his head and started him on a lope. He put his head down, so he could see the wagon track, I think, and never slackened his speed till we came to a house on a little creek that ran into the Elkhorn. We made the thirty miles in a little less than three hours, and how he ever managed to find the way was and is a mystery. The country was very rough and the road wound around the heads of ravines and up over big hills. Sometimes we were facing the wind and I thought he had lost the road, but soon he would make a turn and the wind was on my back.

In the house that I came to lived a German who had a shed built of straw, where he had two horses and a cow. It was a good warm place, and after I got the saddle off my horse I put in about two hours in rubbing him dry. These people lived in a dugout in the bank of a ravine. There was only one room in the house, and they only had one bed. They had a couple of small boys and I slept with them on the floor. We had one featherbed over us and another under us, and slept very comfortably.

The blizzard kept up all night and all of the next day, but cleared up in the evening. I stayed another night and then started for home. I knew that it was about forty-five or fifty miles to Columbus straight across the country, but the country was rough and there was no road, and the snow was now quite deep. For this reason I followed up the Elkhorn River to the mouth of Union Creek, then followed up that stream to a settlement that is now the town called Madison. From there to Columbus was thirty-five miles, and as there was a road to follow I made it that night.

I had ridden somewhere between seventy-five and eighty

miles that day, and much of the way was through snow from a foot to eighteen inches deep. In these days of the automobile it is hard to understand what a lot of endurance a horse had to have to make such a trip.

It was after dark when I got to Columbus, but as I wanted to cross the river to where my brother-in-law lived, I decided to go on that night. At Joe Baker's saloon I asked about the crossing. He said that one team that was hauling wood had broken through the ice that day, and he thought it was pretty dangerous. I learned from him where they were crossing, decided to try it and rode on.

When I was about half way across I came to an open channel, but it was so dark I could not see how wide it was, and had no way of knowing the depth. My horse put his head down and sniffed at the water, but when I spoke to him he jumped off the ice into the water. It came up to the middle of his sides and was full of ice. Nevertheless, he went right on, and although the channel was fifty yards across, he came out on the road on the other side. It was a pretty hard climb up on the ice, but he made it all right, and in a few minutes we had covered the three miles to my brother-in-law's house, where I turned him loose in a warm stall with two feet of straw bedding under him.

People nowadays can hardly understand what our saddle horses meant to us in those days. I doubt if one could find a horse today that even in the daytime would take the plunge into icy water that he took when it was pitch dark, and he never hesitated a moment. This horse was, I think, the best one I ever owned. He was highstrung but gentle, was very fast, and there seemed to be no limit to his endurance. I shall have more to say of him later. I called him Mazeppa,* and the Indians called him ah-kee-kah-toose, buck antelope, because they said his face was like an antelope's.

# SUPPLEMENT

THE PAWNEE VILLAGE (page 77)

In 1871, at the instance of Dr. Ferdinand V. Hayden, who conducted a government geological survey of Nebraska and Wyoming, the noted photographer William H. Jackson made a special trip to photograph the Pawnee and Omaha villages. "The Pawnees were then living in their ancient earth-covered lodges on the Loup Fork. . . . As these were among the last of their kind in the upper Missouri country, and their like would never again be seen, the Doctor was very much interested in having them photographed" (William H. Jackson quoted in Bruce, *The Fighting Norths and Pawnee Scouts*, 4). According to a description based on Jackson's notes:

> The entire village of about 2,500 persons was divided into two parts, one occupied by Skedees, the other by the Chaui, Kitkehahki and Pitahauerat bands living together. Each lodge could hold several families. The earth houses were erected by placing several stout posts (forked at the top) into a circle; cross beams were then laid into the forks and long poles inclined from the outside toward the center against the structure. All was covered with brush and then with dirt, leaving a hole at the top for escaping smoke and a long tunnel-like entrance at the base (5).

The lodges were built on a level plain west of Beaver Creek; the agency lay on the other side, and there was a bridge connecting them. In 1859 "there seem to have been three [villages]—two Skidi villages to the west, and one large village farther east in which the Chauis, Pitahauerats, and Kitkehahkis lived together. The villages were protected after a fashion on the north by high bluffs; but as the Sioux had a trick of slipping across Loup Fork and attacking suddenly from the thickets south of the villages, the Pawnees presently built a high sod wall to defend their settlement on the west, south, and east" (Hyde, *Pawnee Indians*, 123).

## THE HENRY RIFLE (page 79)

This .44 caliber rifle was a forerunner of the Winchester. It was advertised as being capable of sixty shots per minute, and sixteen shots without reloading. During the last year of the Civil War it was described by Confederates as "that damned Yankee rifle that can be loaded on Sunday and fired all the week" (Harold F. Williamson, *Winchester, the Gun That Won the West* [Washington, D. C.: Combat Forces Press, 1952], 36-38).

## INDIAN SIGN LANGUAGE (page 80)

North tells us that he "talked fair Pawnee, but never made much progress with the signs." His brother Frank, however, "by careful study, with constant practice on the reservation, in the field and elsewhere, became very proficient in the Indian sign language." He adds that he never knew a white man who spoke the Pawnee language well except Frank North (Bruce, *The Fighting Norths and Pawnee Scouts*, 56).

## THE OMAHA (page 81)

A Siouan tribe, their name long ago was Maha. With the Ponca and Iowa they migrated from the mouth of the Missouri through present Missouri and Iowa as far north as

Minnesota. Driven off by the Yankton Sioux, the Omaha continued their migration going into the region between the Missouri and the Black Hills. Finally, they turned down river and eventually established themselves in northeastern Nebraska, where they stayed for more than two hundred years. In 1856 they went on to a reservation in Thurston County, Nebraska. The Omaha were the most constantly friendly to the whites of all the Nebraska tribes.

According to North, "The Pawnees and Omahas were friends, and often hunted together. About a thousand Omahas were with the Pawnees when George Bird Grinnell and I hunted with them in 1872, making about 4,000 in all, with probably between 5,000 and 6,000 horses and some 500 tepees—quite a camp . . . . They would break camp about daylight and travel from 10 to 15 miles before eating; then have breakfast and lay over the rest of the day, with another meal about dark. That was all they would eat until after the hunt, when they would have a great feast for two or three days" (Bruce, *The Fighting Norths*, 40).


MAZEPPA (page 91)

In 1861 the actress Adah Isaacs Menken created a sensation in the role of Mazeppa, a Cossack hetman who was punished for a love intrigue by being set adrift strapped naked to a wild horse of Tartary. The play's big scene—in which Menken, clad only in flesh-colored tights, was bound on a charger and carried at the gallop up a wooden runway—was considered the ultimate in daring. Menken played *Mazeppa* in San Francisco and Virginia City in 1864-1865, and whether or not Luther North ever saw the spectacle, undoubtedly he had heard about it. At any rate, it seems probable that the play rather than Lord Byron's poem "Mazeppa" inspired the name of his horse. (See Allen Lesser, *Enchanting Rebel* [New York: The Beechurst Press, 1947], 79 ff., 110, 122.)

# V

## THE CAMPAIGNS OF 1869

[See Map 6; supplement for this chapter begins on page 124.]

I N FEBRUARY 1869 my brother was ordered to recruit a *Febr. 10* [1]
company of scouts, and on the 11th of February we
went to Fort Kearney with fifty men, where we drew clothing, horses and equipment, and marched the men across the
river to Kearney Station, where we loaded the horses in cars
to be shipped to Fort McPherson, where we were to join a
winter campaign into the Republican country. Major Noyes
was in command.[2] This company of scouts was A Company

---

1. The dates in this chapter have been supplied from "The Journal
of an Indian Fighter—the 1869 Diary of Major Frank North," edited
by Donald F. Danker, *Nebraska History*, XXXIX, 2 (June 1958),
87-177.
2. Henry W. Noyes was born in Maine and appointed to West
Point from Massachusetts. He was made brevet major of the Second
Cavalry in 1865 (Thomas H. S. Hammersly, *Complete Regular Army
Register* [Washington, D.C.: 1880], 668).

and I was captain, with Fred Mathews as my lieutenant.

We got to McPherson on the 12th, unloaded the horses, and went over the river to the fort, where we drew arms, ammunition, rations and forage, and went into camp on the river.[3] I was allowed two wagons to carry my forage, rations and camp equipment, but we were not allowed any tents. It rained all day, turning into snow in the evening. We put in a pretty bad night, and in the morning started for the old Jack Morrow ranch,* where we were to turn south toward the Republican.

Major Noyes had been gone several days and we were to follow and join him somewhere on the Republican. It was still snowing when we started, and the wind soon began to blow so hard we could not see much of anything. We managed to get to the John Burke ranch where we got our horses and mules into some sheds and ourselves in some outbuildings, and managed to keep from freezing.*

*Febr. 14*     The next morning my brother went back to Columbus to recruit another company of scouts, and I went on after Major Noyes' command. I met him three days later on the Republican.

We had expected to find plenty of buffalo in the country, but we did not see one, and all of the game we had killed was one antelope. Major Noyes was out of rations and had not killed any game, and so had turned back to the fort. He had two troops of cavalry with him but no tents. I gave him pretty nearly all of the rations I had, and we went into camp with the understanding that we would start for Fort McPherson in the morning.

The next morning it was snowing very hard, but we broke camp and started. By the time we had reached the high table-

3. Fort McPherson, established in 1863, was known successively as Cantonment McKean and Post Cottonwood Springs before it was officially named in 1866 in honor of Major General James B. McPherson. Its cemetery still remains under national supervision.

land the wind was blowing a gale, and we could not see the trail that the cavalry had made ahead of us. The cavalry horses were in much better condition than our ponies, and were making much better time than we were. I kept a man on foot ahead of us to follow the road. About noon it got very cold, and I knew that I was freezing. I had my head well bundled up, but the snow would drift in and my nose, ears and cheeks were frozen pretty badly, while my fingers were also frostbitten so badly that I lost some of my nails.

When we started in the morning Major Noyes said we would camp on the Frenchman's Fork that night. I knew there was no wood on the Frenchman's Fork where the road crossed it, and I was wondering what we would do. About the middle of the afternoon one of my men rode up alongside of me and said, "I think we are near a canyon where there is plenty of wood."

I asked, "Can you find it?", and he said he could. I told him to go ahead and we would follow.

He turned to the left of the trail and was lost to sight in a minute, but we followed in the direction he had taken, and in a few minutes he met us and said he had found the place. We soon came to the head of a canyon where there was plenty of wood and grass, and very good shelter for the horses. The Indian that found this canyon was my first duty sergeant and was a very wonderful man. His name was Co-rux-ah-kah-wah-dee, Traveling Bear.*

As soon as the wagons came he took some men with axes and cut some poles, and stood them up like lodge poles; then took the covers off the wagons and stretched them around the poles, making a tipi. While he with one or two men was doing this, we had the other men scraping the snow off the ground, and as soon as the tipi was up he had men cut grass with their butcher knives and spread it in the lodge for our beds. Then he built a fire in the center. We spread our robes and blankets, and in an hour we were perfectly warm and

[ 97 ]

dry. The men had taken their blankets and some pieces of canvas that we had and had put up lodges for themselves, so we were all comfortable except for our frost bites.

That morning when leaving camp one of my teamsters had stepped in the creek and got his foot wet and had neglected to dry it. When our lodge was finished and he came inside and took off his shoe his foot seemed to be frozen solid. I called Traveling Bear and asked him if he could do anything for it. He got a kettle full of snow and stuck the man's foot in it. Then he took out his medicine bag, put about a teaspoonful of the powdered roots in his mouth, chewed it for some time, then spat into his hand and rubbed it over the foot and ankle. He sat up with this man nearly all night and repeated the treatment several times. Of course I don't know whether it was his treatment or not, but this man only lost the nail off one toe, yet I felt sure, when I first saw it, that he would lose his foot.

The next morning was bright and clear, but very cold. I broke camp early and went down to the Frenchman, where I found Major Noyes in camp on the open prairie. More than fifty of his horses were frozen to death and several of his mules. The Major himself was pretty badly frostbitten. They had burned some of the wagons and a lot of the men were badly frozen. Many of them lost their feet or hands or toes or fingers when we got to Fort McPherson.

My men were all in good shape, so I moved down the river. Where the road crossed, the river had frozen over hard enough to bear a horse, but many of the horses were barefooted, and those with shoes were so smooth that they could not stand up on the ice. I decided that the only thing to do was to chop out the ice and ford the river. I sent some of the men back to Major Noyes to borrow his axes, and set them to work. They were somewhat awkward with the axes, but got along pretty well, and by noon had cut a lane across the river wide enough for the wagons. Then I had two men

[ 98 ]

ride ahead of each mule team and lead the lead mules, and we got across all right. Major Noyes complimented my men for their good work and said to me that he did not know how his men could have done it, as they were so badly frozen.

It took us three days to get to Fort McPherson, but the weather got much warmer, and although we had nothing to eat the last two days, we got through in very good shape. As soon as I got to the fort I drew tents, rations and forage, and went into camp on an island in the Platte, where there was good shelter, and began to build up our horses for the summer campaign, as they were very thin.

Some time in April my brother received orders to re-cruit another company of scouts, and we were ordered to North Platte.[4] After camping at North Platte for a couple of weeks, we were sent to Ogallala.

*April 20*

A few days later, I think some time in May, my brother and I with my company went on a scout up the North Platte River. When we got up the river about opposite Court House Rock,[5] and just as we were camping, we saw two horsemen on the north side of the river. They were just going out of sight behind an island that was covered with willows, and we could not tell whether they were white men or Indians, so my brother told three of my men to ride across and see who they were.

*May 15*

4. North Platte was laid out for the Union Pacific Railroad by General Grenville Dodge in 1866. A boom town during the construction of the U.P., by 1869 it had shrunk to "about 25 wooden and log buildings, including a jail, three stores, nine saloons, and three hotels" (Bill Dadd [pseudonym of John H. Williams], *Great Transcontinental Railroad Guide* [Chicago: 1896], 41).

5. Courthouse Rock, at the eastern terminus of the Wild Cat Hills about five miles southwest of the present town of Bridgeport, Nebraska, was a famed landmark on the Oregon Trail.

We had already unsaddled our horses, so these men jumped on their horses bareback. As they did one of them said, "My horse has a sore back."

My brother called him and said, "Take my mare."

Now this mare was cream in color with white mane and tail. She was a perfect beauty, and Frank only occasionally rode her. She had been led all the time we were out on this trip. The Indian took her and they went across, keeping behind the island until they were near the opposite shore.

When they came in sight of the men they saw they were Sioux, and started after them. The Sioux separated, one running off to the northeast, the other to the northwest. Two of our men went after one and the man riding my brother's mare went after the other. They soon went out of sight over the hills, but were so close to the Sioux that we knew they would soon overtake them.

In a few minutes the two men that followed one of the Sioux came in sight, leading the horse of the man they were after, and made signs that they had killed him. Then they rode off in the direction taken by the man riding my brother's mare. My brother took ten men, and leaving me to finish making camp, he crossed the river.

Just as he got to the hills on the north side he met the three men coming back. The man that had ridden his mare was riding a mule, and had a long gash cut in one of his legs from the thigh almost to the knee, and this is the story the man told; it will give some idea of how superstitious they were.

"I was gaining on my man when he went out of sight over a sand hill. When I rode up on the hill the man was coming back up the hill on the other side with a knife in his hand. I jumped off the mare to shoot him, but the cartridge was bad, and before I could throw in another cartridge he caught the gun and struck at me with his knife. I let go the gun and caught him by the wrist, and threw him to the ground,

[ 100 ]

where I held him till the other men came. I called to them to hurry and shoot him."

Then here is what happened. A man jumped off his horse, ran to where the two were struggling on the ground, put his gun against the Sioux' side and pulled the trigger. I suppose that the Indian squirmed about the time the gun went off and shot went into the ground, but the man that did the shooting took one look and then ran for his horse, calling out that he shot him in the side, and that the bullet bounced back and that the man was "Medicineman" and could not be killed.

The man that had done the fighting jumped up, letting the Sioux go, and the Sioux promptly slashed him with the knife, picked up the gun, jumped on my brother's mare and rode away, while our three men rode for camp.

And now comes the most amazing and incomprehensible part of the story. When my brother met these three men and they told him their story, he sent the wounded man to camp and told the others to come back with him and show him where the fight took place. When they got there the mule that the Indian had been riding was still there. My brother told the men to come on and they rode toward a hill about a half mile away, where the boys said the Indian had gone. When they reached the hill and looked over in the valley beyond, there stood the yellow mare and on the ground near her sat the Indian examining the Spencer carbine he had taken.

When he saw my brother and his party he took out one of his knives, drove it into the mare's heart, and for the first time that day drew his bow from its case and took a handful of arrows from his quiver and prepared to fight.

My brother said, "Now let me show you how much of a medicineman he is," and galloped straight toward him. The Indian fired one or two arrows and then turned to run. My brother shot twice and he rolled over dead.

I have been asked how I account for this Indian's action, but I don't know the answer. He had the fastest horse in the west and all he had to do was to get on her and ride away. I asked my boys what was the matter with him. They said maybe he was crazy.

We went on up the Platte as far as Scotts Bluffs,* but found no sign of Indians there, and went south to the railroad at Kimball, Nebraska,[6] and followed down the railroad to Ogallala. From there we were ordered to North Platte, *June 5* where we joined the other company of scouts.

It was here that we first met William F. Cody, Buffalo Bill. The Fifth Cavalry under General Carr[7] had come up from the south to Fort McPherson, and he was scouting for them. The day we got to North Platte Capt. Brown and Lieut. Hays,[8] of the Fifth Cavalry, and Buffalo Bill had come up from Fort McPherson. As North Platte was a pretty lively town at that time, and Capt. Brown and Cody were taking in the sights, they got somewhat hilarious.

At this time Dave Perry was running a saloon * and dance hall and Capt. Brown and Cody went in to get a drink. Dave was celebrating that day, and after meeting Cody and having a few drinks together they quarrelled and came to blows.

6. Kimball, now the county seat of Kimball County, was known as Antelopeville until 1885 (Lilian L. Fitzpatrick, *Nebraska Place-Names* [Lincoln: University of Nebraska Press, 1960], 87). It was the southern terminus of the old stage route that passed through the Wild Cat Range to Gering on the North Platte River.

7. Eugene Asa Carr (1830-1910), an 1850 West Point graduate, won a Medal of Honor at Pea Ridge during the Civil War. From 1868 to 1891, he served almost continually on the frontier. One of the most experienced of the regular army Indian fighters, he retired in 1892 as a brigadier general.

8. The officer named Brown probably was Major William Henry Brown. He and Lieutenant Edward M. Hays were both friends of Cody.

I did not see the scrap but saw Cody a few minutes after at the hotel, where he was washing the blood from his face, and he looked as if he had gone a few rounds with Jack Dempsey. People who saw it gave Dave the decision. He and Cody afterward became fast friends, but it looked for a while that day as though it would end in a killing.

In the afternoon of that day I was talking to Dave on the street in front of his saloon. He was fairly sober then, and one of his friends came up and told him that Cody was at the hotel and that he was coming up to renew the argument with guns.

Dave said, "You go back and tell that longhaired fellow that I am waiting for him."

I do not think that Cody ever said anything of the kind; at any rate Lieut. Hays and Cody went back to Fort McPherson that afternoon, and that was the end of it.

A few days later we moved our camp to Fort McPherson, and in a couple of weeks we started south with an expedition under General Carr.* He had the Fifth Cavalry and one hundred of the Pawnee scouts. I was in command of the scouts, as my brother had been ordered to enlist another company of scouts, and had gone to the Pawnee Agency to get them. *June 8*

Cody was on this campaign as scout for the cavalry, and he also took along a team and wagon loaded with merchandise and groceries, canned fruit and vegetables, to sell to the soldiers. He had a man to drive his team, and usually made his camp near ours. The day we left Fort McPherson we moved up the river only about five or six miles and went into camp. A little before sundown Cody rode into my camp and said he had to go back to the fort, and asked me to ride down with him and have dinner at his house, and we would

[ 103 ]

then come back to camp. I accepted his invitation and went with him.

We had a very excellent dinner and about ten or eleven o'clock started for camp. It was very dark, and before we had gone two miles there came up such a terrific storm of rain, hail and wind that our horses were about unmanageable. We kept on going, as we thought, in the direction of the camp, but could see nothing. Finally the horses stopped and we could not get them to move any further.

I shouted to Cody that we had better wait for a flash of lightening so we could see where we were. When the flash came we found ourselves on the bank of a pond or slough, and neither of us knew where we were. The bank was perhaps ten feet high, and if we had gone over it I do not know what would have become of us.

We waited till the storm was over and tried to figure out where we were, but could not. Cody said, "Well we are fine scouts, lost within three miles of the fort."

We stayed there until daylight, when we found the road and went on to camp. The boys were just getting up and we told them we had stayed at the fort over night on account of the rain, and to the best of my recollection we never told anyone the truth about that night.

On this expedition the Pawnee scouts always broke camp first and kept about three or four miles ahead of the cavalry all of the time, and we always had small scouting parties still farther ahead. General Carr had two greyhounds that he took along with him, and the first day after leaving the Platte River, he with his adjutant and a couple of other officers and Cody overtook me. He had the greyhounds with him and said that he wanted to give them a run after antelope. I asked him if he thought they could catch an antelope, and he said, "Yes, they could catch anything."

We rode on ahead so that if we saw any antelope we could keep out of sight until we had approached near enough to give the dogs a good start. We soon found a single buck antelope, and by riding down into a ravine and following it for some distance we got within about two hundred yards of him.

We kept out of sight and the General's orderly got off his horse and took the dogs up the bank until they were in sight of the antelope. They saw him at once and started for him. He saw them and instead of running away he trotted toward them. Then we rode up in sight. By this time the dogs were only one hundred feet from him, and he turned and ran the other way.

The General said, "Oh, they will catch him before he gets started."

We all gave a whoop and rode after them as fast as we could, but they were running up quite a hill and our horses could not make very good time, and they went out of sight over the hill. When we came in sight of them they were running across a big flat, and as our horses were pretty well blown we stopped and watched them. The antelope soon went out of sight over a hill about a mile away, with the dogs about two or three hundred yards behind, and when they reached the top of the hill they stopped for a minute and looked, then turned and came trotting back.

No one had said a word up to this time, when Cody spoke. "General," he said, "if anything the antelope is a little bit ahead."

Everybody laughed, I think, but the General, and he grinned and said, "It looks that way," and I never saw him take the dogs out again on that expedition. His orderly took them quite frequently, but I never saw them catch an antelope, though they caught many jack rabbits.

Now here is a curious thing. I have seen some of the fastest packs of greyhounds in the west chase antelope at different times, and never saw them catch one. Col. Clapper's crack dog along with Capt. Woodson's [9] thirteen hounds had a good start after a big buck antelope near Sidney, Nebraska, and he was so far ahead of them at the end of a mile that he stopped and looked back at the dogs, and yet there were many people at Sidney that said this pack of greyhounds caught many antelopes. I saw antelope run away from General George A. Custer's pack of wire-haired Scotch stag or greyhounds in the summer campaign of 1874, when we went to the Black Hills. They chased antelope many times and never caught one, though the General said they had caught many.

My belief is that in the fall of the year, when the antelope were in large bands, the dogs could catch them, for then the antelope were like a flock of sheep and would get in each other's way and run against one another, but I do not believe the dog ever lived that could catch a buck antelope that was in good condition.

A few days after the antelope chase we reached the Republican River and marched down it for about twenty-five miles, and went into camp. I was camped on the river about half a mile below the cavalry, and above my camp about three hundred yards was Cody's camp, and above his wagon was the wagon train. Across the river from Cody's camp was a nice bottom of fine grass, and the wagon boss had sent the mules over there to graze, with two of the teamsters to herd them.

My horses were off to the north of our camp, and just as we were eating our supper we heard a warwhoop across the river, where the muleherd was. We could not see them as

9. Probably Albert Emmett Woodson, assigned to the Fifth Cavalry as lieutenant in 1870 and promoted to captain in 1876. Colonel Clapper has not been identified.

there was a grove of timber on the river. We all ran out toward the horseherd, and the boys ran the horses into the camp as fast as they could.

One of my men caught his horse as they came dashing into camp, and as I could not see my horse in the bunch I told him to stay in camp, and I jumped on his horse bareback, and with about twenty of the men that had caught their horses ran up the river to Cody's wagon, where there was a ford. Cody happened to have his horse saddled and tied to his wagon, so he was the first man across the river, but his horse was not very fast, and a couple of my men on good horses soon passed him.

A party of seven Cheyennes had driven off the muleherd after killing the two herders. One of the herders rode his mule into camp before falling off. He was shot through the body with an arrow and died that night. The other man was killed before he knew the Indians were there.

As soon as the Indians saw us they abandoned the mules and ran south into the hills. I soon overtook Cody, but some of my men had already passed him, and one of them had spoken to him and had reached over and taken his revolver out of his holster. Cody was somewhat uneasy about it and asked me if I thought the Pawnees did not like him very well. It seemed that one of my men that could talk a little English had told Cody that the summer before—1868—a party of Pawnees had gone south to steal horses from the Cheyennes. The Cheyennes had discovered them and in the fight that followed several Pawnees were killed, and this man told Cody that there was a white man with long hair with the Cheyennes, and that my men thought it was Cody. Cody told me this as we were galloping after the Cheyennes.

We soon came to where my men had overtaken and killed two of the Cheyennes, but the rest of them, five in number, had disappeared, and although we rode on several miles farther, we could not find them. It was now dark and

I called the men together and told them we would go back. One of my horses had died from the heat, and we had captured one horse from the Indians. They had killed the two teamsters and we had killed two of their warriors, so it was about a draw.

I asked Cody to point out the man that had taken his revolver, and when he did I told him to give it back, and asked him what he took it for. He said he forgot his own revolver when he left camp, and that when he overtook Cody he saw that his horse was about exhausted, so he grabbed the revolver and told Cody he would bring it back. Cody could not speak any Indian language and so did not know what he said.

I then told them that Cody was not the white man that was with the Cheyennes the year before, and one of the Pawnees said, "I know he is not. I was with that war party and the man with the Cheyennes was much darker than Cody, and his hair was black."

When I told Cody what this man said it made him feel much better, and from that time on the Pawnees and Cody were very good friends. They thought his buffalo killing was miraculous.

We got back to camp that night about midnight, and in the morning I rode up to General Carr's tent to report to him. I thought I had done pretty well to get all of the mules back, and was somewhat surprised when the General, instead of complimenting me reprimanded me for taking so many of my men to chase seven Indians out of the country. I very foolishly talked back and he placed me under arrest, and put Capt. Cushing in command of the scouts.[10]

Next morning shortly after we had started on the march up the Republican, the adjutant overtook us with orders from the General to Capt. Cushing to send a scouting party

10. Sylvanus E. Cushing (1835-1904), captain of Company B of the Scouts, was the husband of Sarah Elizabeth North.

[ 108 ]

south to the Solomon River. Capt. Cushing told him that I was the only white man that could talk Pawnee well enough to make them understand where they were to go.

The adjutant laughed and rode away, but was soon back with word from the General that I was released from arrest, that I should take command again and send the scouting party as directed. This I did, and that was the end of the matter, and I will say here that of all the officers that I served under while with the scouts, I think Carr was the most efficient. Every night when we went into camp he sent his adjutant around to tell us what time to break camp in the morning, and where we were going, and what we were to do.

My scouting party came back from the Solomon with news that they had found an old trail of a few lodges going west, but after following it for a few miles they lost it.

The next day my brother joined us with another company *June 17* of scouts and took command. The following day the whole command moved south to the Solomon River, where we lay in camp for one day and sent scouting parties up and down the river, and also to the south. They found nothing but buffalo, and came into camp with their horses loaded with meat. From this camp we moved back to Prairie Dog Creek, and then went west. We kept scouting parties out both north and south every day, and occasionally ran across the trail of a few horses, probably small war parties, but did not see any lodge pole trails for several days.

One day I was out with several of my boys when we *June 23* found a small band of buffalo. I was riding a sorrel mare that had never chased buffalo, and when we made the dash into the bunch, she was very much frightened and tried to pitch me off. I finally got her straightened out, but after running them for about a quarter of a mile I discovered that while she was pitching with me a pocketbook containing ninety-five dollars that I was carrying in my hip pocket had been jolted out. I gave up the chase and went back to look for it.

[ 109 ]

After hunting for it for some time I gave it up and went to camp, which was about five miles from there.

When the boys that were with me came in I asked one of them if he had noticed my mare bucking. He said he had, and I told him of my loss, and asked him if he could go to the place. He said he could, and although I thought of the saying "hunting for a needle in a haystack," we took our horses and started out. When we got to the hill where the buffalo were lying when we made the charge, he pointed and said, "There is the place," and rode over, got off his horse and picked up the pocketbook. How he could have remembered just where it was I do not know, for I had ridden back and forth over the hill for half an hour before I had gone to camp and couldn't find the place.

*June 26*    A few days after this we crossed the country from Beaver Creek to Driftwood, and from there over to the Republican River, and went up that river. One of our men had shot himself, accidentally, in the hand, the bullet going up his arm and coming out near the elbow, and breaking the bones of his wrist, making a terrible wound. The surgeon attended him, but the arm kept getting worse, and finally the surgeon said the arm would have to be amputated. The man said he might die, but would not have his arm cut off.

*June 30*    About this time a wagon train came out from Fort Mc-Pherson with rations and forage, and we sent the wounded man back to the fort with the train. The weather was very hot and his arm had no care in the five days it took them to get there. Then he was put on a train and sent home. The arm by this time was in an awful condition, badly swollen and full of maggots, but one of the Pawnee doctors took charge of him, and when we got home that fall he was all right, except that his wrist was stiff.

We marched up the Republican for several days, keeping scouting parties out ahead, and off to the north and south, every day. One night we were camped on the south side of

the river about a mile away from the cavalry, and the Indians made a raid on our camp, charging right through it.
This charge was made about midnight and is the only time
that I ever knew of Indians making an attack in the night.
They ran through our bunch of horses, but they were all tied
and none of them got loose. I don't think there were more
than six or seven Indians. We had a guard around our camp,
but they dashed past the man on the east end, went right
past my brother's tent, firing into it, then past my tent, into
which they also fired, and on out of the west end of the
camp. We got out as soon as we could, but they were gone,
and there was no telling which way they went. One of our
men, Co-rux-to-chod-ish (Mad Bear) was shot through the
fleshy part just above the hip joint, but was not hurt much,
and we never did know whether he was shot by the Cheyennes or by one of our own men.*

There was a spring about twenty feet from my tent and
about the same distance back from the river. The water came
up from the bottom and ran off into the river. It had cut a
channel two or three feet deep. Many years afterwards
when the Pawnees had become friendly with the Cheyennes
they told them that one of the men that was in that charge
was thrown from his horse and fell into the spring. He lay
still in that narrow channel, and said that we jumped over
him several times, or that several men jumped over him. He
lay there until everything was quiet, when he crawled down
the channel to the river, then down the river until he was
clear of our camp, and so got away.

The next morning General Carr sent word that we would
lie in camp that day, but that my brother should send out
some scouting parties. With Lieut. Billy Harvey and five
men I rode south, then west, then back to the river, which
we struck about twenty-five miles above camp. We crossed
the river and I said, "Billy, I think we had better ride up on

[ 111 ]

the hill and take a look around before we camp." It was just sundown.

We started up the hill and when we were near the top one of my boys got off his horse and ran up ahead of us, and we stopped our horses to wait for him to look first. When he was high enough to see over, he sat down on the ground and motioned for us to dismount and come to where he was. We did so, and when we crawled up to where we could see over the hill it looked as though all the Indians in the world were there.

About a mile west of where we were the river bent around to the north, and just over the hill where we were lying there was a long draw or swale that led to the river, and strung out going down that draw was the whole of Tall Bull's [11] band of Cheyennes. The ones in the lead had almost reached the point where the trail went out of sight down toward the river, and those in the rear had not passed where we were, and the trail they were following was not more than one hundred yards from us. They were traveling slowly and their horses were loaded with meat and their camp equipage. They looked hot and tired. I expected every minute that some one of them would ride up on the ridge where we were taking a look over the country, but none did so, and finally they all passed by and out of sight to the west end of the valley.

When the last of them had disappeared I turned to Billy and said, "What would we have done if they had seen us?"

Billy replied, "I would have said Kings Ex."

Well, we did not go into camp there, but started down the river for the camp where we had left the cavalry. When we got there we found that another scouting party under Col.

11. The Chief Tall Bull to whom North is referring was the best known of several Cheyenne to bear that name, which was hereditary among them (Frederick Webb Hodge, *Handbook of American Indians North of Mexico*, Part 2, Bureau of American Ethnology Bulletin 30 [Washington: Government Printing Office, 1912], 679).

Royal[12] with ten of our Pawnees and Lieut. Gus Becher in charge had run into a small war party of Cheyennes. The soldiers and scouts chased them for several miles and killed three of them.*

We had to wait at the camp all day for a wagon train that was coming from McPherson, but the following day the whole command moved up the river to where the Indians had camped three days before. We took up the trail there and that day passed one of their camps and came to the *July 10* second one.

We received orders that night to take fifty of our best mounted men and three day rations, and one hundred rounds of ammunition to the man, and be ready to march at daylight in the morning.[13] This we did, and after traveling about fifteen miles we came to another camp that the Indians *July 11* had left the day before. On leaving this camp the Indians had separated into three parties, and General Carr divided his command. He with part of the cavalry and five or six of our scouts under Sergeant Sam Wallace took the left hand trail toward the northwest. Col. Royal with the rest of the cavalry and Cody as guide took the righthand trail toward the northeast, and my brother with myself and Capt. Cushing and thirty-five of our scouts took the middle trail, leading straight north.

The weather was very hot and we could not travel very fast, but went on a slow trot most of the time. When we had gone perhaps fifteen miles farther we were overtaken by one of the boys that we had sent with General Carr, with orders to join him at once, as they had discovered the Cheyenne Village. This boy said that General Carr was concealed be-

12. William Bedford Royall (d. 1895) was a Virginian. He served with the Second Missouri Infantry during the Mexican War and was made a major in the Fifth Cavalry, December 1863.

13. July 10 Frank North noted in his diary: "in the morn we move early . . . and light out for the Indians. we will have a fight tomorrow sure" (*Nebraska History*, XXXIX, 2 [June 1958], 138).

hind a ridge of sandhills and that the Indians had not seen the troops at all.

We immediately turned and started west to join General Carr. We rode at a gallop and came up with him in about half an hour. His men were all dismounted, and we also dismounted, and our men began stripping the saddles from their horses, as they always rode into battle bareback if they had time to unsaddle their horses.

When we got to the General our horses were pretty well blown, and he said he would wait for a while for Colonel Royal to join him, before making the charge on the village. After waiting for perhaps half an hour the General said he would wait no longer, for fear the Indians might discover us and get away.[14]

The men were ordered to mount and we started. The village was about three miles away, and as soon as we passed over the ridge of sandhills we were within sight of their horse herds, but not yet in sight of the lodges. There was a long valley reaching almost to the village, and when we got orders to charge we all broke into a run and, as our men were riding bareback, we outran the soldiers and reached the village a little ahead of them.

My brother, who was riding a very fast horse, was two hundred yards ahead of everyone, and I was just ahead of our men. As my brother rode over the hill he was almost in the village. The Indians were rushing out of their lodges and five or six that had caught horses came up the hill on the opposite side and met him. He stopped his horse and jumping off opened fire on them, but they turned and ran, and he did not hit any of them. By this time I was there, and started to ride up on top of the hill above him, but some

14. North appears to be mistaken about Colonel Royall's participation in the attack. The Journal of the March of the Republican River Expedition for July 11, 1869 indicates that Royall rejoined the main force just before the attack.

Indians came up a draw or low place just above me and took a couple of shots at me, neither of which took effect.

Frank called to me to get off my horse, but by this time the men began to get there and he got on his horse and we all rode down into the edge of the village, and the lodges were scattered along up the creek for half a mile. There were eighty-five lodges in the village. The lodge of the chief, Tall Bull, was at the lower end of the village, and was about the first one we came to. Before we got to it, however, the cavalry came by. They swung to the left and passed on up the valley toward the upper end of the village, while we cut across the lower end toward the other side.

Before going further I want to tell of an incident that happened before we got to the village. About half a mile from the village, and off to one side from our line, a Cheyenne boy was herding horses. He was about fifteen years old and we were very close to him before he saw us. He jumped on his horse, gathered up his herd, and drove them into the village ahead of our men, who were shooting at him. He was mounted on a very good horse and could easily have gotten away if he had left his herd, but he took them all in ahead of him, then at the edge of the village he turned and joined a band of warriors that were trying to hold us back, while the women and children were getting away, and there he died like a warrior. No braver man ever lived than that fifteen year old boy.

As my brother, myself, Capt. Cushing and Sam Wallace rode up to the big lodge near the end of the village, we saw a small two gallon keg of water on the ground, and as we were very hot and thirsty Capt. Cushing got off his horse and after taking a drink handed the keg to my brother who was still on his horse.

About this time a woman came crawling out of the lodge, and running to Capt. Cushing fell on her knees and threw her hands about his legs. We now saw that she was a white woman. She was bleeding from a bullet wound through her breast. She was a Swede and could not talk English, and had been taken prisoner several months before, when this band of Cheyennes had raided a Swedish settlement in Kansas. Tall Bull had taken her for his wife, and when we charged the camp he tried to kill her, but only made a flesh wound through her breast.[15]

We finally made her understand that she was safe and that she should stay where she was. Then we started on across the creek to the west side of the village, but before going on I must tell how I was wounded.

After Frank had drank from the keg he handed it to me. I raised it up to drink, and as I did so an Indian who was lying in the grass about fifty yards away took a shot at me. I felt the bullet strike me in the stomach and come out of my back, and I came near falling off my horse. I was in my shirt sleeves and opened my shirt to look for blood but saw none, then I felt my back and it was all right. I looked around at the other boys, but they were talking to the woman and had not noticed me, so I took a drink of water and said nothing about it, thinking I must have imagined it all.

Before we started across the village I saw a saddled horse up the creek and rode up toward it, thinking that if I could catch it I would turn my mare loose, as she was pretty tired. I had gone only a little way when I came to a dead woman, and upon examination found she was white. She had been killed with a tomahawk. We afterwards learned she had been taken prisoner at the same time the other woman was taken, and when we charged the camp they killed her. When I caught the horse I had gone after I turned and rode

15. Mrs. George Weichell, a German settler of Lincoln County, Kansas, had been captured with Mrs. Alderdice, who was killed in the Summit Springs attack. The husbands of both women were killed when they were captured.

after Frank and overtook him about half way across the camp.

We had been moving slowly up to this time, as the Indians were putting up a fight, but now the soldiers were firing volleys into the camp farther up the creek, and the Indians were running away as fast as they could. We started up the hill out of the village on the west side. My brother and I were a little ahead and to the left of our men when an Indian that was hidden in a ravine stuck his head up and fired at my brother. At first I thought he was hit, as he threw his hand up to his face and stopped his horse. He jumped off his horse and handed me his bridle reins and said, "Ride away and he will stick his head up again."

I started the horses off on a lope and the Indian raised his head to look, but did not get it very high, as my brother was ready for him and shot him in the forehead.

I turned back and dismounted, and just then an Indian woman and little girl climbed up out of the ravine where the Indian had fallen back and came over to us. My brother talked to her as well as he could in the sign language, and pointed over to where he had left the white woman, telling her to go there and wait, which she did.

This woman was Tall Bull's wife, and the Indian killed there was Tall Bull himself, though we did not know this until we got back to Fort Sedgwick three days later, when the interpreter, Leo Palliday,[16] asked the woman if Tall Bull was killed. She said, "yes," and pointing to my brother said, "this man killed him where I came out of the canyon." *

After sending the woman away, we went up toward the head of the canyon where our men were all dismounted. The canyon was about twenty feet deep there, and very

16. Leon F. Palladay testified before a government commission in 1879 that he was forty-seven years old, living at the Pine Ridge Agency, and had spoken the Sioux language for thirty-five years. He had been an interpreter with Spotted Tail's band of Sioux (*Nebraska History*, XV, 1 [January-March 1934], 54).

narrow, with perpendicular sides, and a lot of Cheyenne warriors had run up there. They were armed with bows and arrows and whenever we came near to the edge of the canyon they would let fly with their arrows, and then we would run up to the canyon, stick our guns over the edge, shoot and jump back. After keeping this up for some time and there were no more arrows coming, we looked down into the canyon and found there thirteen dead warriors, and between there and the mouth of the canyon were six or seven more, and in the village were about twenty. These were all warriors but two.

Dr. George Bird Grinnell in *The Fighting Cheyennes* says General Carr reported fifty-two Indians killed, but does not say how many were women and children. I did not see any children killed, but there were two dead women. The fight or chase continued for ten or fifteen miles west and south of the village, and several Indians were killed outside the village, but I do not know how many. I am quite sure that there were more than fifty killed in all.

When we finally turned back toward the village, after giving up the chase, we began to gather up the horses and mules that the Indians had abandoned. There were about five hundred horses and one hundred and twenty mules. The mules they had taken from freighters, and they were extra good ones. We made the charge into the camp at two o'clock and got back to the village about six.

Just as we got back to the village a terrific rain and hail storm came up, and while we were trying to get under shelter in the tipis Cody rode into camp. He had been with Colonel Royal and missed the fight. Later he was given by Ned Buntline the credit for having killed Tall Bull, but he was not in the fight at all.

While we were waiting for the storm to pass over I told the boys about how I supposed I had been shot when we first rode into the village, and that even now I was sore and stiff.

Capt. Cushing picked up my belt, which had a large square buckle on it, and said, "Well you were hit; the buckle is bent where the bullet struck it." I then opened my shirt and found a black and blue spot three or four inches in diameter on my stomach. I also had a cut over my eye where I was struck by an arrow while we were fighting at the head of the canyon. Aside from that none of our men were hurt.

The village was very rich in fancy buckskin shirts, and dresses with beadwork and colored porcupine quills worked into them. There were also several Navajo blankets, and a great many fine buffalo robes, besides quite a little money that they had taken from the colony they had massacred on the Solomon River when they took the white women. In the village our Pawnees found six hundred forty dollars in gold, every dollar of which they turned over to the white woman that we found. This woman, whose name was Weichel, recovered from her wound and was afterward married to a soldier at Fort Sedgwick. The white woman that was killed by the Indians, whose name was said to have been Suzannah Allerdice, was buried on the battlefield, and the battlefield was at first called Suzannah Spring, but was named Summit Springs by General Carr.*

We gave up the day after the fight to destroying the village. The lodges, and, in fact, everything that would burn we burned, and in the afternoon we moved camp about ten or fifteen miles down to the Platte River.

In the fight one of my men, *Co-rux-ah-kah-wah-dee*, Traveling Bear, had left his horse, which was tired out, and pursued four Cheyennes, who were also on foot. They ran into the Canyon that I have before spoken of, and he followed and overtook and killed all four of them, and came back out of the mouth of the canyon with four scalps and four revolvers. My brother reported this to General Carr, and General Carr in his report of the battle mentioned him for his bravery, but in some way got the name confused with the name of the man *Co-rux-te-cha-dish*, Mad Bear, who was wounded in the night attack on the Republican about a week before. Later Congress had a bronze medal struck for him. The name on the medal was Mad Bear, but the medal was given to Traveling Bear by my brother. Mad Bear was in an ambulance the day of the battle, as he was not yet well enough to ride on horseback.

The second day after the fight we moved down the river about twenty-five miles, and that night our men had a good deal of trouble in holding the herd of captured stock. They thought the Indians were trying to stampede them, but they saw no Indians, and managed to hold the herd, and the sec-

*July 15*    ond day after that we reached Fort Sedgwick.

The next day after we reached Sedgwick General Carr allowed each officer of the 5th Cavalry to pick a pony from the herd of captured horses, and then the officers of the scouts were given a pony each, and each of our scouts who took part in the fight was allowed to select a pony. All their ponies were taken across the river and shipped home, my brother going with them. The rest of the herd was turned over to me to take care of, as I was now in command of the battalion.

*July 16*    General Augur came to Fort Sedgwick, and on returning to Omaha took with him the prisoners that we had taken at Summit Springs, four women and thirteen children. They were sent from Omaha to the Spotted Tail Agency on the Missouri River above Fort Randall.

After staying at Fort Sedgwick for about two weeks, the command again started south, under command of Colonel Royal, as I think General Carr was ordered to Washington. We moved south to the head of the Frenchman's Fork of the Republican, where we found the trail of part of the band that had escaped from the Summit Springs fight. They discovered us before we did them and moved down the Frenchman. We followed and they turned north toward the Platte River, crossing a few miles above Ogallala one day ahead of us.

The day we reached the river was very hot and dry; we were traveling as fast as we could, and I kept one or two of my men out ahead as trailers. We were crossing a high tableland covered with buffalo grass, and Cody rode up to me and said, pointing to the man ahead, "Does that Indian think he is following a trail?"

I said, "yes".

He said, "can you see any trail?", and I told him I could not. Then he proposed we ride on and ask the man, which we did.

He replied, "Yes I am following the trail."

I said, "The Long Hair says he doubts if there is a trail."

The Indian pointed ahead, where about three miles away there was a ridge of sand hills, and said, "Tell the Long Hair that when we get there he will see."

We rode on until we came to the sand hills and there were the tracks, plenty of them. Cody said, "Well I take off my hat to him, he is the best I ever saw."

That night we got to the Platte River, after a ride of seventy miles. We were all very tired and hot and thirsty, and as the wagon train did not get in, we went to sleep hungry. One of my men, who had been my orderly took my horse and led him away to find good grass for him, and I lay down with my saddle blanket over my head to keep the mosquitoes from eating me up, and went to sleep.

About midnight my boy came and woke me and said he had some coffee for me. I roused Capt. Cushing and we followed him over to the river bank, where he had a half gallon tin pail full of coffee, and three hard tack for each of us. We ate them and drank the coffee, before I thought to

[ 121 ]

ask the boy where his share was. He said, "I will wait until the wagons get here." I tell this to show how loyal these men were and how devoted to anyone they liked. He had ridden that day as far as I, and had taken care of my horse, then had hunted up fuel enough to make the coffee, and that was no small job, then had given us all he had, when he knew the wagons would not be in until the following day.[17]

When the wagon train did get in the next day the mules were so exhausted that we stayed in camp until the next morning before trying to cross. The Indians had crossed the day before and gone on north towards Ash Hollow. My brother, who had been in Omaha acting as interpreter in a trial where some of the Pawnees were being tried for murdering a man named McMurty,* met us when we crossed the river above Ogallala, and took command of the scouts, and I went home to Columbus.[18]

*Aug. 21* The command under Colonel Royal went on north after the Indians, crossing the North Platte and following them out through the Sand Hills Country beyond the Niobrara River, but they did not overtake them, and finally returned to Fort McPherson where they stayed in camp for about a month to recruit their horses, which were very badly run down.

*Sept. 15* About the first of October an expedition left Fort Mc-Pherson under General Duncan,[19] and, with the Fifth Cav-

17. "Nick Koots *(Bird)* was my striker and like all of my men called me 'Father.' * . . . He was one of the Pawnee killed at Massacre Canyon in the summer of 1873 . . ." (North quoted in Bruce, *The Fighting Norths*, 33, 38).

18. Luther North wrote, "I had a few words with General Carr and when we got to the Fort [Sedgwick] I resigned and came home the first of August" (Luther North Papers, Nebraska State Historical Society).

19. Thomas Duncan (1819-1887) was born in Illinois and at the age of fourteen fought in the Black Hawk War. He entered the

alry and the Pawnee Scouts, moved south to the Republican, where they made a permanent camp and sent out scouting parties up and down the river and south to the Solomon, one party of our men scouting as far south as Ft. Wallace. The country was full of game, buffalo, elk, deer, antelope and thousands of wild turkeys.

One day my brother and Cody were riding alone about *Sept. 26* five or six miles south of camp. They had killed a couple of turkeys and were just tying them on their saddles, when a party of Indians came in sight about a half mile away and started for them. There were eight of them. Frank and Cody jumped on their horses and started for camp. Both were well mounted and there was no danger that the Indians would overtake them, so they galloped along easily and let the Indians gain on them, and so brought them in sight of the camp. When my brother came in sight over the hill, he commenced riding his horse in a circle, which meant the enemy were in sight, so we jumped on our horses and dashed out to meet them, but the Indians had seen the camp and turned back, and as it was nearly dark we returned to camp.*

The next morning we started early and riding south we found the Indians camp on a creek that ran into the Republican. There were only four lodges, and when we charged down on them we found them deserted and the Indians gone. We could not follow their trail as they had scattered and the trails were all so tracked up with buffalo that a horse track could not be followed.

A few days later our men found down the river an old *Oct. 2*

---

regular army in 1846, served with distinction in the Mexican and Civil wars, in 1866 was appointed colonel of the Fifth Cavalry, and in 1868 ordered to the Department of the Platte. Duncan was a brevet brigadier general (Appleton's *Cyclopedia of American Biography*, II [New York: D. Appleton & Co., 1888], 256). William Cody described him as "a blusterer, but a jolly old fellow" who was very fond of hunting (W. F. Cody, *Buffalo Bill's Life Story* [New York: Cosmopolitan Book Corp., 1924], 206).

[ 123 ]

Sioux woman who was pretty nearly starved to death.[20] The men brought her to camp and after a few days a wagon train that was going to Fort McPherson took her in, and I think she was sent from there to the Spotted Tail Reservation at the Whetstone Agency.

About the first of December we were mustered out and sent home.

## SUPPLEMENT

Morrow's road ranch (page 96)

Jack Morrow (1831-1876) came west from Pennsylvania; he sold supplies to freighters and migrants, traded with Indians, and raised cattle. His road ranch was about twelve miles west of Cottonwood Springs on the Oregon Trail (Frank A. Root and William E. Connelly, *The Overland*

20. The woman was questioned through the interpreter, John Y. Nelson, and through a Ponca serving with the Pawnee Scouts. The Ponca talked to her in Sioux and translated her statements into Pawnee, which Frank North translated into English. She said that the band was led by Pawnee Killer, Whistler, and a head soldier named Little Bull. She had lost her way in the flight and was trying to walk to Spotted Tail's camp to the northward. She was merely an old woman, she insisted, and the warriors had not told her their plans. Questioned later at Fort McPherson, she stated that she was Pawnee Killer's mother and that Whistler was responsible for the hostility of the band (Journal of the March, October 3, 1869; General Emory to General Ruggles, October 11, 1869, National Archives and Records Service, Record Group 98).

*Stage to California* [Topeka: 1901], 218-220; Omaha *Daily Bee*, July 7, 1876, 4).

## BURKE'S RANCH (page 96)

In 1864 John Burke established a ranch about seven miles west of Fort McPherson. It was destroyed by the Sioux in 1868, and he bought the Ben Holladay Overland Stage station about two miles west of the fort. Apparently it was here that North found shelter.

## TRAVELING BEAR (page 97)

In a retrospective view of "the great and eventful days of Pawnee history" North had this to say about Traveling Bear: "[He] was about 6 feet in height and very muscular; weight probably about 200 pounds. He had a frank and open countenance, was outspoken, and looked straight at you with his brown eyes (unusual in an Indian). Though apparently rather serious, he was generally pleasant; but in a battle a whirlwind—and I do not think he was ever afraid of anything.

"In 1867, when we had some Union Pacific R.R. officials hunting near Fort Kearny, the Bear shot an arrow entirely through a buffalo—a feat that he probably never duplicated. The only other Indian I ever heard of nearly equaling it was Two Lance, the Sioux warrior . . . I never heard of any white man even killing a buffalo with bow and arrow—much less shooting an arrow through one" (Bruce, *The Fighting Norths and Pawnee Scouts*, 19). Traveling Bear died of wounds received at Massacre Canyon in 1873.

## SCOTTS BLUFF (page 102)

A national monument since 1919, Scotts Bluff, on the south side of the Platte in present-day Scotts Bluff County,

Nebraska, was the first butte of dominating height seen by travelers on the Oregon Trail. Here is how it looked to the explorer and author, Sir Richard Burton, in 1860:

> From a distance of a day's march, it appears in the shape of a large blue mound, distinguished only by its dimensions from the detached fragments of hill around. As you approach within four or five miles, a massive medieval city gradually defines itself, clustering, with a wonderful fulness of detail, around a colossal fortress, and crowned with a royal castle. . . . At a nearer aspect again, the quaint illusion vanishes: the lines of masonry become yellow layers of boulder and pebble imbedded in a mass of stiff, tamped, bald marly clay . . . dwarf cedars and dense shrubs [are] scattered singly over the surface. Travellers have compared this glory of the *mauvaises terres* to the Capitol at Washington, to Stirling Castle . . . .
>
> Scott's Bluffs derive their name from an unfortunate fur-trader there put on shore in the olden time by his boat's crew, who had a grudge against him: the wretch in mortal sickness crawled up the mound to die. The politer guide books call them "Capitol Hills": . . . they are divided into three distinct masses. The largest, which may be 800 [750] feet high, is on the right, or nearest the river. . . . The whole affair is a spur springing from the main range, and closing upon the Platte so as to leave no room for a road. The sharp, sudden torrents which pour from the heights on both sides and the draughty winds— Scott's Bluffs are the permanent headquarters of hurricanes—have cut up the ground into a labyrinth of jagged gulches steeply walled in (*The City of the Saints* [London: Longman, Green, Longman, and Roberts, 1862], 96-97).

## DAVE PERRY'S SALOON (page 102)

The California Exchange Keg House, operated by D. Perry and R. Rowland, advertised "the choicest brands of Wines, Brandies, Gins, Whiskies and Liquors of all kinds to be had west of Chicago" (North Platte, Nebraska, *Platte Valley Independent*, February 19, 1870, 1).

THE REPUBLICAN RIVER EXPEDITION (page 103)

"The Republican River Expedition, like other frontier task forces, was organized for a single specific purpose. In June and July 1869, the Expedition operated in the area of the Republican River Valley in Kansas, Nebraska and Colorado and was charged with the duty of driving the Indian out of his last stronghold on the central plains" (James T. King, "Republican River Expedition, June-July 1869," *Nebraska History*, XLI, 3 [September 1960], 165).

INDIAN NIGHT ATTACK (page 111)

General E. A. Carr reported: "About midnight, an attack was made on our camp by a number of Indians who charged in among the horses, yelling and firing into camp. They did not succeed in getting any animals or injuring anyone. Sergeant Co-rux-to-chod-ish (Mad Bear) Pawnee who was Sergeant of the Pawnee guard, ran out after one of the Indians whose horse had fallen and thrown him and was about to overtake and kill him when he was shot down by a bullet from our own side" (Report of Operations, June 30, 1869, to July 20, 1869, National Archives and Records Service, Record Group 98, Ms., microfilm).

THE SKIRMISH ON JULY 6 (page 113)

In a skirmish on July 6 three Indians were killed by the Pawnee Scouts under the immediate command of Lieutenant Gus Becher. The site was in the sandhills approximately thirty miles north of the north fork of the Republican River (Journal of the March of the Republican River Expedition, July 9, 1869, National Archives and Records Service, Record Group 98, Ms., microfilm).

[ 127 ]

"THIS MAN KILLED TALL BULL" (page 117)

William Cody later claimed he had killed Tall Bull, and Cody's protagonists have stated that Luther North's account of the shooting is an invention. However, while Frank was a partner with Cody in the cattle business, he related the story of the shooting in detail essentially as Luther recollected it. Frank's account is found in the unpublished manuscript cited in Chapter II, footnote 7. See also Appendix A.

THE BATTLE OF SUMMIT SPRINGS (page 119)

General Carr's report of the battle indicates that the Pawnee Scouts played a considerable role:

> We galloped about an hour through low sand hills and loose sand and saw no sign of Indians, and I began to think the whole [affair] was a humbug . . . when some Pawnees beckoned me to come to them, which I did with the command, though I had little hopes of finding anything. . . . The Pawnees pointed out a herd of animals about four miles off in the hills. . . . I thought it were possible it might be Buffalo but of course determined to go and see.
> The Pawnee stripped themselves for the fight, taking off their saddles and as much of their clothing as could be dispensed with and still have something to distinguish themselves from the hostiles. . . . When concealment was no longer possible, I placed the three leading companies in parallel columns of two's, directed Major Crittenden, 5th Cavalry to take command and sounded the charge. We were over a mile from the village and still undiscovered. The leading companies with the Pawnees on their left put their horses at speed while the rest followed at a fast gallop. . . .
> The Pawnees under Major Frank North were of the greatest service to us throughout the campaign. This has been the first time since coming west that we have been supplied with Indian scouts and the results have shown their value.

The place where the battle took place is I believe called Summit Springs. [The Summit Springs site is located about twelve miles south and five miles east of Sterling, Colorado.] This band proved to be "Dog Soldier Cheyennes" commanded by Tatonka Haska or "Tall Bull" who was killed in the engagement after a desperate personal defense (Journal of the March, July 11, 1869).

"Grandfather" Frank North (page 122, footnote 17)

"In 1865 Frank North, then only 25 years of age, was called 'father' by the scouts of that first regular Pawnee company; but after organization of the battalion in '67, every captain became father to his men. So the Major was looked up to and known among them as 'grandfather'—a term of confidence and respect without regard to age, but typical of Indian character where such relations exist. All the Pawnees had absolute faith in him and would do anything he said was right" (Luther North quoted in Bruce, *The Fighting Norths*, 32).

The McMurty murder trial (page 122)

Yellow Sun, Horse Driver, Little Wolf, and Blue Hawk were tried and convicted in the United States District Court in Omaha for the murder of Edward McMurty. On being convicted, Horse Driver and Yellow Sun attempted suicide; Blue Hawk escaped as he was being led from the courtroom and made his way back to the reservation. When he was found there by Frank North, he refused to return to Omaha —a decision in which he was supported by many members of the tribe. Troops sent out from Omaha compelled him to return to jail. The United States Circuit Court of Appeals subsequently reversed the verdict on the grounds that the murder was committed off the reservation and the Indians thus should have been tried by the State of Nebraska. No

[ 129 ]

record has been found indicating that the Indians were tried again. However, Little Wolf died in jail and the others shortly after their release. Several years later another Pawnee, Shooting Star, confessed to the murder of Edward McMurty (Omaha *Weekly Herald,* November 17, 24, 1869; May 11, 1870; Luther North to Robert Bruce, February 9, 1929, Luther North Papers, Nebraska State Historical Society).

MAJOR NORTH, BUFFALO BILL, AND—HOW MANY INDIANS?
(page 123)

In General Duncan's report of this incident, the turkeys become buffalo and the whole affair is projected on a similar scale:

The Indians attacked Major North, the Commander of the Pawnee Scouts, and guide William Cody who were hunting buffalo a short distance ahead of the pioneer detachment. The main column was about a mile and a half in rear of the pioneers. Lt. William J. Volkmar, 5th Cavalry, who was in command of the pioneers at once charged with them to rescue the two men whom the Indians were either trying to kill or capture. . . . The Indians retreated across and up the creek soon showing themselves in considerable force. The pioneer detachment after a charge of about five miles gained an eminence on the south side of the creek, from which a large Indian village was seen among the trees on the stream. The Pawnee scouts joining the pioneer detachment, another charge was made, and the Indians abandoned their village, flying in a westward direction up the creek. Pursuit was continued until dark. One hostile Indian was killed and a number believed to be wounded. A great deal of camp equipage and provisions were captured in the village. No casualties on the side of the command" (Journal of the March, September 26, 1869, National Archives and Record Service, Record Group 98).

[ 130 ]

As Major North saw it: "Sunday 26. today we marched 24 miles and I and Cody came ahead to the Creek and 6 Indians got after us and gave us a lively chase you bet. I got my men out and they killed one Indian and got two ponies a mule and lots of trash" (*Nebraska History*, XXXIX, 2 [June 1958], 158). See also Appendix A.

# VI

## HUNTER AND GUIDE, 1870

[*See Map 7; supplement for this chapter begins on page 157.*]

I N THE SPRING of 1870, Professor Marsh [1] of Yale College
brought a party of students out to make a geological
expedition from Fort McPherson. The Government furnished an escort of one troop of Cavalry, and Prof. Marsh
engaged my brother and two Pawnees to act as guides for
the expedition. They went north from Fort McPherson, and
I think crossed the south and middle loups, and finally followed up the North Loup, and then returned through the
Sand Hill Country to the Platte River at the mouth of Birdwood Creek, and back to Fort McPherson.

1. Othniel Charles Marsh (1831-1899) organized his first Yale Sci-
entific Expedition in 1870. The party explored the Pliocene deposits
in Nebraska and the Miocene of northern Colorado, then continued
westward through Wyoming on to California (*Dictionary of American Biography* [New York: Charles Scribner's Sons, 1949], XII,
302).

While my brother was making this trip I was employed by a man named Cooper to guide a herd of Texas cattle from Wood River, Nebr. to the Whetstone Agency. These cattle were for the Brule Sioux under Chief Spotted Tail. The second day from Wood River we crossed the South Loup, about where St. Paul, Nebraska is now, and the next day we crossed the North Loup a few miles from there. The water was not more than three feet deep at any place, but the quicksands were quite bad.

I had ridden ahead of the herd, and after they were all across had gone back to pilot the wagon over. Mr. Cooper was behind the wagon, and instead of following it he rode down the river on a sand bar for about 100 yards, and then started across. His horse got into a bad quicksand hole and went down, throwing him off. Then the horse struggled to his feet again and went on across, leaving Mr. Cooper afoot. He was wearing a pair of high rubber boots.

The current was pretty swift and he lost his head and called for help, at the same time trying to run for shore. I had got the wagon across and ran down the bank calling to him to get up and stand still until I could get to him, but as soon as he got on his feet he kept plunging ahead and falling down again, all the time calling for help.

I waded out to him, talking to him all the time and telling him that there was no danger. By this time he was panic-stricken and half drowned, and when he got hold of me he threw his arms around me, and as the water was about waist deep, I fell and he fell on top of me. He was a big man, weighing two hundred pounds, and as I weighed one hundred forty, I had my hands full, but I finally managed to get him to the bank.

By this time the cook and one of the cowboys were there, and they dragged us both up the bank, where we lay for several minutes gasping for breath, and Cooper was coughing up water that he had swallowed. When we had somewhat recovered I told him that we had three more pretty streams to cross, the Cedar, the Elkhorn and the Niobrara, and that as far as I was concerned he would get across them by himself; that any fool that didn't know enough to stand up and walk in three feet of water ought to drown, and as far as I was concerned they would.

Mr. Cooper did not make any reply, but the next day when I was riding ahead of the herd he rode up to me and thanked me for saving his life, and of course made me feel pretty small for talking to him as I had.

We had no trouble in crossing the Cedar and Elkhorn, and found the Niobrara low, so we got over that all right, but we were now on the reservation of the Ponca Indians, and a band of about twenty Poncas met us. One of them could talk Pawnee, and he told me that they wanted twenty head of cattle.

Mr. Cooper was somewhat scared, and told me to tell them he would give them ten.

I told them that we would not give them any. They said they would stampede them. I said, "Go on, try it." They bluffed for a while longer, and rode away saying they would send their agent up to see us.

After they had gone Mr. Cooper wanted to know what I had said, and I told him. He thought it would have been better to have given them some of the cattle, and in that way get their good will, but I told him that this was a band of young men and there was no chief with them; that if we had given them any cattle there would have been another party after us in a little while, and, as it was, I doubted if we would be bothered any further.

This proved to be the case, for we saw no more Indians until we reached the Whetstone Agency, where we turned over the cattle, and the next day we started back.

When we got back to the Niobrara River, we found it was very high, as it had been raining hard for two or three days.

[ 134 ]

Where the trail crossed there was an Island with quite a wide channel on each side. In crossing the first channel my horse, which was rather a poor one, got down in the quicksand, and I had to get off and lead him the rest of the way to the island.

When we crossed the island and came to the south channel, it looked so bad that the cowboys that were ahead of me didn't know whether to tackle it or not. I had been walking to get warm, after having waded through the north channel. It was raining and was cold, and I wanted to get across before dark. I got on my horse and road down the bank into the river. I was wearing an overcoat and had a belt with one hundred forty rounds of cartridges in it, and was carrying my ballard rifle in my hand.

Mr. Cooper said, "You had better let one of the boys take your gun, that water looks pretty bad," but I said I could make it all right.

They stayed on the bank and watched me. The channel was about one hundred fifty yards wide, and I had gotten to perhaps fifty feet of the south bank without getting into any water more than belly deep, when suddenly my horse plunged into swimming water. He went to the bottom like a stone, then came up pawing his front feet up into the air, and immediately went down again, and I knew at once that he couldn't swim. Of all the horses that I have ever seen in the water, this horse and one other could not swim. I knew that I must get away from him, so when he came up the second time, I slipped off on the upper side of him, and just as he was sinking for the third time I put my foot against him and pushed myself away as far as I could, and started to swim for the shore.

I was a fairly good swimmer, but an overcoat, 140 rounds of ammunition, and a gun in one hand, constitute a pretty big handicap. I was only a few feet from shore, but the current was taking me down very rapidly, and I was not making any headway toward the bank, and I had to let go of my gun. I raised it up above my head and threw it toward the bank, but it fell short by a few feet and that was the last I ever saw of it.

There was a willow tree that had been washed out by the roots, and had fallen out into the river, and by desperate swimming I managed to catch hold of the top of it and pull myself along the trunk for a little ways, where I got both arms over it and hung there completely exhausted. The current was so swift that I thought it would tear me loose, but I managed to hold on.

In the meantime the men on the other side of the river saw a couple of men come out of the timber on the south side and shouted to them. They came running to the bank and one of them had a rake, which he pushed out to me and I caught hold of it, when he dragged me up the bank, where I lay gasping for breath for about fifteen minutes. The horse had rolled and tumbled down the river, and was finally washed out on to a sandbar, where he lay for a while, when he got up and walked up the bar to the island where the rest of the men were.

After I had rested for a few minutes I took off my clothes and tried to find my rifle, but it was gone for good. This was the rifle that Billie Harvey had given me three years before, and I had done some very good shooting with it.

One day, the winter before I lost it, I was hunting on an island a little east of Columbus, and there was some snow on the ground and the prairie chickens were sitting up in the cottonwood trees. I commenced shooting them out of a big cottonwood; when one would fall the others would sit still and look at it. I shot sixteen out of the tree in succession, missing the next one when they flew. The nearest one from where I stood was seventy yards, and some were nearly one hundred yards away. I was very sorry to lose this gun and it was a good many years before I got a gun that I liked as well as that one.

After I gave up hunting for the gun I went up the river about fifty yards above where I had tried to cross, and found a good ford, but by this time it was dark and I had to cross, and lead my horse and the packhorse across before the other boys would try it. We got over after a while and had some supper, after which I was tired enough to go to sleep. The two young men who pulled me out of the river had just taken up homesteads there, and I think they were probably the first settlers that far up the Niobrara.

The second day after leaving the Niobrara I had fallen behind the crowd. It was near sundown, and when I came over the hill in sight of the Elkhorn River, I saw the boys going into the timber about a mile up the river. I rode down into the valley and turned up toward where they were, and, as I was passing a grove of timber about a quarter of a mile away, a band of six Indians dashed out of the brush, and, giving a warwhoop, started for me.

I was unarmed and my horse was played out, so there was no use trying to run. I saw a stick of wood about five feet long lying on the ground, so I got off my horse, dropped down on my knee, and pointed the stick of wood at them like a gun. They swung their horses around and ran the other way.

I started on up the river leading my horse and carrying my wooden gun. They talked among themselves for a while, and then came again, but this time they scattered and I thought my time had come, but I got behind my horse and, pointing the stick over the saddle, I aimed first at one, then at another, and as I did so each turned back.

It was now getting dark, and before they started another charge I saw where the boys were starting a fire about a half a mile above me, so I got on my horse, and using my dummy gun for a persuader, and letting out a few war-whoops myself, I started for camp. The Indians followed for a little way, and then, seeing the campfire, they turned back. There wasn't much sleep that night, for we did not know how near we might be to a big camp of Indians, but nothing happened and I made up my mind it was just a little war party that was probably going home after stealing horses from the Pawnees or Omahas.

In due time we got home to Columbus without any further trouble.

In 1869 The Indian Department was turned over to the Quakers,* and the agents that were appointed at the different agencies were all Quakers, and their idea was to put a stop to tribal wars.[2]

In the fall of that year a war party of Pawnees made a raid on the southern Cheyennes in the Indian territory, and took about one hundred and fifty head of horses from them. The leader of the party was Uh-sah-wuck-oo-led-ee-hoor, Big Spotted Horse,[3]* and when he brought the horses to the reservation, the agent, Major Troth, took the horses from him and turned them over to the chief, to be taken care of until such time as he could make arrangements to send them back to the Cheyennes.

He [Troth] called a council and told all of the chiefs that

2. President Grant in 1869 hoped to improve the honesty of the Indian service by appointing Quakers to head several superintendencies and agencies. The sect had shown enthusiasm for Indian work. In 1870 the program was expanded to include other denominations. Jacob N. Troth, a Quaker, was appointed agent to the Pawnees (Report of the Commissioner of Indian Affairs, 1869, pp. 332-340, 349-351; 1870, p. 10; George B. Hyde, *Pawnee Indians* [Denver: University of Denver Press, 1951], p. 226).

3. Big Spotted Horse served in the Scouts in 1870. He was recalled as a large, good-natured man, but a brave warrior (Hyde, *Pawnee Indians*, 288).

they were not to go to war any more; that all the different tribes were to be friendly with each other, and that the horses they had taken must be sent back, and that the Pawnees must take them back. The Pawnees balked at taking them back, telling him that the Cheyennes would surely kill them, if they went to their village.

In the meantime winter set in and nothing further was done about it, until the next spring, 1870. Every now and then through the winter the chiefs who had charge of the horses would report to the agent that one of them had died, so that by the time he had made arrangements to return them, only thirty-five of them were left.

Soon after I returned from my trip to the Whetstone Agency, the agent sent for me and employed me to take the horses as far as Fort Harker [4] in Kansas, where I was to turn them over to the quartermaster, who was to send them on to the Cheyenne Agency. I had with me as helpers eight young men that had been soldiers in my company the year before, and one chief Co-rux-ta-puk, Fighting Bear.[5]

We started from Columbus and quite a number of people rode out with us to the Platte River to see us cross. The Platte was bank full, but I was now riding my own horse, and a better swimmer never lived than he, so I took the lead. We crossed about two hundred yards above where the present wagon bridge is situated. We went on and crossed the south channel, and stayed that night on Clear Creek.

The next day we met a herd of Texas cattle out on the hills, near the present site of Osceola. The cattle were strung out on the trail, and the two cowboys that were on the point didn't see us until we were pretty close to them. They

---

4. Fort Harker was on the Smoky Hill River near the crossing of the old Sante Fe Trail.

5. Fighting Bear, born about 1800, was a head-chief of the Pitshauerats (Hyde, *Pawnee Indians*, 255 n.).

wheeled their horses and ran for the rear end of the herd as hard as they could go.

I left the boys to bring on the horses, and I rode ahead. There were ten of the cowboys and as soon as I came to them the foreman wanted to know how many cattle I wanted.

I laughed and told him I wasn't holding up cowboys, and after I had told him my business and where I was going, I gave him a few pointers about crossing the Platte River, and also directed him where to strike the trail for the Whetstone Agency, as that was where he was headed for. He insisted on giving us a yearling steer to kill, and as we had no fresh meat it was very welcome. They cut the yearling out of the herd for us, and I had one of the boys, named Sa-gule-ah-la-shar, Sun Chief,[6] run after it and kill it with bow and arrow, to show them how they killed buffalo. This boy, Sun Chief, was a nephew of Pet-ah-le-shar, and later was head chief of the Pawnee tribe.

The second day after meeting the cowboys we reached a little town in Kansas called Belleville at about noon, and camped on a small stream just at the edge of the town. I rode over to the nearest house and explained to the woman who came to the door that the Indians were friendly, and that we would camp on the creek until toward evening, when it got cooler, and then would move on. After we had eaten I went to sleep under a tree, and in about an hour one of the boys woke me up and said we were surrounded by white men, and that they all had guns.

I got up and looked, and about two hundred yards away I saw several heads sticking up over a hill. I waved my hand at them, and leaned my gun against the tree, and walked up to where they were. There were fourteen of them, and I told them what my business was, and asked them to come

6. Sun Chief was one of the Pawnee leaders at the Massacre Canyon fight between the Sioux and Pawnee, August 5, 1873.

to camp and I would show them my letter of instructions from General Augur, who was in command of the Department of the Platte.

They rode down to camp, and at the same time another party from the other side of the creek came in to our camp; there were thirty of them in all. I got my letter and handed it to a big fat pompous looking man, who seemed to be the leader of the bunch.

He put on his spectacles and looked it over very carefully, and then said: "How am I to know that you didn't write this letter yourself? We don't want any Indians around here; you get out as quick as you can. I think we ought to hang all of you, and you are no better than the Indians, or you would not be with them."

By the time he had finished I was pretty red headed. I grabbed my gun and said: "You get out of my camp, and get out quick." He opened his mouth to answer, but I jumped toward him, and poked the muzzle of my gun into his stomach and said: "Go on now," and he went.

I turned to the others and told them that I was on business for the Government, and that I would move on when I got ready. One of the crowd said that was all right; that the fat man had no right to talk to me as he did. They all shook hands with the Indians, and there was no more trouble.

Several of them had heard of the Pawnee scouts and of my brother. When we got ready to move on, about fifteen of them rode with us for eight or ten miles. That night we camped on the Republican River, and the next day we got to the Saline River near where, the year before, the Cheyennes had captured the two white women that we recaptured from them at Summit Springs, Colorado.

While we were in camp on the Saline two young men came into our camp, and in talking to them I found that one of them was a brother of Mrs. Allerdice that had been killed by the Cheyennes when we attacked their village. I told

[ 141 ]

him that I was the first man to get to his sister, but that she was dead when I got to her. He seemed quite relieved when I told him that they had not tortured or mutilated her. I told him of having seen her buried, and that one of the officers of the Fifth Cavalry had read the burial service at the grave, and this pleased him.

One day when we got to the Solomon River and had gone into camp, one of the boys went up the river, and when he came back to camp there were two soldiers with him. The soldiers told me they were camped up the river about a half mile, on the opposite side of the river. A little way below their camp there was a lot of driftwood that reached across the river. One of the soldiers was hunting in the woods along the river, and came out on the bank just opposite this driftwood, and when he saw the Pawnee boy was coming across on it, he pointed his gun at him and ordered him to halt but the boy kept coming right on and said, "All right me Pawnee Scout."

The soldier knew of the scouts, but he also knew that the scouts should be dressed in uniform, so he took the boy prisoner, and took him to their camp. He could speak only a few words of English, but made the sergeant who was in command of the squad understand that there was a white man with them, so two of the soldiers came down to see. They said they thought the boy was lying to them, because if he was a scout he would know what the command to halt meant.

I asked the boy why he didn't stop when the soldier told him to halt, and he replied, "I thought if I stopped he would think I was going to run and would shoot me, but if I kept on going toward him he would know I was friendly."

We met no one else between there and Fort Harker, and on the seventh day I got there and turned over the horses, and got the quartermaster's receipt for them, and the next morning started back. The boys were all on foot, but Fighting Bear and I had brought our own horses to ride back. It had taken us seven days to go down, but the boys were in a hurry to reach home, as the tribe was about ready to start on the summer buffalo hunt, and we made the return trip in five days. The distance was two hundred fifty miles.

I think it was the second night after we left Fort Harker that we camped on a small creek. We were close to the bank, and just as it was getting dark one of the boys saw some men down the creek. I sent a boy to find out who they were, and how many. He came back soon and said he saw ten and that they were watching our camp. We built up our campfire, took our blankets and lay down a little way from the fire, and as soon as it began to die down a little, we crawled away into the darkness. The boy that took care of my horse saddled him. I mounted, and we moved away about a half a mile and again stopped. In about an hour we could see men around the campfire we had left. I suppose they crept up under the bank of the creek expecting to get a shot at us before we woke up, but we weren't there.

About two o'clock my boy [Nick Koots] woke me and we started on our day's journey. We often started at two or three in the morning, and by six or seven we would have made twenty-five miles, when we would get breakfast, then sleep or loaf till about three in the afternoon, and then make another twenty-five miles, and camp for the night.

The morning I have just spoken of when the sun came up we were perhaps fifteen miles on our way, and in looking over the boys I missed Sun Chief. I asked where he was, and my boy said he guessed he was back where we slept, that he didn't get up when we did, but that he would catch up with us when we stopped for breakfast.

We were now in sight of the Republican River, and we followed it up until it was time to stop for breakfast. After we had eaten I got out my fieldglass and began to look back down the river for Sun Chief, and at last when I was beginning to get really uneasy about him, I saw him coming on a pretty fast run.

When he reached us and had something to eat, he told his story. He said he never woke up until sunrise, and then he started after us. There was a high divide to cross between the creek where we had camped and the Republican River, and he kept up a ravine until he came to the head of it, and then thought he could cross the divide and get into a ravine on the other side, and thus keep out of sight. But, when he was about half way across two men rode out of a ravine facing him. He saw that they had seen him, so he kept on toward them. They were armed with Winchester repeating rifles. When they got to him one of them asked him for his bow. He handed it to him; then he wanted his arrows, and he took off his quiver and gave it to him.

One of the men was talking very excitedly, and he could understand that he was in favor of killing him, but the man that had taken his bow and arrows would not consent, and finally told him to go on. He started, but when he had gone a little way the man called to him, and when he stopped he rode up and gave him his bow and quiver full of arrows. Sun Chief took two of the arrows and gave them to the man as a present, which seemed to please him. They shook hands and said goodbye, and Sun Chief said he never stopped running until he got to our camp.

The last night we camped on a little stream below Fairmont, Nebraska,[7] and just before we got to camp my boy, the one who took care of my horse, put his hand on his knee and limped for two or three steps.

Sun Chief said, "What is the matter, are you getting tired?"

"No, but my knee hurts." Sun Chief laughed and said, "I guess you are tired out."

7. Fairmont, in Fillmore County, Nebraska, was originally known as Hesperia. It was settled in 1871.

My boy, whose name was Pe-isk-ee-la-shar, Boy Chief,[8] finally said, "If you think I am tired, I will race you tomorrow from here home"—about eighty-five miles.

Sun Chief promptly accepted the challenge, and they agreed that they would leave the rest of the party as soon as it got light in the morning, and see which would get to the agency first. I told them I would go with them as far as the Platte River, where I would leave them and go to Columbus. The others were to come on with Fighting Bear.

We started about three in the morning, and before daylight were trotting along the side of a hill. My boy, who was jogging along by my horse touched me and said, "There is a man ahead of us."

I stooped down, and against the skyline and nearly to the top of the hill, I could see a man. He was holding a pair of mules, and his wagon was near him. The mules had probably smelled the Indians and awakened him. They were looking toward us with their ears thrust forward. I turned a little to the left and we went trotting past him about twenty feet away. I suppose he was a homesteader, just taking a claim. I never saw or heard of him again, but I imagine he thought he had a narrow escape that time.

At about sunrise, Sun Chief and Boy Chief increased the pace, and the others slowly dropped behind, for the country was rough—up hill and down—and the day was hot. At ten o'clock we reached the Blue, more than forty miles from the starting point, and here Sun Chief made a mistake. He drank cupful after cupful of water. My boy sipped a little and poured several cupfuls over his head. In a few minutes Sun Chief got very sick and threw up the water that he had drunk, and after lying in the shade for a half hour, he said, he was ready to go on. I wanted to give my horse a little more rest, so we waited a while longer, and then started on.

8. Boy Chief was one of the few Pawnee Scouts to be carried on the roster by his white-man name, Peter Headman.

We crossed the Platte River at Gardner[9] at two o'clock, and from there to the agency was about fifteen miles, and about all the way through the sand hills. I left the boys and rode down the river about eight miles to my sisters, and the boys struck through the sand hills for home.

I saw Sun Chief about a month afterward, and asked him how the race came out. He laughed and said, "He beat me. I had to stop and rest." Boy Chief got home at five o'clock, and we had stopped on the Blue nearly two hours, so the actual running time was twelve hours, and the distance eighty-five miles.

About the first of September 1870 my brother was or- dered to enlist two companies of scouts, and I went with him. My company was sent to Plum Creek to relieve a company of the Fifth Cavalry under Capt. Brown. I was in camp there for about six weeks, and sent or took scouting parties out both north and south, but the Indians were pretty quiet and we had no trouble with them.

About the middle of October I was ordered to Ft. Mc- Pherson to join an expedition into the Republican River country. General Carr was in command, and with him were several Englishmen and three gentlemen from Syracuse, New York. They were with the command for the purpose of hunting buffalo, and they had very good luck, as I think they all killed buffalo on the trip.

When we reached the Republican General Carr sent me with ten men and three days' rations to scout the country south on Beaver Creek, then across to Prairie Dog Creek, and back to the Republican, where I was to meet him. Cody went with me on this trip. We found no Indians nor any

9. Gardner was a Union Pacific Railroad station in Platte County, Nebraska.

sign, but the whole country was alive with game. On every little creek we crossed we found wild turkeys and antelope, and buffalo were in sight pretty much all the time. The afternoon of the third day we got back to the camp, and then moved down the river one day's march.

We lay in camp here one day, and the General sent Cody out to kill some buffalo, as he expected to start back to Ft. McPherson the next day, and we did not know whether any buffalo would be found on the homeward march. A Lieutenant and ten men with two six-mule teams were sent with him to bring in the meat, and one of the gentlemen from Syracuse also went along.

Cody came past my camp as they were starting out, and asked me to go along, so I saddled my horse and went with him. When we had gone about five miles back from the river we found five buffalo, and on running close to them found they were all bulls. Cody killed one three-year-old, but the rest were old and we let them go. We waited until the wagons came up with us.

We were on a hill about half a mile from a small stream that runs into the Republican, and across the stream, west of us about a mile, was a bunch of buffalo lying down. Cody told the lieutenant that while they were cutting up the bull we would ride down and find a crossing for the teams, and then go on and kill enough buffalo to load the wagons, and he asked the New Yorker if he didn't want to go along. Of course he did, and we rode down to the creek together.

Where we struck the creek the banks were so high and steep that there was no chance to cross the wagons, and I told Cody I would ride up the creek, and he could go down, until one of us found a crossing. I had gone quite a distance and had not found a crossing and had ridden into a thicket of willows, when I heard Cody yell, "North, North, Indians!"

I got out of the brush as quickly as I could and saw Cody

[ 147 ]

and his friend riding as hard as they could go in the direction of the wagons on the hill. I followed on a run, but kept looking back and wondering where the Indians were. Pretty soon Cody and friend disappeared in a ravine, and an instant after the New Yorker rode up the other side and continued the race toward the wagons.

When I got to the ravine Cody was waiting for me and laughing fit to kill. I asked him what it was all about, and he said that he hadn't seen any Indians, that he was giving "Mac" a scare. I told him he had evidently succeeded, and that "Mac" would be lucky if he didn't break his neck before he got to the wagons. The country was very rough and broken, and he just plunged down into the canyons at full speed. However, he got safely to the wagons.

We rode along after him slowly, and Bill said, "Now, I must tell some story to the lieutenant."

I said, "You might tell him it was some of my Indians and that I sent them back to camp." He did so, but I was always a little suspicious that the lieutenant did not more than half believe him.

Bill had found a crossing just below when I left him, and after he had pointed it out to the lieutenant we went across to where the buffalo were, and killed six of them. We waited until the wagons came over, when we started for camp. Bill asked "Mac" if he didn't want to go with us, but he preferred to stay with the wagons. It was a very bright sunshiny day and "Mac" had lost his hat, and he was burned to a blister when he got to camp in the evening.

The next day we started for the fort, and when we got there I was ordered back to Plum Creek, and stayed there the rest of the fall.

[ 148 ]

Some time in December of that year my brother took twenty-five of the men from Capt. Cushing's * company at O'Fallon Station,[10] and went to Ogallala for a buffalo hunt. On this hunt my brother had as his guests Mr. James W. Wadsworth [11] of Geneseo, N.Y., who was long representative in Congress and the father of the present U. S. Senator, several railroad men, and a few officers from Ft. McPherson, and Cody was in the party. I was with them, having gone to O'Fallon by rail and joined them there.

We marched up the river to Roscoe, where we crossed to the south side. The night after we crossed, it turned very cold and the river froze over. The next day the railroad men got there and were obliged to cross on the ice. On the south side of the river next to our camp there was an open channel about three feet deep and fifty or seventy-five feet wide. When the men got to this channel we called to them to wait, and we would send some of our men to carry them over. There were eight of them and they were all big men.

We sent the boys over and it happened that the smallest one got the biggest man, a division superintendent named Schanklin. He was six feet six inches high, and the Indian that was carrying him was about five feet eight. The first one across was Con Groner,[12] an engineer, and when he landed

~~~~~~~~~~~~~~~~

10. O'Fallon's station was in Lincoln County on the north side of the South Platte River across from O'Fallons Bluffs, a landmark on the Oregon Trail.

11. James Wolcott Wadsworth (1846-1926) served twelve years in the U.S. House of Representatives between 1881 and 1907. His grandfather pioneered in the Genesee Valley, and his father, who was mortally wounded in the Battle of the Wilderness, commanded the defenses of Washington in 1862. His son, James Wolcott, Jr. (1877-1952), was U.S. senator from New York (1915-1927) and subsequently a member of the House of Representatives.

12. Con Groner (b. 1845) quit railroading in 1876 and became well known as sheriff of Lincoln County. His reputation as a peace officer was such that William F. Cody hired Groner as an attraction for his Wild West Show; he was billed as "The Cowboy Sheriff" (A. T. Andreas, *History of Nebraska* [Chicago: The Western His-

the boy that was carrying Schanklin was about half way over. Con said, "Major tell that boy to fall down."

My brother called to him to fall down, so he tripped and down he went, dumping Schanklin into the ice cold water. He helped him up and motioned for him to get on his back, but Schanklin swore, and said he would walk the rest of the way. We had a wall tent with a stove in it, and Schanklin was soon stripped and dried and was as good as new, and I doubt if he ever found out that his fall wasn't an accident.

The next day we made our hunt and every one that went out had pretty good luck. Mr. Wadsworth killed four buffalo, I think, and Cody gave an exhibition that was the most remarkable I ever saw. He was riding a cavalry horse that had never been used for hunting, and was very much afraid of the buffalo. He rode after a small band and after following them for about a mile, got the horse up to within fifty yards of them, when he commenced to shoot, and in sixteen shots he killed sixteen buffalo, and I want to say here that the man never lived that could equal him at shooting with a rifle from the back of a galloping horse. I have beaten him many times at target shooting at fifty, one hundred and two hundred yards, but on horseback he was in a class by himself. And here is a singular thing; he couldn't hit anything with a revolver; in fact, I never saw him shoot a revolver a dozen times in all the time I was with him.

On the other hand, my brother besides being a crack shot with the rifle, was the best revolver shot in the west. He and Wild Bill Hickock [13] used to meet about twice a week and

torical Co., 1882], 1099; and Don Russell, *The Lives and Legends of Buffalo Bill* [Norman: University of Oklahoma Press, 1960], 306-307).

13. James Butler Hickok (1837-1876) got his start, so to speak, in a shooting affray at Rock Creek Station, Nebraska Territory, in 1861 (Carl Uhlarik, "The Myth of Wild Bill Hickok" [*Prairie Schooner*, XXIV, 2 (Summer 1951)]). He served as a scout and peace officer, and in 1872-1873 toured with William F. Cody. A re-enactment of his murder by Jack McCall in a Deadwood saloon is performed daily during tourist season.

shoot at targets at John Talbot's roadhouse between Cheyenne and Fort Russell, and Talbot would shoot with them. Frank would nearly always win with Talbot second and Wild Bill third. I never saw Wild Bill shoot with his left hand either, although he was always called a two-gun man, and as to shooting from the hip, I never did see a man shoot from the hip, though I have seen such gunmen as Wild Bill, Jack Hays, Doc Midelton, Joe Hall and others.[14]

After returning from our buffalo hunt I went back to my camp at Plum Creek, and did some scouting from there south to the Republican. In one of these scouts I ran across a small party of Indians and chased them for several miles, capturing three horses from them, but didn't get within shooting distance of them. Some time in December we were mustered out, and returned home.

A short time after we were mustered out a party of sixteen of us, with four wagons, went on another buffalo hunt. The only experienced hunters were my brother, Billy Harvey and myself.

14. David C. Middleton was a frontier character and probably the most notorious horse thief in Nebraska history to date. Captured in 1879 after a good deal of gunplay, he did time in the Nebraska penitentiary (1879-1883) and emerged, so he said, "reformed." In 1913 he died in jail at Douglas, Wyoming, where he had been arrested for bootlegging (*Nebraska History*, X [October-December, 1927], 351-352).

Jack Hays may have been John Coffee Hays, Texas Ranger, sheriff of San Francisco, and Indian fighter. Joe Hall may have been Jesse Leigh Hall, Texas Ranger and leader of the Macabebe scouts for the U.S. Army during the Philippine Insurrection (Edward Bartholomew, *Biographical Album of Western Gunfighters* [Houston: Frontier Press of Texas, 1958], n.p.).

We crossed the Platte River at Grand Island, and just before we went into camp my brother and myself were ahead of the wagons on horseback, and off from the road a couple of hundred yards was a sod house. My brother said, "Let's go over and see if we can buy some bread."

We rode over and without getting off our horses knocked on the door. A young woman opened it, and my brother asked her if we could buy some bread.

Instead of answering she said, "Is this Major North?" On being told that it was she said, "I guess you don't know me."

My brother said, "No," and she then said, "I am one of the girls that was captured by the Cheyennes and that you exchanged for at North Platte three years ago."

She wanted us to stay to supper, but we explained to her that the teams were expecting us to find a camping place for them. She gave us a couple of loaves of bread, but would not take any pay for them. She was one of the Martin [Campbell] girls,[15] was married and living with her husband on a homestead. He had gone to one of the neighbors several miles away, and we didn't see him and we never saw her again.

We camped a few miles from there, and the next day moved over to the little Blue, where we found buffalo. I had two saddle horses along, one was a four-year-old that I was just breaking, and the other was Mazeppa or Zep, the horse that I had gone after to the Spotted Tail Agency the year before. I let my brother have him to ride on the first chase we had, and he killed eleven buffalo with the twelve shots from his two revolvers. My colt was so afraid of the buffalo that I couldn't get him near them, so I didn't kill one.

When we were going out with the teams to get the meat, in hunting a crossing of a ravine I found a nearly new lumber wagon, and as there were horse tracks leading away down

---

15. See page 61.

the ravine, my brother said I had better follow them for a way, and see who they were. I took my Zep horse and followed down the canyon for a couple of miles, and then up out of it and across the tableland for eight or ten miles, then up to the ridge overlooking the Republican River. I had my fieldglasses with me and with them I could see a large camp of Indian lodges; there must have been two hundred, I think.

I started back to our camp, and before I got there it began to snow, and by the time I got to camp it had commenced to blow pretty hard. Before morning it had turned into a blizzard, and it kept up for three days. Before we started on the hunt my brother had had a lodge made of heavy canvas, and where we were camped we had pretty good shelter for the horses, and there was plenty of wood, so we didn't suffer much from the cold. We had grain for our horses, but no hay and they could get no grass, so it was rather hard on them, but they came through in pretty good shape. One of the wagons was under the bank of the creek and when the storm was over it was buried out of sight in the snow. It took us all of one day to dig the wagons out and get them up on the bank, and the next day we started for home.

We never found out who the wagon that I found belonged to, but as the horse tracks that I followed went to the Indian camp, we thought probably the man had been killed and his horses taken by the Indians.

On the return trip Frank and I rode ahead and picked out a road for the wagons, for the snow was badly drifted, and in many of the ravines it was twenty feet deep, but packed so hard that we drove the wagons over it without breaking through. The sun came out so bright that about noon the first day Frank became snowblind and had to ride in one of the wagons, and as none of the rest of the party knew the country, I was the only guide. The second day we got to the Platte River and crossed it near Grand Island, and by this time my eyes were so inflamed that I could not see at all, but there was a traveled road from there home, and the teams got along all right.

My eyes were very painful and I stayed in the wagon with a bandage over them all the way home, and for a week or more I was totally blind. All of the party were snowblind, but I was much the worse of any. I suppose it was because I had to use my eyes to follow the trail, long after the others had given up keeping their eyes open all of the time. I don't think that my eyes were any the worse for this experience, as my eyesight was very good afterward.

Two weeks after we got home, I went back to Plum Creek and with a party of four of us went north from there to hunt for elk on Wood River. In the party was Jack McCall,[16] George Belden, a man named Smith and myself, and we had along a man to drive the team and do the cooking. George Belden had spent a good part of his life with the Sioux Indians, and there was a book written of his life called "Belden the White Chief." After living with the Indians he went into the army, serving first in the Second Nebraska Cavalry during the Civil War, and later he got a commission in the regular army as lieutenant, and was courtmarshalled and dismissed. This hunt was perhaps a year or so after that.

When we left Plum Creek Belden and Smith were [not] very good friends, and were quarreling all the time. Smith had a pretty good supply of whiskey along, and kept pretty well loaded. He knew nothing about hunting and was afraid to get out of sight of the wagon for fear he would get lost.

16. It is impossible to say whether or not this man was the Jack McCall who shot Wild Bill Hickok. However, while any comment is purely conjectural, Luther North's letters have a good deal to say about Hickok, and it might be supposed that if he had known his assassin personally he would have mentioned it.

The second day out we were just getting ready to put up
the tent when Belden, who had been hunting, galloped into
camp and said he had seen a band of elk. McCall and I were
putting up the tent, and Belden called to Smith to come
with him and they would get some of them. Smith's horse
was saddled, so he got on him and they rode away together.

McCall said, "That is funny, they have hardly spoken to
each other all day, and now George asks him to go instead
of one of us."

We finished putting the tent up and ate our supper, and
after it had been dark for perhaps an hour, George Belden
came walking into camp.

I said, "Where is Smith, and where is your horse?"

He began to laugh and said Smith was holding the horses.
He hadn't seen any elk at all, and when he got Smith away
far enough from camp and it was nearly dark, he told him
to hold the horses and he would crawl over the hill and get
a shot at the elk. As soon as he was out of sight he came to
camp.

I said, "Where did you leave him? I'll go an get him;
he will freeze out there."

Belden said, "I will not tell you where he is. Let the old
son-of-a-gun stay out there, it will do him good," and he
went to bed.

The next morning he told me about where Smith was and
I went out and got him. He had tied the horses to some brush
in the canyon and had kept himself warm by walking about.
When I told him Belden was in camp, he swore he would kill
him; but I told him he had better go slow, that Belden was a
dead shot himself, and we didn't want any killing on this
trip. He cooled down some before we got to camp and didn't
say anything; in fact, I don't think they spoke to one another
again.

While we were out I ran into a band of elk that day, and
killed three, so we had plenty of meat, and I proposed to

[ 155 ]

Jack McCall that we go home. He was as anxious as I to get away from both Smith and Belden, and the next day we started back from Plum Creek, where we arrived without any further trouble. I went home from there and never saw either Smith or Belden afterwards.

I never knew what became of Smith, but Belden was City Editor on the *Omaha Herald* for some time, and a year or two later he went up the Missouri River and lived with the Indians at the Standing Rock Agency, and was murdered by a halfbreed with whom he had had some trouble. He was a good hearted reckless sort of a fellow, a fine horseman, and a good crack rifle shot. I saw him defeat Cody in a match at Ft. McPherson in 1869. They shot ten shots at 110 and 200 yards, and Belden won at both distances. He was an expert trailer and a good hunter and trapper, and also a good scout and Indian fighter.[17]

17. George P. Phouts Belden, First Lieutenant, Second Cavalry, was cashiered on November 4, 1869. He was at one time employed as a printer on the Omaha *Weekly Herald*. He was killed by an Indian near the Grand River Agency, Dakota Territory (Francis B. Heitman, *Historical Register and Dictionary of the United States Army* [Washington: Government Printing Office, 1903] I, 206; Omaha *Weekly Herald*, September 20, 1871).

# SUPPLEMENT

### THE PAWNEE AGENCY UNDER AGENT TROTH (page 138)

The Quaker regime, however tragically it misunderstood the Indians, was well-meaning, kindly, and honest. Under Major Troth, conditions improved greatly at the agency. "He had put all the old buildings in fine shape and built several new ones. At last, after ten years of longing, Mrs. [Elvira] Platt [the teacher] had the high picket fence around her boarding-school; Troth had even painted the fence white, and he had built at the Indian villages a big, comfortable day-school, where a woman teacher was instructing fifty of the children. The Quakers were supplying clothing for the school children; they had also sent out a matron to live in the Indian villages and care for the sick and aged" (Hyde, *Pawnee Indians*, 240-241).

There was one privilege enjoyed by the Pawnee that Agent Troth did his best to have abolished. "The Union Pacific officials, in acknowledgment of the great service the Pawnee Scouts had rendered . . . , had given orders that all Pawnees should ride free along the line in Nebraska. Some of the Pawnees were having a lovely time, riding on the cars, visiting with fine white people from the East, getting free meals at the stations, selling beadwork, bows and arrows. Agent Troth was annoyed. He wished to keep all the Indians on the reservation . . ." (Hyde, *Pawnee Indians*, 240).

Big Spotted Horse (page 138)

In a reminiscence which appeared in Bruce, *The Fighting North and Pawnee Scouts*, Luther North wrote that since Big Spotted Horse was "left-handed (quite unusual for an Indian) he was also sometimes known as *Left Hand*. He must have been at least two inches more than six feet (slightly taller than Traveling Bear), was generally good natured and laughed a good deal—but was quick-tempered and somewhat restless. Big Spotted Horse was an inveterate gambler and generally broke. He was very fond of his wife, and unlike most Indians, did some of the women's work, often carrying a boy's papoose around on his back. . . . He and Frank White [q.v.] took the lead of the younger Pawnees when, against the advice and wishes of the older chiefs and men, they decided to sell the old Reservation and remove to the Southwest. Though a great warrior, he was not a chief; and making a slight comparison with Crooked Hand, I should say that the Spotted Horse excelled in leading raids into hostile territory, while Crooked Hand rendered his greatest service in fighting off attacks made on the Pawnee villages" (19). Big Spotted Horse was a particularly adept horse thief, and North remarks that he "continued his well-known activities in Indian Territory. My general impression is that he made off with a large number of Cheyenne horses, and was either killed or murdered by officers of the United States, who probably did not appreciate what a skilled performer he was in that line" (20).

Sylvanus B. Cushing (page 149)

Cushing, North tells us, was "over 6 feet and weighed 220 —a giant in strength as in size. One day in the fall of 1870, when Maj. North, William F. Cody, I and others were hunting buffalo near Ogallala, Neb., Cody's horse fell and in some way caught Buffalo Bill. One of Cody's legs was under the horse, and the other up over its side, bringing his crotch against the horse's belly close behind the forelegs, and his face within striking distance of its front feet. To prevent the horse from struggling, Cody took hold of its legs just above the hoofs and began talking.

"Cushing, not far away, was the first man to face the situation. Walking up to the horse on the opposite side from Cody, he stooped over its withers, took the front legs in his hands, and bracing himself against the withers, gave a quick heave and rolled the animal clear over the saddle and off of Bill before it had a chance to try to get up. That was the greatest exhibition of physical strength I ever saw, and probably saved Cody from serious injury, as the horse would very likely have trampled him in the face if it had attempted to get up while holding him fast" (40).

# VII

## SCOUTING WITH THE CAVALRY

[*Supplement for this chapter begins on page 174.*]

IN THE EARLY SPRING of 1871 my brothers, myself and perhaps fifteen or twenty other people went up the Loup
River and located what is now known as Howard County.
I was one of three first County Commissioners of that
county.[1]

J. N. Paul was one of the others, and I have forgotten who
the third man was. People began to settle in the county along
the North Loup, and as that country was on the trail that the
Sioux followed when coming to raid the Pawnees, the
government sent two companies of soldiers one of cavalry
and one of infantry, to a camp on the North Loup to pro-

1. "J. C. Lewis, L. H. North and N. J. Paul were appointed County
Commissioners for Howard County, Nebraska" (Diary of Nicholas
Jay Paul, Monday, April 17, 1871, microfilm, Nebraska State His-
torical Society).

tect the settlers. My brother Frank was employed as scout and guide, and also took a contract to put up hay, and I took some teams and men and put up two or three hundred tons in the fall. I worked with a party that was surveying the Pawnee Reservation.

In the winter of 1872 Frank was transferred to Ft. Russell, Wyo.,[2] and I was employed at the camp on the North Loup. Major Switzer [3] was in command, and in June of that year he made a scout up the south fork of the Loup, about sixty miles above St. Paul, [Nebraska], where I struck the trail of about twenty lodges of Indians. We camped on the South Loup that night, and the next morning started on the trail. It led north through the sand hills, and we followed it to the North Loup.

With three of the soldiers I was riding about three miles ahead of the command, when we came in sight of the Indian camp. They saw us, and while the women began to take down the lodges, the warriors jumped on their horses and came for us. The soldiers started back on a run to meet the command, while I took a look at the camp through my field-glass, to see how many there were of them. The camp was about a mile away, and as I was mounted on my Mazeppa horse, I knew I could run away from them at any time I wanted to.

One of the soldiers, a man named Wentworth, who was a crack shot and a fine hunter, was one of the three with me. He was the hero of one of Ned Buntline's novels, and Buntline called him the Little White Whirlwind. After I had sat-

2. Fort D. A. Russell was established near Cheyenne, Wyoming, in 1867 primarily to protect the Union Pacific Railroad. In 1929 it was renamed Fort Francis E. Warren, honoring the Wyoming senator of that name, the father-in-law of General of the Armies John J. Pershing.

3. Nelson Bowman Sweitzer (d. 1898) was a Pennsylvanian and a West Point graduate. During the Civil War he reached the rank of brevet brigadier general. In 1870 he was Acting Assistant Inspector General of the Department of the Platte.

isfied myself that there were no more than twenty-five or thirty warriors in the bunch, I started back towards the command. I soon overtook Wentworth, whose horse was not much good. He asked me to stay with him, and I told him that as the command was only a short distance behind, and the other two soldiers would soon meet them, there was not much danger, even if the Indians did overtake us, as we could stand them off until the soldiers came.[4]

About this time we came to quite a deep ravine on Dry Creek that ran into the North Loup, and as we rode down the bank I stopped my horse, thinking that this would be a good place to put up a fight. I got off my horse and left him in the bottom of the ravine, and climbed up the bank to wait for the Indians.

I could see three or four that had crossed the river; they were on top of a high hill, and I think they must have been in sight of the soldiers, and one of them began to ride his horse in a circle and waved his blanket at the same time. I think he was signaling to the Indians that were following me. At any rate, they all stopped, and after talking together, they turned and rode down and crossed the river, and joined the warriors on the hill. I took a couple of shots at them, but as they were about half a mile from me, I did no damage.

By this time the women had packed their horses and crossed the river. I was expecting the troops would come every minute, but when the women had all passed out of sight behind some hills across the river, I rode on back to

---

4. Captain North's memory of this incident mellowed over the years. The soldier in question was Conrad Wentworth, on whom Buntline modeled the hero of a dime novel. On January 22, 1876, North wrote to his uncle that as Wentworth's horse tired "The hero of a hundred battles, on paper, was bawling like a calf and begged me not to run off and leave him" (Luther H. North to John Calvin North, January 22, 1875, Luther North Papers, Nebraska State Historical Society). See Appendix A.

Ned Buntline was the pseudonym used by Edward Zane Carroll Judson (1823-1866).

find the troops. They were back some two miles and were dismounted, when the soldiers that had been with me got back to the command, and told Major Switzer of the Indians. He halted and dismounted his men, and waited for the wagons, which were about a mile behind, to come up. Then he issued one hundred rounds of ammunition to each man, all of which took time and gave the Indians a chance to get away.[5]

When I got to the command he asked me what tribe the Indians were, and how many there were. I told him I thought they were Brule Sioux from the Spotted Tail Agency, and that there were probably one hundred, including women and children, and that it was probably a hunting party.

By this time some of the Indians had ridden up on the hills opposite to us on the north side of the river, and about a half a mile away, and the Major told me to ride down to the river and tell them to come over, that he wanted to talk with them. He seemed surprised when I told him I could not talk the Sioux language, but would try to make them understand.

Wentworth and I went down to the river and motioned for them, and six or seven of them came across. One of them knew a few words of English, and when asked what they wanted he said, "Sugar, coffee and flour." The Major made a speech to them that they could not understand. He told them they must go home and be good Indians, gave them sugar, coffee and hardtack, and they went away rejoicing, and that was the last we saw of them. A few days later we reached our camp on the North Loup.

5. North was still indignant in 1876. "Now what do you suppose the old whisky bloat that was in command of our party done, he halted and dismounted his men and right there we staid for two hours and the Indians walked off. That's about the way the Regular Army officers fight Indians" (Luther North Papers, Nebraska State Historical Society).

While in camp I put in a good deal of my time in hunting, and furnished meat for the Infantry Company, while Wentworth did most of the hunting for the Cavalry Company. One morning I had started out a little after sunrise with a couple of soldiers and one of the teamsters and a wagon, to get a load of elk meat, and when out ten miles from camp I was overtaken by a messenger from Major Switzer. He ordered me to return to camp. When I got there he said he had some dispatches to send to Grand Island, and that I was to get the answer to them and return to camp as soon as possible.

It was eleven o'clock when I left the camp, and he sent a lieutenant and twenty-five men with me the first twenty miles, as he had gotten word that the country was full of Indians. It was sixty miles to Grand Island, and after the soldiers turned back at the end of twenty miles, I rode the rest of the way alone. I saw no Indians, but crossed the trail of a war party of perhaps fifty mounted Indians, and it was so fresh that where they crossed a creek the bank was still wet where the water had splashed as the horses climbed out. I left the traveled road and kept in the ravine as much as I could, and crossed the South Loup a little west of St. Paul, and reached Grand Island a little before seven o'clock. I had ridden eighty miles in all that day.

I took my horse to a livery barn, and had him fed and given a good rubdown, but while the man was taking care of him I took the dispatches to the telegraph office, and got me some supper. In about an hour the answers came, and at nine o'clock I saddled my horse and started back.

Just after crossing the South Loup at St. Paul I was caught in a terrific thunderstorm, and the wind blew so hard, and it was so dark that I had to turn my back to it and wait until it was over, then started on, and at a little before four o'clock I was at the camp, having ridden one hundred forty miles in twenty hours on one horse, the best I ever owned.

Pretty much all of this ride was made on a trot, though occasionally I would break into a canter for a mile or two. The wild west pictures of scouts dashing madly on a long ride on a gallop are not faithful. A scout who was starting on a long ride had to be as careful as possible of his horse, and keep him in as good condition as he could, so that if he had to make a run for it, his horse was ready.

After taking care of my horse I delivered my package to the Major's orderly, and went over to my tent to get something to eat. I was drinking a cup of coffee when Major Switzer sent for me.

When I got to his tent he said, "I am very much surprised to see you back so soon, how do you feel?"

I told him I was all right.

He said, "I hate to ask you to start out again now, but I must send someone down to St. Paul at once."

I replied, "If you will furnish me with a horse I will go."

He then said the quartermaster would furnish the horse, and in a few minutes I was again on my way, and before eleven o'clock was back to St. Paul, where I was to stay until the next day.

The weather was pretty warm and about three o'clock I took my blanket and went out on the east side of the house, and thought I would take a nap before supper. I had ridden one hundred eighty miles, and had gone without sleep for nearly thirty-six hours, as I had gotten up about four o'clock the morning before. I went to sleep all right, and the next I knew the lady of the house was calling me and the sun was shining in my face. It was morning and she was calling me to breakfast. She said she had come to call me for supper the night before, but I was sleeping so soundly she hated to wake me up. It was after six o'clock and I had slept for fifteen hours straight. I ate my breakfast and afterward went out into the hills and killed an antelope.

Shortly after I got back the mail carrier came from Grand

Island and I got the mail for the camp, and that afternoon started back. About fifteen miles out I saw some horse tracks crossing the road and followed them for four or five miles, when I came in sight of Indians. There were eight of them, and as I wanted to know whether they were Sioux or Pawnees, I rode down in a canyon that ran parallel to the course they were taking, and by riding pretty fast I managed to get ahead of them. By the time I got to the head of the ravine I fastened my horse and crept up to the top of the bank. They were about a quarter of a mile away, and I could see through my glasses that they were Pawnees. I then stood up and shouted to them, and they came over.

I saw they were surprised to see me, and told me a small party of Sioux had been down to the Pawnee Agency and stolen a lot of horses, and they had followed them, but had given up overtaking them and were now on their way home. I told them of the trail I had crossed two days before, and they said that was the party they were after. We sat down on the hill and smoked and talked for a half hour or so, when they started for home. I went on to camp, where I arrived about sundown.

I told Major Switzer about meeting the Pawnees and he said, "If you run across any more of them in this country, tell them to go back to their reservation and stay there; that any Indians found away from their reservation would be considered hostile, and would be treated as such."

I thought of telling him that if he treated all the hostiles as he did the party of Sioux we met a short time before, by giving them sugar, coffee and hardtack, they would all be hostile, but I had another thought that beat that and so kept still.

While I was in this camp we caught five young elk, and raised them on a bottle. Captain Munson [6] had a pair of them broken to drive, and I believe later took them to Omaha,

6. Probably Captain Samuel Munson of the Ninth Cavalry.

where he drove them through the street, but they caused several teams to run away, and he gave up driving them. I don't know what became of them.

The latter part of June we started out on a scout with the cavalry company, and after going up the North Loup one day, we crossed over to the Cedar River and marched down it one day, and after laying in camp one day the Major asked me if we could cross the country from there to our camp in one day. I told him we could, but that the country was pretty rough for wagons, and the trail would not be very straight. He said we would try it, so we started the next morning and traveled until noon, when we came to some waterholes, where we camped for dinner.

After eating we started on, and when we got over within a few miles of the Loup River, we got into the rough hills, and I had to zig zag back and forth among the heads of the canyons to find a road for the wagons. Two or three times the Major had said to me, "Can't you find a straighter road than this?" I tried to explain to him that as soon as I could get down off the hills we were following on to the little stream to our right, we would follow the valley of the creek right down to the river, and would be just opposite our camp, and that the road would be good all of the way.

Finally, as I was making another turn, around the head of a canyon he said, "I think if we went off to the left here, we would find a much straighter and better road."

I said to him, "If you know so much about this country you don't need a guide," and I started off on a gallop and was soon out of sight.

In an hour I was in camp and went to the quartermaster and told him I was through. He settled with me and then said, "Couldn't you and the old man get along together?"

When I told him what had happened he was very much

amused, and said, "It is a wonder he didn't put you under arrest, he is such an old crank."

I said, "He did not have time as I left suddenly."

He then asked me when the command would get to camp. I told him if they kept on in the direction they were going when I left them, they would never get to camp with the wagons, as they were heading for some canyons; that they never would get them out.

This proved to be the case, as he got to the head of a canyon where he could go no further, and in trying to turn back one of the wagons rolled over into the canyon and was completely demolished, and they abandoned it. The command finally made a dry camp and came in the next day. I had gone down the river a few miles and stopped with a settler friend of mine, and it was a couple of months before I was in that part of the country again.

The next day after leaving the camp I rode down to Spring Creek, where there was quite a colony of Columbus people, who had taken homesteads there, and in their settlement were my two sisters and their husbands. I stayed there with them for a week or two, and then started for Columbus.

Three or four miles below Spring Creek there were the ruins of an old Pawnee village, and the walls of their earth houses were still plainly to be seen. I got off my horse and was walking through it, when I came to one great circle that was seventy yards in diameter.[7] I was somewhat puzzled over it, as I had never seen or heard of a house that size, and when I got to the Pawnee village that day, I stopped at

7. The village was in Howard County about four miles north of the present town of Palmer, in Merrick County. It covered about fifteen acres, and according to John Dunbar, a missionary who visited it in 1836, the village contained seventy lodges. Confirming North's observation, an archeological report states that "Formerly there is said to have been a great circle over 200 feet across in the center of the site but this has been obliterated" (Waldo Wedel, *An Introduction to Pawnee Archeology*, Smithsonian Institution Bureau of Ethnology Bulletin 112 [Washington: 1936], 25-26).

Eagle Chief's lodge and asked him about it, and about the village.*

He said the Skee-dees lived there a long time ago, and that the big lodge was probably a public building and was used for all public gatherings, councils and religious ceremonies. He also said that it was while living at that village that the Skee-dees became separated. They were going on their summer hunt and part of them started ahead of the others. They went north, probably as far as the Niobrara, when they were attacked by the Sioux, and were defeated in the battle that followed, and as the Sioux were south of them, they retreated to the north until they came to the Missouri River. They followed up the Missouri until they met the Mandan Indians, with whom they made a treaty and built houses there, and have lived near or with them ever since. They are called the A-rik-a-ree.*

I had supper with Eagle Chief and we sat up until nearly morning talking. He said that before this separation the Skee-dees were a very large tribe and could hold their own with any of their enemies, but after that they had rather a hard time, and at last were conquered by the Lak-tata-oo-led-u-hoor—the Chaw-we, the Kit-kah-hawk, the Pete-ah-how-u-rat. This was a long time after the separation of the Skee-dees. Several writers tell of the return of the A-rik-a-rees in 1833, and say they lived with the Skee-dees for two or three years, and that they were so quarrelsome and dirty that the Skee-dees drove them away, and they went back to the Man-dans.* Eagle Chief must have been past twenty years old in 1833, and he was quite positive in saying that the A-rik-a-ree had never come back. Some of them had been back to visit the Skee-dees, but I do not believe they ever all came back, or that more than perhaps a dozen ever came at one time.

[ 169 ]

The next day after my visit with Eagle Chief I went on to Columbus, and a short time after that my brother Frank had a letter from George Bird Grinnell of New York, asking him to take him and a Mr. James M. Russell of Kentucky on a buffalo hunt.* The both men knew my brother, having been in the group of students from Yale College that Professor Marsh had brought out two years before, when my brother acted as guide for him in his expedition from Ft. McPherson north to the Loup River country. As my brother was at Ft. Russell and could not go, he referred them to me, and when they let me know at what time they would be here, I went to Plum Creek, Nebraska, where I hired a team and man to drive it and cook for us. I also got saddle horses and provisions enough to last a couple of weeks.

When the two men arrived we started south to overtake the Pawnees, who had gone on their annual summer hunt. This was the beginning of my friendship with Mr. Grinnell, and it has lasted until now. It is now fifty-two years since that buffalo hunt, and he still journeys out here every year to see me.

I think it was about the third day from Plum Creek that Mr. Grinnell killed an old bull buffalo. About the sixth day we overtook the Pawnees and traveled with them until they made a big surround and killed perhaps a thousand buffalo.

When the Pawnees were about to start on one of their hunts, the chiefs of the different bands had a meeting and agreed on four men, one from each band, who were to be leaders of the hunt, and these four men had absolute command, even the chiefs being subject to their orders. They rode ahead of the tribe on the march and picked out the camping grounds; they carried a staff or pole an inch in diameter and seven or eight feet long, to the end of which was fastened a strip of cloth, and the feathers of a hawk or an eagle, and the skin of some animal or bird that was the medicine of the beaver. This staff was held in an upright position while on the march.

Each day these leaders chose certain men to scout ahead and off to each side of the line of march, and when they came in to where they had made camp, they reported to the leaders what they had discovered. The leaders in turn reported to the crier, who in turn shouted the news to the camp. The crier came out in front of his lodge at sundown and called out in a loud voice, "Listen, listen, all of you people." Instantly everything was still; when he would begin to tell the news of the day.

It was perhaps like this, "Blue Hawk was riding far ahead today, and found on Prairie Dog Creek a large band of buffalo. Tomorrow will be the big hunt; we will move camp at daylight." Or, again, "Little Wolf saw the tracks of seven men north of here. They wore Sioux moccasins. You had better have your horses close to camp tonight, or they may be taken." In this way, every evening the camp was informed of what had taken place during the day, and of what to expect on the morrow.

The day we overtook the Pawnees and camped with them, I took the two young men over and introduced them to Pete-ah-le-shar, Chief Man, the head chief of the tribe, and told him what we were there for; that these men wanted to see how the Pawnees killed buffalo. He said it was good, and that the next day they would make a big killing. After smoking with him we returned to our camp and took a good rest and sleep.

The next morning the Indians broke camp early and moved south across the hills to Driftwood Creek, where they went into camp, and the hunters mounted their fastest horses and started for the big hunt. There were about one thousand mounted men, and the leaders or captains of the hunt rode in front, and no man, not even one of the chiefs, dared ride ahead of them or attempt to kill a buffalo, until they

[ 171 ]

gave the word. The reason for this was that, if individual hunting was permitted the men who had the best and fastest horses would be the only ones who would get any meat, and they would scare out of the country the buffalo that they didn't kill, and those people who had slower horses would kill nothing and get no meat. Another reason was that the Pawnees had so many enemies that they dared not scatter out widely for fear of being attacked. So they always tried to make a big killing at one time, and as close together as possible.

When all was ready, we left camp and rode for a mile or two on a trot, and then broke into a slow canter. Many of the Indians, in fact the great majority of the younger warriors, ran on foot and led their horses, so that these would be fresh for the run when we reached the buffalo. They were stripped down to the breechclout, and all were riding bareback, and all were armed with bow and arrows. Men and horses were both excited, especially the horses. To them a hunt was like a race to a thoroughbred.

After riding for about ten miles the leaders stopped and everybody dismounted and gave the horses a chance to breathe. Then all mounted and formed in a line, or rather three or four lines. The leaders rode slowly ahead up a hill, on the other side of which the buffalo were lying down. When the leaders reached the top of the hill in sight of the buffalo, they leaned forward on their horses and shouted, *now-wah*, and the hunt was on.

There was a mad race, and before the buffalo were fairly on their feet we were among them. The dust from a thousand buffalo and a thousand horses was so thick that we could hardly see anything, but as they began to scatter, we saw small groups of buffalo, with a few hunters pursuing each band, and in an hour or so the hunt was over, so far as the killing was concerned, and there were a thousand dead buffalo to be taken care of.

The camp had moved from where we had started on the hunt, and we were now camped within two or three miles of where the buffalo were killed. In killing them the Indians kept circling them so they would be as near together as possible, and as near to the camping ground as they could keep them, for all the work of skinning and cutting up, taking to camp and drying the meat, had still to be done. This part was all done by the women.

The young men that were with me were very much interested in the hunt, and both of them had very good luck. Russell I believe killed some buffalo, and Grinnell killed several, and I believe I killed one. That night after we reached camp Pete-ah-le-shar invited us to a feast at which many of the chiefs were present. The meal served was kah-wis,[8] a sort of a sausage that the boys thought was very good. After this meal came an invitation from La-sharo-too-ri-hoy, Good Chief, where we had roast ribs. We were served by the wife of Good Chief, who was the most beautiful woman in the Pawnee tribe. After eating and smoking with him we went to our camp.

For several days more we traveled with the Pawnees, but at last the young men's time was up, and we said goodbye to the Pawnees and started back for Plum Creek, where we arrived safely about a week later. This was the next to the last buffalo hunt that the Pawnees ever had, before they were removed to the Indian territory; in fact, it was the last hunt in which the whole tribe took part.

The following year, 1873, part of the tribe, with John Williamson [9] in charge, while hunting on the Republican

8. *Ka wis* was a Pawnee delicacy consisting of a thin strip of tender meat placed with some water in a section of intestine, with both ends tied. It was roasted in the coals and was not unlike a frankfurter both in appearance and popularity (Letter of Gene Weltfish to Donald F. Danker, April 5, 1958).

9. John William Williamson (1850-1927) moved to Genoa in 1871. He was employed at the Pawnee Agency, and because of his

near where we had joined them the year before, were attacked and defeated by a large band of Sioux from the Whetstone Agency, and about one hundred fifty of them were killed. The spot where this battle took place is still called Massacre Canyon; it is in Hitchcock County, Nebr., and is near the town of Trenton.[10] *

# SUPPLEMENT

EAGLE CHIEF (page 169)

"A nice old fellow. I knew him very well; in fact every one of those 16 Pawnee chiefs. While I was clerking in the trading post on the reservation in 1868, Eagle Chief often came in the store to visit. I sometimes gave him tobacco, sugar or coffee, and he would tell me the legends of the Skeedee band . . .–L.H.N." (Comment under a picture of Eagle Chief in Bruce, *The Fighting Norths*, 35). According to the same source (35), he died near Pawnee in or about 1884.

wavy shoulder-length brown hair the Pawnees named him *Buk-skariwi* (Curly Head). The agent, John Burgess, picked him as trail-agent on the ill-fated buffalo hunt. His duties were "to keep the Pawnees in order and to protect them from white men and, if possible, from the Sioux" (Hyde, *Pawnee Indians*, 244). He barely escaped the Sioux at Massacre Canyon. In 1874, Williamson helped to escort the Pawnee on their way to Indian Territory.

10. The Sioux were Oglala and Brûlé from the Red Cloud and Spotted Tail agencies; the date was August 5, 1873. Estimates of the dead vary from 69 to 156 (Hyde, *Pawnee Indians*, 245-246).

THE ARIKARA (page 169)

This tribe of the Caddoan language group is seemingly related to the Pawnee. When the first white explorers came to Dakota, they encountered the Arikara between the Big Bend of the Missouri and the Cheyenne River. The fur traders called them Rees. In 1823 they opposed a force sent up from Fort Atkinson under General W. H. Ashley's command, and clashed with the whites on several other occasions. The Arikara live near Fort Berthold, North Dakota, owning their land in severalty (Hodge, *Handbook of American Indians*, 72-73).

THE MANDAN (page 169)

The Mandan, who belonged to the Siouan language group, were not nomadic. An agricultural tribe, they lived in villages. A smallpox epidemic devastated them in 1837, and in the period between 1845 and 1848 they settled in the Fort Berthold area (Hodge, *Handbook of American Indians*, 83-86, 797-798).

REPUBLICAN VALLEY HUNTING GROUNDS (page 170)

". . . I took Mr. George Bird Grinnell on a buffalo hunt. We joined the Pawnees on the Republican River. . . . As far back as records are available, the valley of the Republican River was a famous hunting ground for the Indians—particularly the Pawnees; and after white men learned of the game to be found there, it became the region most favored for buffalo hunting on the Great Plains. As railroads were built up the Platte Valley and across Kansas, the buffalo were gradually driven from the sections they traversed; but there were still plenty of them in the great valley between the pioneer railways. Both William F. Cody ('Buffalo Bill') and the late Dr. W. F. Carver are said to have considered that the best game district of the early 60s and 70s in the United States.

"Many famous buffalo hunting expeditions visited the Republican Valley region, of which probably the most celebrated was that of the Grand Duke Alexis and a party of distinguished men of the Russian Empire of that time. The hunt was an international event planned by Gen. P. H. Sheridan as the representative of our Government, and under the immediate command of Gen. George A. Custer. . . . 'Buffalo Bill,' then a scout at Fort McPherson, Neb., where the huntsmen were outfitted, was in actual charge of the details; and Spotted Tail, war chief of the Brule Sioux, accompanied the party with a band of some 300 Sioux warriors and buffalo hunters" (Luther North in Bruce, *The Fighting Norths*, 39).

MASSACRE CANYON (page 174)

The following is excerpted from an account by Luther North in Bruce, *The Fighting Norths*, 38-40:

> The last tribal battle between [the Sioux and the Pawnee] was really due to circumstances that could—and should—have been easily prevented. In 1869, the authorities in Washington turned the Indian Department over to the Quakers; [11] and the Pawnees among others were supervised by an agent sent out from the East. He was William Burgess, who began teaching the Pawnees to love their enemies; they were told not to war with the Sioux, and that the Sioux would not be allowed to molest them.

11. There had been a great deal of dishonesty in the Indian service reaching up to some high officials in Washington and elsewhere, for which reason President Grant either originated or listened to the idea of appointing Quakers as Indian agents, to eliminate such practices. Some gain was made in personnel and morale, but there were many serious mistakes of judgment; and the whole Indian question was in turmoil during the 1870's. (*Author's note*)

[ 176 ]

Prior to 1873, the Pawnees had two annual hunts, and the whole tribe of 2,700 or more hunted together, protecting themselves as best they could against their enemies. In 1873, for some reason, part of the tribe was ready to go on the hunt before the rest, and the agent told them it would be all right—that the Sioux would not molest them.

So about 700 Pawnees went up the Republican River and its tributaries. They had a leave of absence for 60 days from their reservation in Nebraska to allow for the hunt; and Mr. Burgess sent John Williamson with them to notify the few settlers that those Pawnees were really friendly. But it happened that about the same time the agents of the Red Cloud and Spotted Tail bands gave those tribes permission to hunt in the same country, and they started out in the charge of Nick Janis. There were from 1,000 to 1,200 warriors in the Sioux camp, and about 150 warriors in the Pawnee camp (among the total of about 700).

On August 6 [5], as the Pawnees were crossing from the Republican to the Frenchman's Fork where the Sioux were camped, the Sioux warriors met them at the head of the ravine, to which the name Massacre Canyon was afterward given. The Pawnees had their squaws and children take shelter in the canyon, and then put up as good a fight as they could holding off the Sioux for about two hours, when they ran out of ammunition. Soon all their arrows were shot away, and they had only a few guns.

It was then necessary to cut the packs off their horses and make a run down the canyon, where many more were killed. Williamson escaped with part of them, and some months later was sent back to bury the remains of those who could be found, a total he told me of 156, mostly women and children. My belief is that there were at least 200 killed; Ralph Weeks [Warrior Chief, a Pawnee Scout], who had some education, and was one of the Pawnee boys in the fight, told me he thought that was about the number. He said that when they saw the Sioux coming, they thought some white soldiers must be with them; so he and Williamson rode out to meet them.

But the Sioux opened fire and shot Williamson's horse, which fell dead just as they reached the ravine; they ran back, and the Sioux chased them some two or three miles.

[ 177 ]

When they came out of the canyon, the Sioux turned away; and as the Pawnees ran on toward the Republican, they saw a cavalry troop coming up the river. The Pawnees always believed that the Sioux turned back when they saw the soldiers; and said if it had not been for that, more of their number would have been killed. . . .

In addition to Ogallala Sioux from Red Cloud Agency and Brule Sioux from Spotted Tail Agency, I believe there were some Cheyennes and Arapahos who were visiting Red Cloud and accompanied his band on that hunt. My impression is that it was the Ogallalas who had the permission to hunt on the Republican River, and that the other Indians accompanied them only as their guests, one might say.

Among the Pawnee Scouts killed in the fight, North mentions his striker, or batman, Nick Koots. Traveling Bear, who had distinguished himself at Summit Springs, lost his whole family—a wife and four children—and was himself left for dead. When a Sioux stooped over to scalp him, "Traveling Bear threw his arm around the neck of the Sioux, pulled him down, took his knife away from him and killed him. Though very seriously wounded, the Bear made his escape across country about 150 miles to Plum Creek Station, Neb., and finally reached the Pawnee reservation at Genoa, but died a few months later " (39).

Today a granite monument at Massacre Canyon commemorates the last battle between the Pawnee and the Sioux. Carved on it are the faces of a Sioux, John Grass, and Sun Chief of the Pawnee.

# VIII

## THE BLACK HILLS EXPEDITION
## OF 1874

*[See Map 8; supplement for this chapter begins on page 191.]*

JUST AFTER RETURNING from the buffalo hunt, Joe Tiffany, Wesley Rhone [1] and myself started from Columbus to Spring Creek in Howard County. Joe and I had each a team and were intending to bridge several little creeks on the road. On the way to Genoa, we were joined by an old gentleman with a team, who was going to Howard County with the intention of locating there. When we passed through the Pawnee village some of the Indians went out with us to the Cedar River, where Fullerton now is, and they told me we had better go back, as the Sioux were in the country. We concluded to go on, however, and they went back.

1. Tiffany and Rhone were Platte County farmers.

I had a saddle horse with me that I led behind the wagon, or turned loose—as she would follow—when I thought there were no Indians around. The next morning after the Pawnees turned back I rode her and got Wesley to drive my team, and I went on ahead.

We found no sign of Indians and that day built a small bridge across a sort of dry gully and camped on a creek about four or five miles from Spring Creek, where we intended to build a bridge. This work of building took us all day, and the old gentleman who was with us said, "I will help you with the bridge, if you will help me get some young cottonwood trees to put out on my place, when we are on the way back."

Joe said, "All right," that he knew where there were a lot of them between the Cedar and the Pawnee village.

The next day we drove up to Spring Creek, where there was quite a settlement of Columbus people. We stayed there for a few days, and then started back for Columbus.

We drove to the Cedar the first day, and the next morning when we had gone about three miles Wesley Rhone discovered that he had left his gun back at our camp on the Cedar. I told him to take my mare and go back after it, which he did.

He had hardly got out of sight, when I saw two Indians just riding out of sight into a ravine about a mile down the valley below us. I stopped my team and told Joe Tiffany to drive his team ahead and I would tie mine to the tailboard of his wagon and ride with him. The old gentleman was very much excited, and as he had no gun he got a butcher knife out of the mess chest. Joe and I got out our extra cartridges and laid them in a box in the front end of the wagon, where we could easily get at them, and then started on.

When we crossed the next canyon and came up on the bank, we saw about one hundred mounted Indians off on the hill to our left about a half mile away, and at the same time

[ 180 ]

I saw a wagon just going out of sight about a mile down the valley from us.

I said to Joe, "We are all right; they are Pawnees. The boys from the agency have come up here after oak wood, and the Indians came along to guard them."

The Indians were riding down toward us and were about a quarter of a mile away. Joe stopped his team and looked back toward the old gentleman. He said, "Mr. Blank would you like to stop here and get some of these little trees?"

Blank stood up in his wagon and shook the butcher knife at him and shouted, "No, no, drive on, drive on."

Joe grinned at me and drove on.

About this time Wesley overtook us, and the Indians also rode alongside the wagons. They asked me if I had seen any sign of Indians, and when I said "no," they said that the day before two of the schoolboys who were hauling wood had been killed within a quarter of a mile of where we were now.

We stayed at the agency for dinner that day, and drove on home that afternoon.

Later in the fall a crowd of about fifteen of us went hunting up the Loup above St. Paul in Howard County, and saw no Indians; but one night while in camp there we heard the galloping of a band of horses, and the next day some Pawnees came to our camp and said the Sioux had run off a lot of their horses.

On this trip with us was a young Welshman named Thomas. He was just over from the old country and was very much astonished when I packed the hindquarters of an elk on my Mazeppa horse, then got on him myself and forded the South Loup River. This boy, Davie Thomas, got lost one day, and I found him and gave him a ride to camp on my horse.

I must tell here about these two horses, Mazeppa and the mare Trifle. Trifle was the one that would follow the wagon, and when in camp I never tied her up, but let her run loose, and at night if I lay out on the ground, when she was ready to lie down she would come to where I was sleeping and lie down within five or six feet of me. Mezeppa would do the same thing. This pair of horses were the best and most intelligent camp and hunting horses that I ever owned.

Mezeppa caught that incurable disease glanders, and I had to kill him. It was like killing ones best friend. I owned many good horses afterward, but none that I ever thought equaled him. He was small, weighing a little less than nine hundred pounds, yet he could carry me and my equipments weighing over one hundred eighty pounds farther and faster than any horse I ever rode. I carried dispatches from Columbus to the Pawnee Agency, a distance of twenty two miles, in one hour and fifteen minutes, and was ready for the return trip in less than an hour afterward, and I rode him back in two hours.

Late in the fall of 1872 I was hunting for a party of workmen, who were putting up telegraph wires from Cheyenne to Rawlins, Wyoming. When we got to Fort Steele [2] I found my friend Major Switzer in command. This was the first time I had seen him since I left him in the hills of the North Loup. He was talking to the boss of the linemen when I rode into camp with an antelope behind my saddle. He shook hands with me and I offered him the hindquarters of the antelope, which he accepted, and that was the last time I ever saw him.

I spent the winter at home in Columbus, and in the spring joined a surveying party that was sectionizing a part of the Pawnee Reservation. In the summer Mr. Grinnell came out and we went on an elk hunt together, and he killed his first elk on the Cedar River not far from Fullerton.

2. Fort Fred Steele, on the North Platte River approximately thirteen miles east of Rawlins, Wyoming, was established in 1868. The post was abandoned in 1886.

In the fall of 1873 I went to Denver to meet Professor Marsh of the Peabody Museum of Yale College, and from Denver we went to Greeley, Colorado, and from there the Professor went back home. With four other men and a team I then went out into the Pawnee Butte country east of Greeley to gather fossils for the Yale Museum. We put in two months there, when I returned to Columbus and went into the livery business with my brother-in-law, C. E. Morse.

In the spring of 1874 an expedition started from Ft. Lincoln[3] in Dakota to explore the Black Hills country,* and Mr. Grinnell was to go along as one of the geologists, and I went as his assistant. Of course I knew nothing about geology, but was glad of the chance to go. General George A. Custer was in command,[4] and he had his full regiment, the Seventh Cavalry, and two or three companies of Infantry under Major Tilford.

Besides the officers of his regiment there were Colonel William Ludlow of the Engineer Corps, and Colonel Fred Grand and Major Forsyth of General Sheridan's staff, together with a number of civilians, among whom were Professors Donaldson and N. K. Winchell of Minnesota, with several newspaper men, one from a Minneapolis paper, one from the *Chicago Interocean*, and I don't know who the others were. There was a photographer, two miners, named Ross and McKay, besides a number of Indian scouts from the Santee Sioux and the Arik-a-ree tribes. Charley Reynolds

---

3. Fort Abraham Lincoln, at the juncture of the Missouri and Heart rivers in present-day North Dakota, was built in 1873 by forces under the command of General George A. Custer.

4. George A. Custer (1839-1876) was an Ohioan and a West Point graduate. He served throughout the Civil War, but it is in connection with "Custer's Last Stand" that he is known to nearly every American.

was chief of scouts, with a couple of Frenchmen as his assistants. I believe that Charley Reynolds was the best scout in the west.[5] He was killed two years afterward with Reno at the battle of the Little Big Horn, when also Custer was killed with his entire command.*

I met Mr. Grinnell at St. Paul, Minnesota, and we went over the Northern Pacific Railroad to Bismarck, Dakota, which was then the end of the Northern Pacific road. While we were waiting there for the ambulance to take us across the river to Ft. Lincoln, some Indians that were standing on the sidewalk near us commenced to talk, and I said to Mr. Grinnell, "They are talking Pawnee," and I asked one of them in Pawnee if he could understand me. He said, "yes," and commenced to talk to me.

They were A-rik-a-rees, and while they spoke the same language that the Skee-dee band of Pawnees did, and could understand me very well, it was hard for me to make out what they said. Their dialect was so different that I could hardly understand them. They asked me many questions about the Pawnees, and told me in turn that they were going on the expedition with Custer. They were part of his Indian scouts. The leader, a chief named Bloody Knife, was killed with Custer two years later.

We were taken over to the fort, where we were detained about thirty days, when we started for the Black Hills.

*July 2, 1874*
We left the fort with the band of sixteen men mounted on white horses playing Garry Owen, Custer's favorite tune. This was the first and last expedition that I was ever on in an Indian country that had a band along. Every morning upon leaving camp the band would play for two or three miles, and nearly every evening after supper the general

5. Charles Alexander Reynolds (1842-1876) came west to the Dakota frontier after being discharged from the army. In 1873 and 1874 he scouted for Custer as well as for Forsyth and Ludlow.

[ 184 ]

would have them come over in front of his tent and play for an hour or so.

The tent that Mr. Grinnell and I occupied was always pitched in the headquarter row, not very far from Custer's, and often of an evening, when he would have a big campfire in front of his tent, we would join the crowd of officers and civilians that gathered there.

Custer was quite sociable and did a good deal of talking. He was a very enthusiastic hunter, and was always telling of the good shooting he had done. He had along a pack of Scotch stag hounds, and nearly every day there would be a chase after jack rabbits or antelope, and though they frequently caught the jack rabbits, I never saw them catch an antelope. While General Custer was always telling of the great shots he made each day that he hunted, he didn't seem to care much about hearing of any one else doing good shooting.

One day Mr. Grinnell and myself were hunting off to the right of the command. We were perhaps a mile away and up the side of a big hill, when three blacktail deer that were frightened by the command came running up the hill toward where we were. We got off our horses and when they ran past us about one hundred yards away, I killed them all with three shots.

Mr. Grinnell thought it was quite wonderful shooting, and when we got to camp he took the saddle of one of the deer and carried it over to the general's tent. When he gave it to him he said, "Capt. North did some very good shooting, he killed three running deer with three shots."

The general said, "Huh, I found two more horned toads today," and that was his only comment on the shooting.

Capt. Tom Custer [6] on several occasions caught live rattle-

6. Thomas W. Custer (1845-1876), Captain, Seventh Cavalry, was a brother of General Custer. Another brother, Boston, who had come west for his health, also was at the Little Big Horn and died with George and Thomas.

snakes and carried them on his horse for miles. He would take a forked stick and put it down on the snake's neck just back of the head, then seize the snake by the neck with his right hand and pull the stick away. At first his horse was terrorstricken and he had difficulty in mounting, but after he had caught two or three the horse became used to it and didn't mind them.

We became quite well acquainted with Major Forsythe, who was in command of the scouts that fought with the Cheyennes on the A-rik-a-ree fork of the Republican River in 1868. The battleground is now called Beecher Island. Lieut. Beecher was killed in the fight, and the Cheyenne brave Roman Nose was also killed. Forsythe was wounded the first day having his leg badly broken below the knee. They were surrounded for nine days before relief came from Ft. Wallace.[7] Major Forsythe was a very interesting talker and I liked him very much.

After reaching the hills, I think we spent a couple of weeks in exploring them. We came into them from the north, and traveled south to what is now Custer City, where we camped for several days. The miners, Ross and McKay, here prospected for gold and found some, but not a great deal. General Custer sent Charley Reynolds to Ft. Laramie with mail. The newspaper men sent to their papers glowing accounts, saying we found gold from the grass roots down. This started a stampede for the Black Hills that fall, and for the next two years that had a great deal to do with the Indian wars of 1876-7. The Sioux and Cheyennes looked upon that region as about the last hunting country that they

7. The Battle of Beecher Island took place September 17, 1868, on the Arikaree Fork of the Republican in northeastern Colorado. The fifty men commanded by Forsythe and Beecher were attacked by about a thousand Indians, mostly Cheyenne and Sioux under the leadership of Roman Nose. The whites dug in on a small island and repulsed several horseback assaults.

had, and resented it when the whitemen began to go in there.

We found it a wonderful hunting country; deer, elk, grizzly bears, mountain lions, bighorn and other smaller game were plentiful. One day the General killed a big grizzly, a battle scared veteran. The General sent liberal pieces of the meat to the different messes, and we got our share, but a very little of it went a long way with most of us, for it was tough and very strong. Bear meat from a young animal is good, but from an old one is hardly fit to eat.

On the return trip to Ft. Lincoln we passed through a portion of the bad land of the Little Missouri River. One day while riding with General Custer ahead of the command, we came to a small pond of water near which a duck had nested. She had seven or eight young ones about half grown. The General got off his horse saying, "I will knock the heads off a few of them."

Mr. Grinnell looked at me and made a gesture. I dismounted and sat down on the ground behind the General. He shot and missed; then I shot and cut the head off one of the birds.

He shot again and missed, and I cut the head off another. He looked around at me, then shot again and missed, and I cut the head off a third one.

Just then an officer rode up in sight on the opposite bank of the pond and said that our bullets after skipping off the water were singing over the heads of his troops. The General said, "We had better stop shooting," and got on his horse and rode away without saying a word to me; but I don't think he liked it very well.*

When we got to the Little Missouri River we found the abandoned camp of an immense village of Indians, and in conversation that evening in front of the General's tent, I said to someone that it was perhaps just as well that they were gone before we got there, as there were a lot of them.

Custer said, "I could whip all the Indians in the northwest with the Seventh Cavalry."

I suppose he felt that way about it when he found the village on the Little Big Horn two years later. I know he thought the Indians were very inferior fighters, and there is no doubt in my mind that he thought he would have a great victory over them when he charged the village. He was a great fighter, but like most white men he underrated the Indians.

I do not think that any braver men ever lived than the Cheyenne or Pawnee Indians. My brother defeated the Cheyennes at Plum Creek, when they outnumbered him more than four to one, but his men were armed with Spencer repeating carbines, seven shooters, while the Cheyennes had mostly bows and arrows. The Pawnees were somewhat disciplined and fought as a unit, while the Cheyennes fought each man for himself, as, in fact, all Indians fought.

Much has been written about the great chiefs Sitting Bull, Red Cloud, Spotted Tail, Crazy Horse and American Horse of the Sioux, and Tall Bull, Dull Knife and Roman Nose of the Cheyennes; of what great leaders they were; and in some respects this is true. These men were orators and were looked up to with much respect, and some of them were great warriors; but in battle not one of them could have given an order that would have been obeyed, for there was no such thing as discipline among them. If some great warrior wanted to charge the enemy, he would say, "Now I am going," and if a band of young men felt so inclined they would follow him; but if Red Cloud or Sitting Bull had picked out two or three hundred men and ordered them to charge the enemy in a body, no attention would have been paid to the order. The individual Indians just fought in their own way and took orders from no one, and it was for this reason that they so seldom conquered disciplined troops. I am told, however, that the Cheyenne Old Little Wolf gave orders to his men and enforced them.

The A-rik-a-ree scouts under Bloody Knife seemed greatly to enjoy talking to me about the Pawnees, and we became pretty good friends. One very hot, dry day as we were marching through the bad lands and all were tired and thirsty, Mr. Grinnell and I were riding by ourselves off to one side of the command, when looking back we saw about a mile behind us one of the A-rik-a-ree scouts. He was on foot, and when he saw we were looking his way he motioned to us and started toward us on a run.

Mr. Grinnell said, "Shall we wait for him?"

I replied, "No, he just wants to ask some fool questions," and we rode on.

He kept following us on a dog trot, gaining on us, of course, and every time we looked around he motioned for us to stop, but the sun was blazing hot, and I guess we were both cross, and we kept on until at last he got near enough to call.

Then I said, "We had better stop and see what he wants."

When he came up to us the sweat was streaming down his face from long run. I asked, "What do you want?"

He said, "Nothing, I found a pond of good water over yonder, and when I saw you I thought you might want a drink," and he handed us his canteen ful of good cool water.

Mr. Grinnell and I looked at each other, took a long drink of water, and looked at each other again, but neither of us seemed to have much to say, and I guess we felt pretty small. Finally I said in Pawnee, "It is good water all right."

The boy laughed and said, "goodbye," and started away toward the command, and Grinnell and I rode on our way. Had a white boy tried to stop us for our own benefit and been ignored in this way, he might well enough have said, "Well, Mr. Smart Aleck, you can hunt for water for yourself," but this boy ran for two miles to give us a drink.

Just as we were leaving the Black Hills two of the Indian scouts, an A-rik-a-ree and a crippled Sioux started an old she bear with two cubs out of the hills, and after a long run of seven or eight miles killed the two cubs and finally overtook the old bear, and so got all three of them.

We reached Ft. Lincoln about the first of September, and the following day took the train for St. Paul, where Grinnell and I separated, he going on to New York and I to Columbus.

This was the grasshopper year and the country between Omaha and Columbus looked desolate enough. Not a green thing was left in the fields; the leaves were eaten from the trees, and in Columbus the paint was partially eaten off some of the houses. Some of the people had tried to save their gardens by covering the vegetables with sheets and other bed clothing, but the grasshoppers ate up the bed clothes as well as the vegetables. This was a gloomy time for everybody, and some of the settlers abandoned their claims and moved back farther east, but the most of them stuck it out and got through in some way.

For the remainder of that year and in 1875 I was in partnership with my brother-in-law, C. E. Morse, in the livery sale and feed business, and spent most of my time in Columbus.

# SUPPLEMENT

THE BLACK HILLS EXPEDITION (page 183)

The first white men to see the Black Hills probably were the La Verendrye brothers and their party, January 1, 1743. Before Custer's official exploration in 1874 several parties had entered the area, and in 1852 John Evans made a reconnaissance of the Badlands. F. V. Hayden also had explored along the foot trail from Fort Pierre to Laramie. In 1856-1857 Lieutenant G. K. Warren was commissioned by General W. S. Harney to explore the Hills and look for a site for a military post. This was a violation of Harney's promise to the Sioux not to cross this terrain without their permission. It was the sacred hunting ground of the Tetons; possession of the Black Hills signified freedom to them.

The 1868 Treaty of Fort Laramie guaranteed that the land north of Nebraska and west of the Missouri was to be kept inviolable Sioux territory, but rumors of gold had drawn attention to the region and as early as 1861 a Yankton group organized a Black Hills Exploring and Mining Association. However, first the Minnesota uprising and then Generals Sherman and Terry had put a stop to invasion of the Hills by gold seekers.

It remained for the expedition of Lieutenant Colonel (better known as General) George A. Custer into the Hills to open the gates for a great flood of illegal immigrants. . . . Before long the members of the expedition were finding gold in many places, and for weeks the discovery of the ore occupied the headlines from coast to coast. . . .

Once Custer had discovered gold, the American government began to treat with the Indians to obtain this rich region. . . . The Black Hills were relinquished, but not opened for legal settlement until February 28, 1877 (Hurt and Lass, *Frontier Photographer* [Lincoln: University of Nebraska Press, 1956], 87-91).

CHARLIE REYNOLDS (page 184)

In the foreword originally written for the Luther North recollections, part of which was omitted from this book because of its similarity to the introduction to *Two Great Scouts*, George Bird Grinnell wrote:

> . . . Charlie Reynolds, one of the great scouts of old times, killed on the Little Big Horn River in 1876, gave his life in order that the men of Reno's command might have an opportunity to save themselves. Almost his last words to the few civilian scouts with him, spoken while Reno's men were seeking safety by rushing toward the crossing of the river, were: "Come boys, lets try to hold these Indians while the soldiers get across." The charging Indians were too many; and a moment later he fell (Luther North Papers, Nebraska State Historical Society).

CUSTER AS A MARKSMAN (page 187)

Some fifty years later Luther North was more complimentary about the General's shooting. On being shown a photograph, taken on the Black Hills expedition, of Custer, Colonel William Ludlow, Bloody Knife, and a dead grizzly, Captain North said that all three were "shooting at the bear, and there were several bullet holes in the hide. I believe the General claimed the honor, and as he was an expert with the rifle, am inclined to think he did. Grinnell and I were eating red raspberries up on the side of a nearby hill, and could hear the bombardment; but the bear was dead before we reached the spot—so I didn't have a chance to get in a shot and claim that I killed it!" (Bruce, *The Fighting Norths*, 20).

# IX

## *THE POWDER RIVER CAMPAIGN*
## *OF 1876*

*[See Map 9; supplement for this chapter begins on page 233.]*

I N THE SPRING of 1876, the Indians began to get pretty restless and two expeditions were sent out against them, one
under General George A. Crook,[1] and the other under General Alfred Terry. General George A. Custer was with the
Terry command and found and fought the Indians on the
Little Big Horn River. Custer was defeated and killed with
two hundred sixty-five men. General Crook had been defeated on the Rosebud River eight days earlier—June 17th.

1. George Crook (1829-1890) was an Ohioan and a West Point
graduate. After seeing action against Indians in the Pacific Northwest, he distinguished himself in the Civil War. In 1876 he was in
command of the Department of the Platte. He was said to have more
understanding of the Indians, and sympathy for them, than many
of his fellow officers.

General Custer was killed June 25th, and in August General Sheridan sent for my brother to come to Chicago.

When he reached there, the General told him that he wanted him to go to the Pawnee Indian Agency [2] and enlist one hundred of them to join General Crook on a winter campaign in the Powder River country. He gave him transportation to Ft. Sill in the Indian territory, and at the same time had transportation sent to me from Columbus to Ft. Sill, where I was to join my brother. [3]

I was much puzzled to know why we were sent to Ft. Sill, as that was a long way from the Pawnees, but I started the next day, and when I got to the fort I found my brother had gone on to the Wichita Agency, but the commander of the fort said he would be back that night. When he did come he explained it all in this way.

When he got to Chicago General Sheridan said, "Major I want you to go to Ft. Sill, where you will be furnished transportation to the Wichita Agency. There you will find the Pawnees, and you will enlist one hundred of them. Have them furnish their own horses and march them across country to Sidney, Nebraska, where they will be furnished clothing, arms and equipment. You will be furnished rations at the different posts that you pass on the way."

Frank said that he had not had a chance to say a word until the General got this far. Then he said, "I don't think the Pawnees can furnish their own horses."

Sheridan interrupted him before he could say any more and said, "Then ship them to Sidney and buy horses for them there."

Frank said, "But, General, the Pawnees are not with the

---

2. In 1874-1875 the Pawnee had been moved from the Loup to a new reservation, west of the Arkansas River and north of the Cimmaron, in Indian Territory.

3. Fort Sill, originally established as Camp Wichita in 1869, was at the foot of the Wichita Mountains in Indian Territory.

Wichitas, and I don't think we should go to Ft. Sill to get to their agency."

The General again interrupted him and said, "I know where the Pawnees are, and you go to Ft. Sill. I have ordered transportation for you and your brother. You better start at once; goodbye."

There was nothing more to say, so Frank started.

After he left Chicago he sent a telegram to General Sheridan saying, "I have been informed that the nearest way to the Pawnee Agency is to leave the railroad at Coffeeville, Kansas." About an hour after he received an answer saying, "Go as your orders direct." All we could do was to go to Ft. Sill.

The officer in command there said that the previous autumn Sheridan was at Ft. Sill and went out to the Wichita Agency, where a band of the Pawnees were then visiting, and that he must have thought that they were located there. Frank telegraphed him that the Pawnees were not with the Wichita, and that we would have to go to Coffeeville, Kansas, and a telegram soon came from Sheridan to the commander of the post to furnish us with transportation to Coffeeville.

The next morning we started back for the railroad, and two or three days later we reached Coffeeville, where we hired a team to take us to the agency. The distance was one hundred twenty miles. The roads were very bad and there were several streams to ford, but we got through all right, and about midnight on the third night we reached the agency.

Frank was very ill with ague and also was suffering from asthma, and had scarcely slept for two or three nights. We went to the government farmhouse and got a bed. Frank said he hoped the Indians would not learn that he was there until he had got some sleep. Just at daylight the next morning I woke up and heard some Indians outside talking. I opened the window and signed to them to keep still. A few of them came to the window and I told them that Frank was sick, and that he had just gone to sleep, and asked everyone to keep still until he woke up. They said all right, and I pulled the curtain down. Frank woke up about an hour after, and when we got up we found the whole tribe outside, waiting to see him.

I hadn't heard a sound from the time I talked to the boys at the window until we got up, but when they saw Frank a great shout went up from them, *ah-ti-us Pawnee Lashar* (Father, the Pawnee Chief), and they fairly climbed over each other trying to get to him. He soon told them what he had come for, and also told them to come to the agency council house in an hour, as he wanted to talk to them, and also to the agent.

We met at the council house at ten o'clock, and Frank told them what General Sheridan had said to him about their furnishing their own horses. They said that so many of their horses had died that they could not do that, but they were all eager to enlist, and before noon, or in about an hour, we had the one hundred men we needed.* We stayed there the rest of that day, and the next morning started back to Coffeeville.

Many of the men that had enlisted had ague, but when we tried to persuade them that they were too sick to go, they declared that they were all right. Eight or ten more than the authorized one hundred wanted to go, and when Frank told them that he could only take one hundred, those we were obliged to reject said they would go as far as Coffeeville; that a great many people were dying from the ague; that maybe some of the boys would be too sick to go before they got to Coffeeville, and then they would take their places. The tribe was in very bad shape. They were miserably poor, nearly all of them had ague, and many of them were dying. They were very much discouraged and many of them were longing to get back to Nebraska.

The morning we left, great numbers of them followed us for miles. Some went ten or fifteen miles on foot, and then reluctantly turned back. We reached Coffeeville in three days, making forty miles per day. Many of the boys had such hard shaking spells from the ague that they were obliged to lie down by the road until it was over. Then they would get up and come on after us on a run. Many of them were so sick that I was afraid they would die before we got to Coffeeville, but they all said that as soon as they got back to their old home they would be well. This proved to be true. Two men died at Sidney, after we had been there for a couple of weeks, but the rest of them soon became well and strong.

By the time we got to Coffeeville Frank was very ill. He shook until it sometimes seemed that he would shake to pieces; then he had a terrible fever and was delirious.

From Coffeeville I telegraphed to General Sheridan, and the next day the cars came to take us to Sidney. We had to change cars at Kansas City, and while waiting there in the station, I had a doctor for Frank, who talked continually about what should be done. The doctor said he would have to stay there and be taken to a hospital, but before the train that we were going on left, Frank came out of his fever and told the doctor that he was going on, and he did so. He was pretty sick for several days, but began to get better as soon as we got to Omaha, which was the morning after we left Kansas City.

When we started out from Omaha the boys were wild with joy, and pointed out to one another the different points along the Platte River where they used to live. They sang and danced and told stories of war parties and buffalo hunts.

When we got to Fremont they pointed out to me the hill called *Pah-huk,* which means the place where the *nah-hoo-*

*kach* (spirit animals) live. This hill is on the bank of the Platte River, and the cut bank is perhaps two hundred feet high, and is perpendicular, and in those early days the water was quite deep. The entrance to the spirit house is supposed to be under the water, and the Pawnees who had been in the house or lodge said that they had followed a little bird which acted as guide, and that they jumped off the bank into the water where they found the opening, a sort of tunnel that led into [the] lodge.

At the end of the tunnel next to the entrance are the guards. On one side of the door is a large grizzly bear, and on the other side is a great rattlesnake. The little bird warns the man that he must not be afraid or something terrible will happen to him. When the young man went in the snake raised its head and rattled loud, and the grizzly bear stood up on its hind legs and growled terribly, but the young man made his mind strong, and passed between them as if they were not there, and found himself in a great lodge with a fire in the center, and all of the different animals sitting about it.

The leader was a great beaver, and there were elk and deer, antelope, foxes, coyotes, big wolves and birds, such as swans, sand hill cranes, wild geese and many other animals and birds. The beaver was the spokesman and welcomed the young man, and called him brother. He stayed with them for some time, and they taught him how to do many wonderful things.

The young man I knew, who said he had been in the lodge, could certainly do things that no one who ever saw him do them could account for. He was a scout in my company in 1869, and was one of their great medicine men. He died soon after the Pawnees moved south.

When we enlisted this last company of scouts one of the men was a Ponca Indian, who had married a Pawnee woman and had lived with the Pawnees for years. The Pawnees and

[ 199 ]

Poncas had been friends for a long time, but there was a time several generations ago when they were enemies. About the time they made a treaty of peace one band of the Pawnees lived on Shell Creek, north of Schuyler, and one day they saw a large band of Ponca warriors coming to their village. They went out to meet and welcome them, but when they got to them the Poncas suddenly threw back their buffalo robes, drew their bows and arrows, and commenced killing the Pawnees. The Pawnees ran to their lodges, got their arms and, after a desperate battle defeated the Poncas, and drove them back to their home, which took the Pawnees three days. On their return to their village they had a great scalp dance and composed a song to commemorate the victory. Interpreted it would be something like this:

> "Oh you Poncas, you came visiting, yes you came
> with smiling faces, did you get what you were
> laughing about when you changed it to a war party."

This was such a wonderful victory and the Pawnees liked the song so well that they were still singing it in our day, and whenever we had a battle and conquered the enemy and had a scalp dance, they would sing that song.

On our way north, after we had gotten as far as Shell Creek, and the boys were still talking about their old home there, I spoke of the Shell Creek Village and said, "Now let us have the Ponca song." In an instant the talking ceased and not a word was said by anyone.

I waited for a minute, and just as I was going to ask again for the song, one of the head men came over to my seat and said to me, "Father we have a Ponca with us. It would make him feel badly if we sang that song." [4] This shows the

---

4. This incident is also recounted in Bruce, *The Fighting Norths*, page 42, and the speaker is identified as Sergeant Frank White, also known on the Powder River Expedition as *Li-Heris-oo-la-shar*, or Leading Chief.*

finer feeling of the Indian. It had probably been two hundred years since that battle, but now this Ponca was their comrade and they would not do anything to hurt his feelings.

When we reached Columbus, which was our home town, I think a majority of the residents were at the station to see us. Frank stopped off to have medical attendance, and my brother-in-law, Capt. S. E. Cushing went with me to Sidney, Nebraska, where I drew arms, ammunition, clothing and camp equipment, and went into camp on Lodgepole Creek, about a mile below the town.

In about a week Frank and my older brother, J. E. North, came up. I had been notified to meet them at Julesburg, forty miles east of Sidney, and went down on the train. When they got there J. E. got off, and Frank went on to Sidney leaving us at Julesburg to buy horses to mount our men.

A great many cattle were driven up the trail from Texas that year, and with each herd there was a pretty big band of cow ponies. There were about three hundred of these near Julesburg, and we got one hundred before night. I was a pretty good judge of horses, and I think I got a fairly good lot. They were thin in flesh, but we were expecting to stay in Sidney for about a month, and thought they would put on some flesh in that time, as they would have a government ration of corn. The most of them learned to eat corn and oats in a few days, but some of them were a long time learning and were still pretty thin when we were ordered to Ft. Robinson.[5]

We left Sidney some time in October and moved by easy *Oct. 14* marches across the country on the Black Hills stage line past Court House Rock, and crossed the North Platte River on what was then called Clarks Bridge, then on north to Snake *Oct. 16* Creek, where we spent one day. The next day about sun- *Oct. 19* down a courier from Ft. Robinson met us, with orders to

5. Fort Robinson was established in northwestern Nebraska in 1874 and remained an army post until the end of World War II.

move the camp to Ft. Robinson, and with forty or fifty of our best mounted men to follow the guide that had brought the orders to us, and join General McKenzie,[6] who was sent by General Crook to round up Red Cloud and his band and compel him to come in to the agency at Ft. Robinson.[7]

*Oct. 22*    We started at once. Frank picked out forty-four of the best horses and, taking me with him, he left Capt. Cushing with the rest of the men and the wagons to go on over to Ft. Robinson. The guide, a halfbreed named Billy Hunter, started ahead with us to overtake General McKenzie, who was to leave the fort about sundown, and make a night ride to Red Cloud's camp on Chadron Creek. We rode at a steady trot for about five hours, when we made the junction with McKenzie, and after a few minute's rest, started on again, and rode on the same steady trot until about four o'clock in the morning, when the guides told us we were near the village, or rather two camps, that were about a mile apart on the creek.

In one camp was Red Cloud, and in the other were two lesser chiefs, Yellow Leaf and Swift Bear.[8] McKenzie divided

6. Ranald Slidell Mackenzie (1840-1889) of New York City graduated from West Point as first in the class of 1862. He was immediately put on active service and at the Civil War's end was commanding a cavalry division. Mackenzie was relieved of the command of Fort Sill to take part in the Powder River expedition and ordered up with six companies of the Fourth Cavalry. Subsequently he served in the Southwest and held the rank of brigadier general at his death. Because of a Civil War wound, Mackenzie was known to the Indians as Bad Hand.

7. Frank North's diary indicates that the courier arrived with orders to go to Fort Robinson on November 22. They had proceeded about ten miles when word came to join Mackenzie in capturing Red Cloud, and North took "42 men and Lute and lit out" (Frank North Diary, October 22, 1876).

8. Red Cloud (1822-1909) was an Oglala sub-chief until the 1866 crisis in the Powder River country. At that time he became the acknowledged chief of hostile elements among the Oglala, and many discontented hostiles from other Sioux, Cheyenne, and Arapaho tribes joined his war party. He refused to sign the Laramie Treaty of 1868 until the government actually had withdrawn its troops from the specified area. In later years he became more friendly to the

his force, he himself taking command of the part of the regiment that was to surround the Red Cloud camp, and sending the rest of the men under Major Gordon to the Yellow Leaf camp. Frank went with McKenzie, taking half of the scouts, and I went with Major Gordon,[9] taking the rest of the Pawnees.

We were to surround the camp as soon as it got light enough, and Major Gordon's order to me was to dash through the camp and gather up all of the horses in the camp and around it, and hold them together, while he would surround the camp with soldiers. He gave strict orders that not a shot should be fired, unless the Indians first fired on us.

When daylight came, we moved up as near as we could and as quietly as possible, and then I made my dash, giving the war whoop as we went into the camp, and driving all the horses before us. Some of the horses were tied, but we stopped long enough to untie or cut the ropes, and took them all with us. Not a single Indian showed his face outside the lodges until we were through the camp and were gathering up the horses that were scattered up and down the creek and out in the hills. It must have been an hour before we got them together, and when I counted them, I found I had four hundred.

In the meantime Major Gordon surrounded the village, and when I got back the Indians had come out and he was talking with them, and telling them through the interpreter

government, and in assenting to the Treaty of 1876, which relinquished the Indian claim to the Black Hills, opposed Crazy Horse and Chief Gall. He became influential through his active support of the U.S. government and made several trips to Washington (Hurt and Lass, *Frontier Photographer*, 59-60).

Red Leaf and Swift Bear, both Brûlé chiefs of some importance, were in charge of the camp.

9. George A. Gordon (1837-1878) was a Virginian and West Point graduate. He served with distinction during the Civil War, and in 1873 was appointed major of the Fifth Cavalry. He was commander of Fort Sidney, Nebraska, 1877-1878.

[ 203 ]

what they must do. After waiting for some time McKenzie came over, and Frank was with him.

The Indians began to take down their lodges and McKenzie allowed them to take enough of the horses to pack their camp, and for the old and feeble ones to ride on, but he made the young warriors walk, and we started on the march for Ft. Robinson.

We got there a little before sundown. There the Indians were disarmed and the horses again taken from them and *Oct. 24* turned over to us, and after we had eaten supper, Frank took twenty men and started to take the herd to Ft. Laramie. He had been in the saddle almost constantly for twenty-four hours, and yet he started on the ninety mile ride to Laramie that night, and at nine o'clock the next morning he turned the horses over to the quartermaster there, and got his receipt for seven hundred and twenty-two head.

The next morning after Frank started with the horses I was breaking camp to start on the march to Ft. Laramie, when California Joe came down to my camp.[10] His camp was about a mile from mine, and he had just come from Deadwood in the Black Hills. He knew Frank and had been to our camp the night before and eaten supper with us, and then gone back to his own camp. He had come in the morning to see Frank again. I told him Frank had gone on to Laramie with the horses, and that we were starting for that place. He talked with me for a few minutes, and started back to his camp, and I set out for Laramie.

There were several troops of cavalry and two companies of infantry that had been ordered to Laramie, and they started ahead of me. When I had gone about ten miles I was overtaken by a lieutenant of one of the infantry companies, who had stayed behind at the post when his company started, and he rode with me for some little distance.

10. Moses E. Milner, a well-known scout.

When he first overtook me, he said, "California Joe has been murdered."

I said, "I guess that is a mistake; I was talking to him just before I started."

The lieutenant said, "It was when he was on the road from your camp to his own that he was killed. Some fellow shot him in the back."

Joe was quite a noted scout and guide, and was a very close friend of Wild Bill Hickok, and well known by Jim Bridger and Kit Carson. He was in Deadwood at the time Wild Bill was murdered, or soon after, and was very outspoken as to what he thought of the gang of gamblers that he seemed to think responsible for Hickok's death. It was thought by some people that the same gang had Joe murdered. I believe nothing was ever done about it.

The second day's march from Ft. Robinson, a little before noon I heard a lot of rifle firing ahead of me, but out of sight, over a hill about half a mile away. I felt sure it was the infantry companies that were ahead of me, and thought they had been attacked by Indians. I at once ordered a charge and we soon came to the top of the hill, but before we got there the firing ceased, and when we came in sight the men were resting at ease.

I was told that as they were marching along a band of antelope had dashed over the hill to their right. The animals were evidently badly frightened at something behind them, for they ran straight for the soldiers and passed right through the center of the company, dodging between the men. There were ten or twelve of them, and after they got through the ranks all the men fired at them. There must have been two hundred shots fired, but only one antelope was killed.

These troops had been on the summer campaign with General George Crook, and had marched hundreds of miles through Wyoming and Dakota, and they were in the finest kind of condition.* They marched from Ft. Robinson to Ft.

Laramie in three days, a distance of ninety miles, and didn't seem to mind it at all. They could outwalk my horses. General Crook himself, with an escort of ten men, made the distance in one and a half days; the escort was cavalry, of course.

*Oct. 25, 8 p.m.*  When we got to Ft. Laramie we went into camp on the Laramie River below the fort, and we stayed there for about two weeks. After we had been there two or three days General Crook told Frank to bring the men that took part in the capture of Red Cloud's band over to the government corral, and when we got there he said, "I want you and your brother, and each of these men, to have a horse from the band that was taken from the Sioux.

After we had chosen our horses he said, "Now, Major, I want you to pick out seventy more of the best horses in the bunch and take charge of them, and take them along as a reserve to take the place of any horses that may die or give out on the campaign." After these had been taken out, the bal-

*Nov. 3*  ance of the confiscated horses were sold at public auction. They were bought by traders, cattlemen and miners.

The horse that Frank had chosen for himself was a dark bay, and was said to be the fastest horse in the Sioux tribe, and the one he picked out for me was a gray horse, and he also was a very fast horse. These two horses later came near causing a clash between the Sioux scouts and our Pawnees.

After we left Ft. Robinson General Crook organized a company of Sioux Indians from Red Cloud's band, to be used as scouts, and they joined the expedition at Ft. Laramie. They were in charge of Major Clark, and when they came to Ft. Laramie they were mounted on their own horses, so that we evidently didn't get all of their horses when we brought Red Cloud into Ft. Robinson.

The weather turned cold and stormy after we had been in camp at Ft. Laramie for a week or so, and one morning it was snowing and the wind was blowing pretty hard. We had our tent tied shut and a fire in our stove, and were pretty comfortable, when someone rode up to the tent and called Frank. I untied the tent and saw it was Major Clark.

He said, "Hello Major, are you going on the expedition? The General has already gone."

Frank said we had no orders to move.[11]                              *Nov. 4*

Clark laughed and said, "Well, you had better follow along, the General has started for Ft. Fetterman and General McKenzie is just starting."

All we could do was to break camp and follow, and from   *Nov. 5* that time until the return of the expedition in the latter part of January, we never knew when we were to move camp. The General would break camp in the morning, and with his bodyguard would start out, and we would follow. When he went into camp, we tried to find a good place somewhere within a mile and camp.

On every expedition we had ever before served on the commanding officer used to send his adjutant around in the evening with orders as to when we would break camp in the morning, and where our position would be in the marching line, but this was entirely different. The first night out from Ft. Laramie the General with his bodyguard camped on a small stream that ran into the North Platte River; General McKenzie with his regiment camped three miles below him on the river; we were a couple of miles from McKenzie, and the wagon train was somewhere below us. The next day, I think, the General went clear through to Ft. Fetterman, General McKenzie with his regiment got into Fetterman the third day about noon, and we got there in the evening, and  *Nov. 8* the wagon train the next day.[12]

11. Although Frank North complained of short notice from Crook, he recorded that it was received on November 4 (Frank North Diary, November 4, 1876).

12. Fort Fetterman, established in 1867 and abandoned in 1882, was on the south side of the North Platte River on the Bozeman Trail.

We were camped on the North Platte River north of the fort, and the Sioux scouts were in camp between our camp and the fort.

After lying in camp for perhaps a week, one day about noon one of our men who had been herding the horses some distance from the camp, came galloping into camp and said that Major Clark and one of the Sioux scouts had come to the herd and that they had caught Frank's bay horse and had started to take him away. Of course our men hardly knew what to do about it, but one of them asked Major Clark to come to our camp with the horse, which he said he would do, and in a few minutes he and a Sioux chief called Three Bears rode into camp. Three Bears was leading Frank's bay horse.

Frank walked out to the Indian and took the rope from him, and said, "Major, this horse belongs to me."

Major Clark said, "Isn't this one of the horses that was taken from Red Cloud's band?" On being told that it was, he said the General said that those horses were to be used as a reserve, and as Three Bears' horse has given out I came to get one for him, and he wants that one.

Frank said, "Well, he can't have him." He then explained to Clark about the horses that the General had given to our men, and about the seventy extra horses that we had, and that Three Bears could have any one of them. But, as both Clark and Three Bears seemed to think that they would get this horse, Frank lost patience and said, "Major, you can tell your Indian that this horse belongs to me, and I am going to keep him."

Major Clark said, "Well, I will see the General about it."

Frank said, "Do so, and I also will see him."

Clark and Three Bears then rode away and Frank told his man to saddle the bay horse. He said he would go over to the post and see the General. I told him if he would wait until I could send for my horse I would go with him, and he said he would wait.

I sent my boy after the gray horse, and while we were waiting for him, one of the teamsters from the wagon train that was camped near us came over to the camp and said, "Major the Sioux are on the warpath; they say they are coming over to clean out the Pawnees."

This made Frank pretty indignant, and he told our men to be prepared for them, if they came. As there were only seventy of the Sioux and we had a hundred men, we were not much worried about the outcome.

When my boy came with the gray horse, I saddled him and Frank and I started for the fort. When we came in sight of the Sioux scout camp, we found them standing in a group, and Three Bears was talking to them. We couldn't understand what he was saying, but we thought he was telling them about Frank taking the horse from him. The road passed within thirty or forty feet of them, and as we got near them Three Bears quit talking, and they all stood looking at us.

Frank touched his horse with the spur, and as he was highspirited he commenced to dance. Frank began to sing the Pawnee war song and I joined in with him, and we danced our horses and sang our song past them. No one spoke a word, nor did any of them make a move, and we rode on to the fort, where Frank found Major Clark, and asked him to go with him to see the General.

We found the General at the sutter store, and Major Clark told him that he had taken Three Bears to our herd to get a horse and that Frank had refused to let him have it.

Frank interrupted him and said, "No, Major, I didn't refuse him a horse, but the horse he chose was the one that the General allowed me to choose for myself at Ft. Laramie."

The General then told Major Clark that he should have

come to our camp before going to the horse herd, and have found out which horses we were holding for the Sioux scouts; that the horses he had given our men were not included in that bunch.

Frank then said, "General, why not have the Sioux scouts take all the horses that were kept out as extras?"

The General said that would be a good plan, so when we went back to camp, we cut out the seventy head of horses and turned them over to Major Clark. The Sioux scouts were not very well pleased, because we were given the best horses, and we heard through some of the white scouts that they said they would kill the horses that Frank and I had chosen; but they never tried it, and we had no more trouble about them.

On the fourteenth of November Frank crossed the river to see if there were any orders to move, and left word with me that if the command started to break camp I should do so also. Not long after he had gone General Crook with his bodyguard broke camp, and I followed them. We marched out about twelve miles and camped on Sage Creek. The thermometer registered 14° below zero, and there was some snow on the ground.

Frank overtook us about five miles out from Fetterman, but could find out nothing about where we were going, except that we were following the same road taken by the Connor command in 1865. We had no orders from General Crook, and just tagged along after him, and when we saw him go into camp, we found a good place and we made our camp.

*Nov. 18*  When we got to Ft. Reno on Powder River, the General called a council of all the scouts.[13] There were the Sioux, the Cheyennes, the Arapaho, the Shoshones and the Pawnees.

13. Fort Reno, the scene of the council, was a post established in 1865 but abandoned in accordance with Sioux demands in 1868. It was temporarily reactivated in 1876.

[ 210 ]

The General made a speech to them. He told them they were now all soldiers together, and should be friends. After the General's speech some of the Indians made speeches, and finally Three Bears, the Sioux chief, walked across to our men and, speaking through an interpreter to one of our sergeants, gave him a horse and called him brother. Our men also made speeches and gave the Sioux some horses, and the council was dismissed.

From Ft. Reno the command moved over to the Crazy  *Nov. 21*
Womans Fork, and from there General McKenzie, with eight hundred cavalrymen and nearly all of the Indian scouts, was sent into the Big Horn Mountains in search of the Cheyennes. Frank and I with part of our Pawnees went with him.

We left the camp on Crazy Woman on the twenty-third  *Nov. 23*
of November, marched about ten or fifteen miles, and camped on a small stream, a branch of Powder River. The weather was cold and we had no tents. The next morning we made a start, but before going very far we met some Arapaho scouts that the General had sent out ahead, and they reported having found the Cheyenne Village.[14] We went into camp in a ravine out of sight, and lay there until nearly night, when we got orders to prepare to move, and about sundown the command started.

This was about the hardest march that we ever had. We climbed up and up, it seemed for miles, then over a ridge, and down again. In many places the trail was so narrow along the side of the mountain that we could march only in single file, and the command was strung out for perhaps a couple of miles; then if the valley or canyon spread out, we would trot our horses and close up the ranks. The night was very dark and it was quite cold. The men had orders not to smoke, but some time after midnight Frank told me to stop and let

14. Frank North believed that Sioux scouts found the village (Frank North's Diary, November 24, 1876).

the men pass by me, and try to get a count on them, and see if they were all there.

While they were passing me I saw a good many cavalrymen that had fallen out of ranks also pass, and many of them were smoking. I noticed another thing and that was that a great many men were sick at the stomach; even some of the Pawnees were so. I don't know why this was so; perhaps the high altitude and the cold had something to do with it. After following along in the rear of the company for some time, I rode on and joined Frank.

*Nov. 25*  Just before daylight in the morning we could hear the beating of Indian drums, and knew we were near the village. General McKenzie halted and dismounted the whole command. The canyon through which for some time we had been riding widened out a little at this point. The General gave us orders to keep up the lefthand side of the creek; when he gave the order to charge the Shoshone scouts were to follow us up that side of the creek, and the cavalry was to keep up the righthand side. Our scouts with the Shoshones were to pass around to the left of the village, and the soldiers to the right, and we would have the village surrounded.

Our men unsaddled their horses, as they always rode bareback when making a charge. I had brought along the gray horse that we had gotten at the Red Cloud Village, and had one of the men leading him. While we were waiting for daylight I told the man to take my saddle off the horse I had been riding, and put it on the gray. I was pretty tired and cold, and as the wind was blowing pretty hard, I walked off to one side among the rocks, and found a sheltered place behind a big rock, where I sat down. I leaned back against the rock and went to sleep, and I came very near missing the fight.

When it began to get light the General sent word to Frank to get ready for the charge, and Frank began to look for me. He found the man who had my horse, but he did not know where I had gone. Frank sent some of the men to hunt for me, but none of them happened to come to where I was, and they told him they couldn't find me. The cavalry were all mounted, and Frank was just ready to mount my horse, when I woke up and came stumbling out of the rocks, and by the time we were mounted the bugler blew the charge.

The trail on our side of the creek ran along the side of the mountain, and was so narrow that we had to ride in single file. Frank took the lead; I was next to him, our men were strung out behind us, and after our men came the Shoshone scouts. We were to ride past the village to the left and swing round the upper end; the cavalry was to pass to the right and meet us at the upper end of the village as said.

General McKenzie had taken a half dozen of our scouts with him, and among them was a boy that had been educated at Carlisle, Pennsylvania. When we were within a quarter of a mile of the village, this boy, Ralph Weeks,* who was riding at the head of the company commanded by Lieutenant McKinney, who was across the creek from us, called to Frank and said, "The General says for you to cross the creek to this side, that there is no trail up that side."

We had been riding at a gallop, but, of course, had to stop and look for a place where we could get down the steep bank to the creek. This took a few minutes, and then we found a muddy bottom, and about half the horses mired down and we lost time in getting them out, and I think that this gave the Indians a chance to get their women and children out of the village and up among the rocks, where they could hide. This was the only pass by which they could get away, and if we had gone around on the left of the village, we could have cut them off from the pass.

Of course, we would have had only our own men, about fifty of our Pawnees, as the Shoshones had taken a trail leading up to the top of the mountain to the left, and there was no way down except the way they had gone up, for the

[ 213 ]

mountain ended in a cliff at the upper end. This cliff over-looked the village and the pass beyond where the Cheyennes escaped, and the Shoshones stayed up there all day, and kept up a rifle fire on the Cheyennes who were holding the pass, but as the distance was about half a mile I don't think they did much damage. Had we got to this pass I doubt if we could have held it, for the Cheyennes were bound to go out that way, and would probably have gotten the best of us.

At all events, we didn't get there, and after we had crossed the creek we charged alongside the soldiers into the village. As we came to the lower end of the village, the Cheyennes opened fire on us, and a small party of warriors that had run up a canyon to the right of the village poured a volley into Lieutenant McKinney's troop, and McKinney was killed and some of his men were wounded.

The valley where the village was located was quite wide, and the stream was shallow, with fairly good bottom, and we crossed back into the village, but before we had gone far we found ourselves between two fires, the Cheyennes, who had taken up a position behind a ridge of rocks were in front of us, and the Sioux scouts were behind us, and as they were none too friendly to our men, they were not very particular whether they shot at us or the Cheyennes.

We rode on through the first group of tipis, but found them deserted, then crossed back again to the right bank of the stream and dismounted, and leaving our horses at the foot of a butte, or hill, we went up to its top, and lying down there, began to shoot across the valley at the Chey-ennes that were behind the rocky ridge. As this was about a quarter of a mile distant and the Indians were all pretty well hidden, I don't think we did them much harm.

Here we were joined by eight or ten soldiers and the scouts Frank Grouard and old Bill Hamilton.[15] These two

15. Grouard's account of the battle, in which he claimed to have killed the Cheyenne chief, Little Wolf, is given in Joe DeBarthe,

would pump five or six shots apiece at the Cheyenne breast-works as fast as they could, and then clap their hands over their mouths and give the Indian war whoop, and pretend they had killed several Indians; but, although I was watching through a pair of field glasses, I saw no Indians killed there, and after the first charge into the village I doubt if there were many Indians killed, although we were exchanging shots with them all day.

I walked up the canyon where McKinney was killed and counted fourteen dead warriors, and several more were killed on the other side of the creek, but how many I don't know. We lost five men killed, besides Lieut. McKinney, and forty or fifty wounded. We kept up a skirmishing fire back and forth pretty much all day, but did not succeed in driving the Cheyennes out of gunshot of the village.

In the valley just under the ridge where the Cheyennes were making their stand was a band of about ninety or one hundred ponies, and four or five of the Arapahoe scouts made a dash for them, but were driven back. A few minutes later some of the Shoshone scouts tried it, and they failed, and one of them was shot through the body. Then Three Bears of the Sioux scouts and three of his men tried for the horses, and they also failed. As soon as a party started for the horses, the Cheyennes concentrated their fire on them. Each of the parties that tried and failed were jeered at by the other scouts on their return.

After Three Bears return I asked Frank to let me try for them. He didn't want me to go, but I said, "All of the other scouts have tried it, why shouldn't the Pawnees?"

He said, "if the Pawnees try it I shall expect them to bring in the horses. How many men do you want?"

*Life and Adventures of Frank Grouard* (Norman: University of Oklahoma Press, 1958), 168-169. See also Appendix A.

William T. Hamilton (1822-1908) was a fur trader and scout who had lived on the frontier since 1842. He served at various times from 1858 to 1876 as scout and interpreter for the U.S. Army.

I told him one, and I chose a man that had been with me when I was surrounded on the Driftwood ten years before, and had served in my company in 1867, 1869 and 1870. His name in those years was *Pe-isk-le-shar*, Boy Chief, but he had taken a white man's name, Pete Headman.

The creek came down past the ridge within a hundred yards of where the horses were feeding, and there was a bunch of quaking aspen growing on the bank. We got behind that and followed up the stream; each of us carried a blanket over his arm, and we had our revolvers, but left our guns.

When we got as near the horses as we could without being seen, we rode out of the brush on a run, and as we came to the horses we shook out the blankets and yelled at them. They were scattered over a good deal of ground and didn't scare very easily; but we finally got them together, and drove them down through the village and across the creek, and behind the butte where our men were. Three or four of the horses were killed, but Pete and I came through untouched, and a few days afterward General McKenzie gave us the whole bunch to be divided among our men.

Towards evening General McKenzie called a council of his officers and talked over the advisability of charging up the mountain, and driving the Indians out of the rocks, but it was decided that as we had taken all of their winter supplies, and all of their camp equipage, it was not worth the lives it would cost to get them out, so we went into camp.

The Pawnees were ordered to camp in the village, and as there was no shelter there from the sharpshooters upon the side of the mountain, they made it pretty warm for us. While the men were getting supper Frank and I were sitting on a log facing the fire, with our backs to the mountain, and some Indian about a half mile away was shooting what I think must have been a sharps buffalo gun. Pretty soon a

[ 216 ]

bullet whizzed over our heads and killed a mule on the other side of the fire from us.

I said, "If that fellow lowers his sights a little he will make us move," and sure enough the next shot struck a tin cup full of coffee that was on the log between us. We then got busy, and taking a lot of packages of dried buffalo meat, we built a breastwork and got behind it. He took one or two more shots at us, and then gave it up and left us in peace.[16]

This fellow must have been a crack shot, for in the afternoon a couple of soldiers started across a little valley from one hill to another, and they were at least six hundred yards from where he was hiding behind a rock. The soldiers were about one hundred yards apart, and were running. When the first man got about half way across, the Indian shot and the soldier dropped. The other soldier ran on, and when he was within twenty feet of the first man the big gun boomed out again, and he went down. Neither one of them was killed, though I believe one of them died later.

As soon as it got dark, we put out a guard and went to sleep, and when I awoke I felt as if I was smothering, and when I pushed the buffalo robe off my face, about half a bushel of snow fell down my neck. It was daylight and still snowing, and about eight inches of snow lay on the ground. After destroying the village and burning what we could, we started on the return march.[17]                                    *Nov. 26*

~~~~~~~~~~~~~~~

16. The entry in Frank North's Diary for the day of battle reads: Saturday 25th. Had a hard night march and at 7 a.m. struck Little Wolf's village of Cheyenne 173 Lodges and had a hard fight which lasted all day and part of the night. We are camped in the village tonight and bullets are dropping all around us. We have burned all the lodges. 18 dead Indians are lying around us. One Lieutenant and four men are killed on our side and 17 soldiers and one Snake Indian wounded. A stray bullet just killed a mule within 30 paces of Lute and I.

17. Many years later Luther North wrote to Dr. Richard Tanner: "The thermometer never got higher than 25 below. . . . Those poor Cheyennes were out in that weather with nothing to eat, no shelter (we had burned their village) and hardly any clothing. It

The wounded men were carried on travois. Lieutenant, afterward Colonel, Homer W. Wheeler, had charge of the travois men, and he must have been a genius to have succeeded in getting them out safely, for in many places the trail was so narrow and steep that one could hardly ride a horse, and how he ever got the travois over it without dumping the wounded men down the mountainside, is more than I could understand.*

*Nov. 28* The second day after we left the village we were camped near the Sioux scouts. They had twenty or thirty horses that they had captured, and General McKenzie gave them to the chiefs to divide among them. They didn't seem to agree about the division, and got into a fight over it. One Indian knocked another down with his gun and jumped on his stomach with both feet, and that settled it, as the fallen man didn't fight back. Our men saw the fight and were very much disgusted with the beaten man because he didn't fight back.

A couple of days later we got back to General Crook's camp on Crazy Womans Fork, where it was said we would rest for a few days, but when we were eating supper an order came from the General to send a scouting party over to Clear Creek to see if the Cheyennes had come out of the mountains there. It was a thirty mile ride, and the weather was very cold, but there was a full moon. As soon as I finished my supper Frank told me to take four men and go.

*Nov. 30* I selected the men I wanted and we started. There was no snow on the ground where we were camped, and we had a fairly good road, and made good time for the first fifteen miles. Then we struck snow and the farther we went the deeper it got, and when we got to Clear Creek the horses were almost belly deep in snow, and it was so cold that I was pretty nearly frozen.

<hr />

was said that many children died. It makes me sort of sick to think of it" (Richard Tanner Papers, Nebraska State Historical Society).

We found a thicket of willows, and I told the men to start a fire. One of the boys said that if the Indians are here they might see a fire, and I told him that I would as soon be killed by Indians as to freeze to death. He laughed and they all got off their horses, and while one was hunting for dry wood the other three kicked the snow away from a space about six or seven feet in diameter, then cut a lot of small green willow, and made a bed to lay our blankets on.

While they were doing this I sat on my horse, but when the fire got to burning I dismounted and tried to get warm. One of the boys had a quart tin cup and melted snow and made coffee, which helped some, and we put in the rest of the night huddled over the fire. The poor horses had nothing to eat but willow twigs.

In the morning we went up the creek about a mile, but the snow was so deep we could go no farther, and as there was no sign of the Indians having come out of the mountains there, we started back for camp on Crazy Woman. We had to go pretty slowly and it was almost dark when we got there.

Frank had been over to General Crook's tent, and just as he was leaving the General remarked, "We will move back to Powder River tomorrow."

Frank said, "My brother hasn't come back from Clear Creek yet."

The General replied, "Well if he doesn't get here before we start in the morning, you can leave some men to tell him to follow us." Frank said he acted as though he had forgotten that he had sent us.

When Frank told me that I said, "Well I guess it isn't worth while to report to him, if he has forgotten about it," but Frank told me to go ahead; so I went to his tent and reported that I had seen no sign, but that it was possible that part of the snow might have fallen after they had passed there and covered the trail.

[ 219 ]

The next day we started back to Powder River, and reached it that night. The weather was getting colder every day; the horses were getting thinner all the time, and some of them were giving out and had to be abandoned. We lay in camp on Powder River one day, and then started on the road to Ft. Fetterman.

The first day we marched about twenty miles and camped on the dry fork of Powder River. There was very little water in the stream we camped on; no wood except grease wood and sage brush, and no shelter where we camped. We were on a high hill, and across the creek from us was General McKenzie's camp, while General Crook was camping about a mile down the creek below us. He had some wood in his camp.

That night was very cold, the thermometer showing thirty below zero in the morning. After breakfast we saw that McKenzie's command were taking down their tents and saddling their horses, and we did likewise, and then waited for General Crook to make a move. We waited until noon, then we saw General McKenzie ride down toward General Crook's camp. When he returned he came through our camp and told us we were not going to move camp that day, so we unpacked our wagons and went into camp again.[18] The same thing happened the next day, and on the third day we waited until we saw General Crook pulling out of camp before we took down our tents; then we followed him.

*Dec. 5*  We camped near Pumpkin Butte on a poor camping ground with little feed for the horses, and little wood for fires. The next day we moved a few miles, and camped on the Belle Fourche River. The weather was very cold; we were losing horses every day, and no one seemed to know

18. "Got our wagons all loaded ready to move when I learned by accident that we were not to move. I never saw such an outfit in my life nobody knows five minutes beforehand what is to be done. 40 teams started for Fetterman today. I sent some mail home" (Frank North Diary, December 4, 1876).

where we were going. General McKenzie came over to our camp in the evening, and visited with us for an hour or more. He thought he would probably move down the river the next day, but was not sure.

We moved down the Belle Fowrche a few miles into a good camping ground. Just after we were settled in camp a party of seven miners from Deadwood passed through our camp on their way to the Big Horn Mountains to prospect for gold. They had a wagon and several saddle horses, and were pretty well armed. Frank advised them to give up their trip, as the country was full of hostile Indians, but they said they could take care of themselves, and went on up the river.

About four o'clock the next morning one of the men came *Dec. 11* into our camp half naked and pretty badly frozen. He said the Indians had attacked their camp, and he didn't know where the rest of the party were. The poor fellow was about half crazy, and was suffering terribly with his frozen feet. Frank told me to take ten men and go up the river and look for the rest of the men.

I started before it was light, and hadn't gone far until I met three more of the miners on foot. They were not quite so badly off as the one that first came into the camp, but were somewhat frozen. I told them to follow the road to camp and I would look for the rest of the party. I hurried on as fast as I could to where they had camped, and there I found one man dead, and everything taken from the wagon.

It had snowed a little in the night, and I found where the Indians had come down the creek Belle Fowrche on the ice. They were on foot and there were only six of them. They had probably been following our command ever since we had the fight with them. They had come within about thirty feet of the miners' wagon, and were behind a thicket of willow brush when they fired into the camp, and broke the leg of one man. The other evidently ran away and left him, and the Indians found him there and killed him with an axe they found in the camp. They then took everything they could carry, such as provisions and bedding, and all of the horses except one, and then started off toward the southeast.

I found their trail, and just as we were starting to follow it, we saw a man coming toward us on horseback. It proved to be one of the miners. He had jumped on one of the horses when they were attacked and ran away, and had been lost until after daylight, when he had struck the road made by our wagon train and was following it. I sent him on to camp and followed the Indians, but after an hour's ride I turned back, for our horses were so weak I knew there was no chance to overtake the Indians.

When I got back to within about two miles of camp, I met Frank with twenty-five men. I had been gone so long he thought I might have run into a big war party, and he was coming to my relief. He told me that all of the miners were in camp except the one that was killed at the wagon. We went back to camp, and that night it snowed a little and turned very cold.

Next morning I went with the boys that were detailed to take care of the horses to find a good grazing ground, and a couple of miles from camp we found a canyon that looked pretty good, with grass and good shelter. It was about a hundred yards wide and ran back at that width for a quarter of a mile, where it closed up until it was only about twenty feet wide, with perpendicular sides.

I left the men here with the horses, and taking one man with me rode into the narrow neck of the canyon to see how far back it went. It didn't run straight back, but turned first to the right, then to the left. It was snowing all of the time and our horses made no noise, and as we came around a corner of the canyon it opened out into a little park of two or three acres, which was enclosed with high cliffs, and no way out except where we had come in. In this park were about fifty elk.

When they saw us they ran around the enclosure, and then came straight for us. We got out of the way and let them go by. I killed one big bull as they ran past. They went on out to the larger park, where the boys were with the horses, and they killed two more as they went by. We dressed them and packed the meat on a couple of horses and took it to camp. I stopped at General McKenzie's tent and gave him some of the meat, then went on to our camp, where we had a feast.

We stayed in this camp for several days. Then one morning, when the thermometer was forty below zero, we started *Dec. 20* back up the Belle Fourche, and when within a few miles of Pumpkin Buttes went into camp. There was no wood except sage brush, and the creek was frozen over so hard that the boys had difficulty in getting water for the horses. One of the teamsters had his fingers pretty badly frozen, and Frank was pretty sick with asthma, but both he and I got through without freezing. Capt. Cushing froze badly his fingers and one of his toes.

The next day we started for the dry fork of Powder River. When we got to the Pumpkin Buttes we found the road so icy that the teams couldn't pull the wagons up the hill. Capt. Cushing and I had been walking all the way to keep warm, but on account of his asthma Frank could not walk, and he suffered from the cold. There was some pine wood at the foot of the buttes, so I had a fire built and Frank got warmed up. I told him to take his man as soon as he got warm, and ride over to Dry Fork as fast as he could, and I would stay where we were, and when our wagons came I would help them up the mountain.

Frank soon started, and when the wagons got there, I had the men take their lariat ropes and tie them on the side of the wagons and, taking all of our hundred men to one wagon, we just walked them up the mountain in short order. Each company had two wagons, and when we got ours up

[ 223 ]

the top, the road from there to camp was almost level, and we made the journey in a couple of hours, getting into camp about two o'clock.

After we got our tents up and had fires going, several of the officers of the cavalry came over and wanted to know how we got our wagons there so soon. They had just come on ahead and left their teams to get up the mountain as best they could, and some of them didn't get up until the next morning. We had about a dozen of the officers with us for supper that night, and as I had killed a couple of antelope on the way over, we had plenty of meat, fried bread and coffee for them.

*Dec. 22-29*   The next day we started on the return trip to Ft. Fetterman, which we reached the latter part of December, and stayed there until the first of January 1877, when we were ordered to Ft. Laramie.

The Sioux scouts were sent home to Ft. Robinson from our camp on the Dry Fork of Powder River, and the Shoshone scouts from Ft. Reno. Before the Sioux scouts left us a lot of them came over to our camp and danced to our boys. The boys made them presents of about twenty-five head of horses, and then they gambled with them all night, and won about fifteen horses from them. They parted pretty good friends.

*Dec. 31*   We mustered the men for pay at Ft. Fetterman. Lieut. Robinson was mustering officer. It was bitter cold and he did not inspect the arms very carefully, which was lucky for us all, I guess, as I do not think they were in very good shape.

We left Fetterman the afternoon of the first, and it took us six days to go to Ft. Laramie. The roads were very bad, with much snow and ice. One of the horses gave out and we left it. On the fifth day Frank took one man and rode on into the fort, and the next day Capt. Cushing and I got in with the scouts. Cushing had a bad time with his hands and

feet, which were severely frozen when we had such bad
weather on the Belle Fourche.

After staying for a few days at Ft. Laramie, we were ordered to Sidney, Nebraska. The day we got to Scotts Bluffs *Jan. 11,*
I took two of the boys and went into the hills to try and get *1876*
some game, but had no luck, and in the evening we came
back towards the river, where Frank said he would camp,
but when we got to the top of the hill we found it was perpendicular on the side, and we had to go back to hunt a path
down on the east side. One of the men was riding a spotted
mule that he bought at Ft. Laramie, and when we found a
place where we thought we could get down the hill, I sent
him ahead.

The hill was pretty steep and quite slippery, and we all got
off and led our horses. We were following down a ravine,
and when within about a hundred yards of the foot of the
hill, we came to a jumping off place where the melting snow
or rain had cut a deep gulley from there to the foot of the
hill. It was about six feet wide at the top, and narrowed
down to perhaps three feet at the bottom. The hill on either
side above the cut, or washout, was very steep and slippery,
but we thought we could make it.

The man with the spotted mule, *Koot-tah-we-coots-oo-
lel-la-hoo-la-shar*, Big Hawk Chief,[19] started to climb along
the righthand side, and the other man took the lefthand side,
while I stayed at the head of the cut to see how they got
along, before myself starting down. They had only gone a
few steps when the mule's feet slipped from under him and
he fell on his side, and commenced to slide toward the gulley.
His owner caught hold of a small pine tree with one hand,

19. Luther North believed that Big Hawk Chief died in Pawnee
County, Oklahoma, around 1893, in his early forties.

and held to the bridle with the other, and stopped him for a moment, but when he tried to get up the bridle broke and he slipped over the bank, tail first, and disappeared.

It was about fifteen feet to the bottom of the ravine. The Indian climbed carefully down to the edge and looked over. I asked him what he saw and he said, "Oh father the spotted mule is broken in two."

The Indian on the other side had reached the mouth of the ravine successfull, and I took my horse down on that side, and we all three went up the gulley to the mule. It took us some time to get there as the washout was full of small pine trees that had been carried down.

When we finally got to him we found the mule lying on his back. A log about a foot in diameter lay crosswise of the gulley and the saddle was fitted across the log, and the mule's feet were sticking up in the air. The ravine was too narrow for him to roll down on his side, and his head was up the canyon. We managed to crawl over him and get hold of his head and neck, and as he was balanced over the log, we tipped him over endwise on to his feet.

He was pretty stiff and sore for a while, but soon got so he could walk pretty well, and in a day or two was entirely well.

We were late getting into camp and Frank was getting uneasy about us, but as he didn't know where to look for us he could do nothing. The next day we got through the pass at Scotts Bluffs and camped about north of Chimney Rock,* and our next camp was at the foot of Court House Rock.

We got there early in the afternoon, and in the evening with some of the boys I climbed to the top. We went up from the north side, and did not find it very hard climbing, but the south side was perpendicular. The Pawnees tell a story of a war party of Pawnees that was driven up there by the Sioux, and after having been kept there for several

[ 226 ]

days escaped down the cliff side by tying their ropes to-gether and sliding down.

The same story is told of the Pawnee Buttes in Colorado, but I am doubtful if it happened at either place. When the Pawnees went to take horses from the enemy they carried very light hair ropes, and as the cliff at Court House Rock must be more than two hundred feet high, it would take at least ten of their ropes to reach down, and I am quite sure that the hair ropes that they used in the early days would have broken with the weight of a man before he had gone fifty feet. Besides that, the men that we asked about it didn't seem to know who it was that led the party nor the names of men who were with it.

Two days after leaving Court House Rock we reached *Jan. 20* [20] Sidney. The whole town was out to watch the Pawnee scouts return. The boys were carrying the scalps they had taken fastened on the ends of poles, which were held upright over their heads, and as we marched down the main street they sang their war songs.

We went into camp about a mile down the stream below the barracks, where we fixed up our tents for a permanent camp. Frank had ridden ahead of us the day before, and had rations and forage taken down to the camp, and our horses were certainly glad to get a good feed of hay and corn. The ground had been covered with snow all the way from Ft. Laramie, and all the feed they had was what grass they could get from under the snow, and about two pounds of corn per day for each horse.

At this time there was a stage line running from Sidney to the Black Hills, and many ox and mule trains outfitted there. The town was full of saloons and dance halls, and gamblers and gunmen were very plentiful. Several men were killed there that winter, and a number of gun battles took place,

20. This is the last entry in Frank North's Diary.

where neither of the parties engaged was very badly hurt.

I was in a saloon one night when a gambler and a teamster quarreled. They pulled their guns and commenced shooting at each other. They were at opposite ends of a billiard table, and one of them fired six and the other five shots. The gambler was hit once, losing the lower tip of his ear, and the other man wasn't touched.

The saloon was full of men when the shooting began, and in one minute it was empty. There were two doors from the saloon to the street, one at the front at the east, and one on the south side opening on another street. The side door was on a line with the shooting, and as he was going through the door one man was shot through the leg.

These two men were considered fairly good shots, but neither of them was still for a second; they jumped and dodged continually, and, of course, took no aim. Of course this was rather an unusual ending to a gun battle, but it shows that all gunmen were not so deadly as some writers would have us believe.

One of the officers at Sidney barracks, a Capt. Woodson, had a pack of greyhounds, and we put in some of the time chasing jack rabbits. There were thirteen of the hounds, and one day as we started out, some one made the remark that there were thirteen of us on horseback, and that we would have bad luck. The dogs caught thirteen jacks that day, proving that thirteen is an unlucky number—for jack rabbits.

In the spring of 1877 we were mustered out, and the Indians, who had nearly two hundred horses, were sent home. The government furnished them with rations, and Frank and I went with them to see that they didn't get into trouble with or frighten any settlers that we might pass on the way.

A short time before leaving Sidney W. F. Cody, Buffalo

Bill, stopped off to see us. He was on his way to California with his theatrical troup, and while we were visiting with him we made arrangements to go into the cattle business together.

When we left Sidney we came down to Julesburg, and then followed the railroad down to Ogallala, where we crossed the river to the south side. The night after we crossed the horses stampeded, and we were there three days finding them. Some of them had gone back up the river as far as old Ft. Sedgewick. We had drawn rations at Ft. Sidney to last us to Ft. McPherson, where we were to get a fresh supply. The night before we got to McPherson we camped on the river opposite North Platte, and had nothing to eat.

We had gone into camp pretty early, and the boys took the horses over to an island in the Platte River, as the grass there was very good. The next morning we started early and reached Ft. McPherson before noon, and after drawing rations went into camp on the river.

In the evening two men drove into our camp, the sheriff from North Platte and a man named Joe Mackel,[21] who lived on the south side of the river from the town of North Platte. Mackel said that our boys had killed one of his cows when they were on the island the day before, and he had sworn out a warrant for the arrest of all of them, but if they would pay for the cow he would do nothing more about it.

Frank told him that they had not killed the cow, and that the sheriff should arrest them, and we would go back to North Platte with them.

The sheriff didn't know what to do, and told Frank so, but said he hoped we would settle it in some way.

Frank told him that these men were not killing people's cattle, and he didn't propose to pay for the cow.

21. Joseph Mackle was an Irish immigrant and Civil War veteran who raised cattle near North Platte. He was elected county clerk of Lincoln County in 1879 (A. T. Andreas, *History of Nebraska*, 1100).

Some of our men could understand English and they told Frank that they would rather pay for the cow than to go back to North Platte with all their horses and luggage. One of the men named *Pawnee Puk-oot*, Old Horn, said, "We want to get home. I will give this man one of my horses."

Mackel said he would take the horse or forty dollars, and the men soon made up a purse of forty dollars and paid him.

Frank told the men that they ought not to do it; that the white man would say they had killed the cow, or they would not have paid for her, but they said they didn't care, they wanted to get home. So it was settled and the sheriff and Mackel went back to North Platte.

The next day we started south, going out through Cottonwood canyon. When we had gone about fifteen miles *Pawnee Puk-oot* rode up to the head of the column where Frank and I were riding and said, "Father I have done a wrong thing." He then said that he had killed Mackel's cow and told us how it happened.

Before leaving Sidney he had bought a little thirty-two caliber rifle, and when the boys had taken the horses to the island at North Platte, he had taken his rifle with him. There were six of these boys and they were all sitting together smoking, when one boy picked up the rifle and said to its owner, "What do you think you could kill with this gun? It shoots too small a bullet."

Old Horn promptly put a cartridge in the gun and said, "Point it toward yourself and pull the trigger, and let's see if it is any good."

The boy handed it back and said, "I didn't mean that close." Just then a cow walked out of some brush about a hundred yards away, and the boy said, "Shoot at that cow, and see if it will hurt her."

"No," said Old Horn, "I should kill her."

"You could not even wound her," said the other.

Finally, after more bantery Old Horn pointed the gun

toward the cow and pulled it off. The bullet struck the cow in the center of the forehead, instantly killing her, much to the surprise of Old Horn. "You know father," he said in telling of it, "I am a poor shot and had no idea that I would hit her."

The men were all frightened and didn't know what to do. At first they thought they would come to camp and tell Frank what had happened, but finally one of them suggested that they drag the cow out into the river and leave her where they was some quicksand, and the owner would think she got stuck there and had drowned. This they did, but Mackel had found where they had dragged her, and going out to where she was partly burried in the sand and water had found the bullet hole in her forehead.

When *Pawnee Puk-oot* began to tell his story Frank was very angry and started to reprimand him, but he talked so fast that Frank couldn't stop him, and before we finished we were both roaring with laughter. He was a good talker, and when he told of his surprise and dismay when the cow fell, it was too funny, and we had to laugh.

Nothing of importance occurred on the way through Kansas, until one night we camped near some town the name of which I have forgotten. Some of the boys went into the town, and in some way got into trouble, and one of them was shot, I think by the town marshall. Several of the boys went up to town to find out what became of the boy that was shot, and the people there, I think, were very much frightened.

Frank was very sick that night with asthma, and I had told the boys early in the evening not to bother him, and they didn't come to our tent to tell about the shooting for some time after it happened. When they finally told us Frank called some of the men that had been sargents in the company and sent them after the boys that had gone up to town, telling them to come to camp and we would see about it in the morning. They were soon all in camp, and the next morning we found the wounded man in the hospital, where he died a couple of days later.[22]

In the meantime we had moved on toward their reservation. Frank was so ill that when we got to Arkansas City we concluded they could go the rest of the way by themselves, and we bade them all goodbye and took the train for home. They were very sorry to see us go, and we were sorry to part with them.

This was the end of the organization of the Pawnee Indian scouts. They were true and loyal soldiers; brave as any body of men I ever saw; as good trailers as ever lived, and on every campaign that we took part in it was the Pawnee scouts that always located the hostile Indians. The single exception to this was in the case of the Dull Knife Village of Cheyennes in 1876. This was found by the Arapahoe scouts.

22. The shooting occurred in Hays, Kansas, May 19, 1877. A deputy sheriff shot a Pawnee named Red Willow who was suspected of attempting to break into a store. According to the local newspaper, the comrades of the wounded man "mounted their ponies and came stringing into the town single file, and it was then that the lights went out and our citizens went for their side arms. . . . They said, 'Pawnee kill white man—Pawnee bad Indian, when made mad by white man—Red Willow die—heap trouble.' . . . as to the necessity of shooting the Indian we shall not venture an opinion . . . but our citizens certainly owe Major North a debt of gratitude for holding the revengeful and blood-thirsty red skins in check" (*Ellis County Star*, Hays, Kansas, May 24, 1877).

# SUPPLEMENT

ENROLLING THE LAST PAWNEE SCOUT COMPANY (page 197)

The following description was written by Robert Bruce from Captain North's letters and after examinations of official records, newspapers, and related data:

The Norths were seated at a table on the porch of the building, about which the Pawnee warriors crowded, every youth and man anxious to offer his services, and hoping that his name would be placed on the list. Eagle Chief (*La-tah cots La Shar*, Skedee), Sun Chief (*Sacco Roo La Shar*, Chawee), Curly Chief (*Tec La Shar cod dic*, Kitkahakee), Ruling His Sun (*Ke wuck-oo-lah La Shar*, Pitahauerat), and Baptiste Bayhayle the well-known interpreter, were among those on hand to witness the proceedings.

Maj. North looked carefully over them, and then called one Indian at a time to the front. If he passed still closer scrutiny, his name was placed on the roll for the adventurous trip. They were not required to give affirmations, as enlistment into service was to be later, at Sidney Barracks (Bruce, *The Fighting Norths*, 42).

SERGEANT FRANK WHITE (page 200, footnote 4)

Li-heris-oo-La-Shar—the name was translated variously as Traveling Chief and Leading Chief—was "not only a warrior, but something of an orator and man of affairs—what might be called a progressive Indian, who could take care of himself on almost any occasion" (Luther North in Bruce, *The Fighting Norths*, 20). The same source includes a description of Frank White from an account by Captain John G. Bourke, one of the participants in the Dull Knife fight.

> Li-heris-oo-La-Shar . . . of the Pawnees had a good face, prominent cheek bones, aquiline nose, large mouth and frank open eyes, though not as piercing as those usually noticed among aborigines. He had the air of a far-seeing, judicious lawgiver, who took note of all he saw and whose advice could be relied upon; yet the outlines of his countenance showed plainly that, if aroused, he could be a bad enemy.
>
> At a "great talk" held while the expedition was resting at Fort Reno on the way from Fort Fetterman to the Big Horn Mountains, Li-heris-oo-La-Shar, who had enlisted under the English name of Frank White, made the most of the occasion to impress upon the other tribesmen that he was nothing more or less than a white man, determined to follow the white man's road (53).

THE "HORSEMEAT MARCH" (page 205)

Crook and his men had recently completed a fifty-two day march through the gumbo flats and Black Hills of western Dakota Territory. This force was a part of the Yellowstone and Big Horn Expedition organized by General Sheridan to harass the Sioux. Crook fought one engagement at Slim Buttes on September 9, the battle in which the Oglala chief, American Horse, met his death. Early in September the rations ran out and the men were forced to eat some of the cavalry horses; at the same time they were beset by eleven consecutive days of rain. On September 13 supplies arrived and the troops marched on to Fort Robinson, where they arrived on October 23 (Hurt and Lass, *Frontier Photographer*, 99-110; Martin F. Schmitt, ed., *General Crook: His Autobiography* [Norman: University of Oklahoma Press, 1946], 201-212).

RALPH WEEKS (page 213)

"One of our sergeants in the Dull Knife fight counted coup on a live Cheyenne youth, who was hiding in a clump of bushes, then killed and scalped him. After the usual ceremonies, his name was changed to Lah-we-lah coo-La Shar (meaning *Warrior Chief*). He was also known as See re ri root Kah We (the meaning of which is 'conspicuous in esteem'), probably having both those names at different times, though on the 1876 muster rolls he appeared as Ralph Weeks. I somewhat lost track of him after the removal to Indian Territory, but understand that he studied law and became quite a prominent character in the early days of Oklahoma" (Luther North in Bruce, *The Fighting Norths*, 20).

EVACUATION OF THE WOUNDED (page 218)

Colonel Homer W. Wheeler described the evacuation of the wounded in *The Frontier Trail* (Los Angeles: Times-Mirror Press, 1923).

An incident worth relating shows that Indian scouts were valuable allies and could be depended upon. The wounded were behind what is known as "Hospital Hill." From some rocks a little way up the mountainside, the hostiles were firing upon them and on a number of led horses, making it very uncomfortable. Col. Mackenzie asked Maj. North in my presence at the Hospital Hill, if he could drive the Indians away from there. North replied that he thought so, if there were only a few of them.

★          ★          ★          ★

In a short time half a dozen Pawnees with a non-commissioned officer appeared. When told what they were to do, they stripped down to their "gee strings," removed their heavy boots and substituted moccasins (they were wearing uniforms). Then tying handkerchiefs around their heads so that they might not be mistaken for the

[ 235 ]

hostiles, they quickly disappeared up the mountainside. The firing soon ceased. I was later informed that the Pawnee scouts had killed and scalped one or two of the hostiles.

CHIMNEY ROCK (page 226)

This spectacular Oregon Trail landmark is a narrow shaft rising approximately one hundred fifty feet from a conical mound of reddish sandstone which covers some forty acres. It has been worn down by the action of the wind and rain, and—if early explorers did not exaggerate—a hundred and fifty years ago stood more than twice as high.

Courthouse Rock and Jail Rock are buttes lying to the southeast on the Oregon Trail. One story says that the former was so named by early travelers who thought it resembled a county building, and that the nearby Jail Rock was given its name by cowboys because where there's a courthouse there's usually a jail close by. The upper part of the buttes is composed of a banded formation of sandstone, clay, and lime so malleable that one heavy storm can change the contour of the formation. Early explorers estimated the height of Courthouse Rock at from three to five hundred feet and its circumference one mile (*Nebraska: A Guide to the Cornhusker State* [New York: Hastings House, 1939], 384-389).

# X

## *THE CODY-NORTH RANCH*

*[Supplement for this chapter begins on page 280.]*

O N OUR RETURN to Columbus we made arrangements to start a cattle ranch on the head of the Dismal River. Colonel Cody, Buffalo Bill, was one of the partners in this company, and the ranch was known as the Cody and North Ranch. Frank took a party of men and went northwest from North Platte to the head of the Dismal River, where he built a log ranchhouse, a sod stable, and a big cedar pole corral.[1]

1. The ranch headquarters was said to be located in the south-western corner of Hooker County, Nebraska (*Nebraska History*, XXI, 2 [April-June 1940], 114). The log ranchhouse was purchased about 1894 by Nathan E. Trego. He dismantled it and moved it to his own ranch in what was then called Cottonwood Valley in McPherson County. Two rooms were added to the original building which still stands about 17 miles straight west of Tryon, Nebraska, on Highway 92 (information from Mrs. Harry Yost, Maxwell, Nebraska).

I had made a trip to Ohio and New York State to visit my birthplace and relatives and friends, and on my return, the latter part of July, I joined my two brothers at North Platte, and with Colonel Cody we all went to Ogallala to buy our cattle. On our arrival there we found the cattle that had been brought up from Texas were being held on the south side of the river.

There were several large herds there, and as we looked across the river at them, I said to Frank, "How do they compare in number with the buffalo we saw over there seven years ago, when we came up here to hunt?"

He replied, "I think there were ten times as many buffalo in sight then as there are cattle."

When we crossed the river we found there were forty thousand head of cattle there, which would mean that seven years before there had probably been four or five hundred thousand buffalo in sight at one time from that point, and that in seven years they had been almost exterminated. There were thousands of hunters that were killing them for the skins alone. I was at Ft. Wallace, Kansas, in the fall of 1873, and there was a stack of dried hides piled up along the railroad there that I think must have contained over one hundred thousand skins, and that was just one shipping point on the Kansas Pacific. There were certainly many millions killed for the hides alone.*

The next day after reaching Ogallala we bought fifteen hundred head of cattle and hired six of the men that had driven them up from Texas * to help us take them to our range. Two of these cowboys were the Taylor brothers, Baxter and Buck. Baxter, the older brother, was six feet three inches tall, and weighed two hundred twenty pounds; Buck, who was nineteen years old, was six foot four and of about the same weight. They were born in Texas and had handled cattle all their lives. Bax Taylor was the best broncho buster that I ever saw, and Buck, a few years later, joined

Buffalo Bill's Wild West Show, and was known as the king
of the cowboys while with the organization.

It took us about ten days to brand and drive our cattle
to the range, and we spent the next two months in building
fences, putting up hay, and preparing for winter. The country was full of game; elk, white tail and mule deer antelope,
and many prairie chickens, and the lakes west from the head
of the Dismal River were alive with wild fowl; swans, sand
hill cranes, geese and ducks by the millions. We had to keep
a couple of men riding range all of the time, and that job
fell to me, and that gave me plenty of time to hunt. The
cattle were tired and thin from their long trip from Texas;
the grass was good and they didn't travel far from water.

For a few days after reaching the ranch we closeherded
the cattle and rounded them up on a flat near the house at
night, and they soon got so they would start for the bedground themselves about sundown. Then we stopped herding them, but still rode every day, and when we found any
cattle that we thought were getting too far out in the sand
hills, we would turn them back toward the creek.

One day while riding on the North Dismal I found some
horse tracks and following them discovered an Indian camp.
There were quite a number of lodges, but none of the Indians
had seen me, and I lost no time in getting back to our camp.
One of the boys had gone after our horse herd, and didn't
get in until after dark, and then he didn't bring the horses.
They had never gone far from the ranch before. We had
part of the horses in a small pasture that we had built, but
thought the Indians had taken them. We felt sure the Indians
were from the Rosebud Agency,[2] Chief Spotted Tail's band
of Brule Sioux, and Frank said he would send a telegram to
General Crook, who was in command of the department of

2. It was to this agency, established in 1878, that the Brûlé came
from the Whetstone Agency, led by Spotted Tail, who was trying
to remove them from easy access to the white man's whiskey.

the Platte, telling him of our loss, and that the Sioux were off their reservation.

I was to take the dispatch to North Platte and send it from there. I told Frank that in my rides south I had discovered some valleys that would be a better and nearer road to the Platte than the one we had come out on, and that I would go that way, and could make it through in one day. Frank said he would ride out with me for a few miles.

We started the next morning at sunrise, on Sunday morning, Frank, Buck Taylor, Billy Jaiger and myself, leaving one man Adam Shiek, at the ranche. When we had gone about ten miles Frank and the boys turned back, and I went on alone.

Shortly after Frank got back to the ranch the Indians showed up on a hill across the creek, and made signs that they wanted to talk. Frank motioned them to come to the house, and when they did so he went out and had a talk with them. They said they were friendly and wanted to go in the house.

Frank could not talk the Sioux language but was an expert sign talker, and he asked them why they had their war paint on, if they were friendly? He told them that they couldn't come in the house, and accused them of taking our horses. They denied having the horses and soon rode away. There were twenty-eight of them.

After they had gone Frank told Billy Jaiger he was going to send him to North Platte the next day, and that he could meet me at the forks of Birdwood Creek, where I would camp that night. We had a man and team in town that was to start out on Monday morning, and I was coming back with him.

On Monday morning Frank started with Billy, and rode out with him for several miles and put him on the wagon road. Billy asked, "Why can't I go the way your brother went yesterday?"

Frank answered, "You would get lost, so you stick to the road."

Frank then went back to the ranch, and as soon as he left him Billy left the road and tried to follow where I had gone the day before. He had gone but a short distance when he got off his horse to shoot at an antelope. His horse got away from him and he was soon out of sight in the sand hills, and Billy was lost.

In the meantime I had started from North Platte that same morning for the ranch. With me was our man Wesley Rhone and a Dr. Stull, who was coming to the ranch to hunt. We got to the forks of the Birdwood, about half way to the ranch, Monday night, and the next day when we got to the head of the Birdwood we saw the track of a man on foot in the road going in the same direction we were. This puzzled me; first because there was no one in the country but our men, and nobody in a cattle country ever went on foot.

We kept seeing the tracks all afternoon, and at dark when we were about three miles from the camp we heard someone shout, and then an answer in front of us.

I said, "There are some of the boys from the ranch coming out to meet us, but when we had gone a quarter of a mile further and no one came, it struck me that perhaps the Indians had attacked the ranch and that the tracks we had seen were made by one of the men who had got away and was lost.

I took the saddle horse that I had been leading behind the wagon, and telling Wes. to come on with the team, I started for the ranch on a gallop. When a half mile from the ranch I could see a light in the window, and knew that they were all right. When I got there Frank asked me about Billy. I told him I hadn't seen him, but that he was lost and on foot. Then I told him about the tracks in the road, and he told me about starting Billy to town. I was going to start out again to hunt him, but it was so dark and a thunderstorm came up, so I put it off until morning. The weather changed and the next morning was very cold.

I started at daylight and when I got to where we had heard the shouting the night before, I sent off Wes Rhone, who was with me, to the west, to the cattle trail leading south to Birdwood, and told him to follow it and to look out for the man's tracks. I went east a mile, to where another trail came in from the south, and followed it about five miles. Farther south the two trails came together, and just before I got to the junction of the trails I found the tracks in the trail, and they were going south. The trail soon led into the wagon road, and then we could follow on a lope, and about four o'clock in the afternoon we came in sight of Billy at the head of the Birdwood.

When we got near enough for him to hear I hollowed to him. He stopped, looked around and then started on a run away from us. I yelled again, and he turned around and came slowly toward us. At first he did not seem to know who we were, but when I told him we were looking for him and would take him to the ranch, he seemed to come to himself and told us how it all happened. The day we found him was Wednesday, and he had been walking since Monday morning with not a bite to eat, for everything he had was tied on his saddle, even his coat. He was in his shirt-sleeves when we overtook him.

I put him on my horse and gave him my overcoat, then we started for the ranch. He only rode a mile, when he said he could not stand it any longer, and wanted to get off and walk. He was riding behind me on my horse. I told him to hang on to me and I started the horse on a lope, but after going a couple of miles further he begged so that I stopped.

Just then some antelope came over a sand hill about a hundred yards away, and I killed one of them. We found some dry roots of the sand cherry in a blowout, and built a fire and broiled some of the meat. Billy ate about two pounds and wanted more, but I wouldn't give it to him. He felt better after that, and after resting for a while we started on, and a little after dark got to the ranch.

I asked him who it was that shouted to him the night before; he said he didn't know; that he was walking along the road and saw a man off to his left on a hill—it was then pretty dark—he called to the man and the man said, "Come over here." Billy went to the hill and when he got there the man was gone, and we never did find out who it was.

That was one of several mysterious things that happened while we were in the cattle business that we never could account for. It was while Billy was going to the hill to meet this man that we had driven past him the night before. Billy said that when the storm came up he got into a sand blow-out[3] to keep warm, but soon a band of cattle came drifting past; they were bawling, and he got out of the hole and ran with them and bawled too. I guess he was delirious; he was very nervous the night we got to the ranch, and got up and started for the door, and once got clear out, but I headed him off and brought him back.

This boy was afterward working on a cattle ranch in Wyoming, and was lost in a blizzard for five days, with the temperature twenty below zero. He was so badly frozen that both of his legs were taken off below the knees, and he lost all of the fingers and thumbs off both hands. He finally located at Chadron, Nebraska, where he was elected Clerk of the District Court, and was re-elected and served for thirty years.[4]

3. A crater scooped out by the wind.

4. "Billy's" name correctly was Louis John Frederick Iaeger. He had been a performer in Cody's Wild West Show, where he was known as Billy the Bear. After his misfortune in Wyoming, he worked for Cody as a bookkeeper before settling in Chadron (A. E. Sheldon, *History of Nebraska* [Chicago: The Lewis Publishing Co., 1931], III, 371-372). For another reminiscence, see James H. Clark, "Early Days in Ogallala," *Nebraska History*, XIV (April-June 1933).

Two days after finding Billy, I found the horse he had been riding. The saddle and bridle were still on him, but a pair of fieldglasses that belonged to me was gone. The next day after finding the horse Frank and I went over to the North Dismal where I had seen the Indian camp, but they were gone, and on the return trip we found the horses that were missing, so the Indians hadn't taken them at all.

At this time we had a man getting out logs to build a house. His name was Adam Sheik. He was a great talker and was always telling what a good hunter he was. One day in January 1878, or perhaps a little later, Adam and I were riding down the creek and saw a big white tail buck standing at the head of a deep canyon. I told Adam to shoot him. He got off his horse and shot, and the deer fell. Adam dropped his gun and ran to him. He caught the buck by one of his antlers and pulled his head back to cut his throat, when the deer got up and in the struggle they both went over the bank into the canyon.

I rode over, and when I got where I could look down in the canyon Adam was sitting on the ground with one of the deer's antlers in each hand. It was just about shedding time, and in the struggle they had come off and the deer ran away. I think the bullet just struck the animal hard enough to stun him for a while. It was probably the first deer that Adam shot and he felt very badly about it.

In the winter of 1878, Frank went to Columbus, and while there someone gave him a dog. I think he was a cross between a great dane and a newfoundland. He was an immense brute and was of a sullen disposition, but seemed to like Frank.

When Frank came back to the ranch some time in January, he brought him out with him. When Frank got on the train at Columbus he took the dog in the smoking car with him, and soon after starting the brakeman came in, and seeing the dog said, "Major, dogs are not allowed in here. I'll take him to the baggage car for you."

Frank said, "All right, do so."

The brakeman came over where the dog was lying at Frank's feet and stooped down to take hold of his collar. The dog growled in a deep bass tone, and the brakeman stepped back, looked around at the other passengers, and said, "Does anyone object to having this dog ride here? I guess not, so you can keep him here."

Major Frank laughed and the dog stayed in the smoking car until they got to North Platte, where I met Frank with a team, and we took him to the Ranch.

Not long after we got him, we heard one night the howl of a gray wolf, and in the morning the dog was gone. There had been a light snow in the night, and I soon found the tracks of the gray wolf and the dog, and followed them for seven or eight miles. After going two or three miles they were joined by one or two other wolves, and there were signs of a battle, but I saw nothing of either dog or wolves, and after the snow had melted I gave up trying to follow them. We never saw the dog again, and concluded the wolves must have killed him.

The next summer one of our men, Albert Pratt, while riding the range came across a female gray wolf with seven puppies; three of them were gray like the mother and four were black like the dog. Al gave chase and managed to kill two of them, both black, and late that fall the three gray puppies were killed, two of them by Bill Burke, a cowboy working for the John Bratt Cattle Company,[5] and the third

5. John Bratt (1842-1918) emigrated from England and came to Nebraska Territory in 1866. After working as a bullwhacker and freighter, in 1869 he established the John Bratt Cattle Company with Isaac Coe and Levi Carter as partners. Bratt became one of the best known ranchmen in Nebraska; his herds ranged over a vast area south of the Platte and west of Fort McPherson.

by a trapper named Jim Carson, who was a nephew of the famous scout Kit Carson.

This left two black puppies and the old mother wolf, and for the next two years they roamed the sand hills killing cattle whenever they were hungry, and sometimes apparently for fun, as I found four animals that they had killed in one day. The three were always together, and they were so cunning that no one could get a shot at them, and they would never feed more than once from one of their kills, so there was no use trying to poison them. A band of six or eight coyotes always followed them to get the animals that they had killed. Some times for several days at a time we would see them every day, then they would disappear and be gone for a month or two.

An Englishman, named Smith, who had a cattle ranch on the Middle Loup got three Siberian wolf hounds, and hunted them for several weeks before getting sight of them, but finally found them and put the dogs after them. They ran through the roughest sand hills in the country, and his horse was soon so blown that he could only walk. He told me that he saw the wolves and dogs go over a high hill about a mile away, with the dogs close to the wolves, and that when he got to the hill, he saw the wolves about a half mile away. They were about two hundred yards apart, each sitting on a sand hill, and between him and the wolves was a valley about a quarter mile wide. When he came in sight the wolves trotted off, and when he rode down into the valley he found his dogs about two hundred yards apart and almost torn to pieces. He said it looked as though they had gotten the dogs separated, and had attacked them one at a time, but, of course, that was a guess.

At another time I was down on the Dismal River, and just as I rode out into a flat about a mile long, I saw the three rush out from the sand hills and catch a three-year-old heifer. They were nearly a mile from me, but I ran my horse as fast as I could go. They had her down but saw me when about a quarter mile from them, and left her. I jumped from my horse and took a shot at them, but they were too far away. When I got to the heifer I found her throat terribly torn, and a hole in her flank from which the entrails were hanging. I put a bullet in her head to end her misery.

I spent many days hunting these three, but they seemed always to see me first, and I could not get within rifle shot of them. One day while lying behind a hill watching a big buck deer, I saw the three wolves together on a sand hill a mile or more away. It was a warm October day, and I watched them until they lay down.

I had my horse in a low place behind a ridge of sand hills, and going back to him and taking a roundabout way, I kept out of sight of the hill where the wolves were, until I got within about four hundred yards of them. I then left the horse and crawled to the hill. The side that I came to was very steep, and when I had climbed up to within about fifty feet of the top, I stopped to get my breath.

I sat down and turned to look toward the top of the hill, and saw the head of the old mother wolf. She was in a sand blowout about three feet deep, and was standing with her front feet on the bank, and was looking over the country. I swung my gun around, and just as she saw me I fired, and she disappeared. I scrambled up the hill as fast as I could, and when I got to where I could look over, I saw the two black ones about a hundred yards away. They were standing still and looking back toward me.

Just as I saw them one of them stood up on his hind feet to get a better look. I took another step up and as they started to run shot at one of them. They went out of sight, but in a moment one of them came in sight again around the shoulder of the hill, and I shot at him. He kept on running, and as he was in sight of me I sat down and watched

[ 247 ]

him. He hadn't gone very far until he slowed up, and finally came down to a walk, and then passed out of sight.

I then went over to the blowout and found the old mother wolf dead. She was the biggest wolf I ever saw. I am sure she weighed more than one hundred fifty pounds. I went back and got my horse and followed after the wounded one. When I got to where he went out of sight, I found a little blood, and followed it, but it was slow work, and when it was nearly sundown, I got on my horse to go to the ranch. Just then the wounded wolf got up about fifty yards away, and ran out on a flat about a mile long. I gave chase and over-took and killed him. I skinned him and when I got to the ranch nailed the hide up on the side of the house, it was seven feet and over in length.

The next day we started on the beef roundup, and I never went back to the hill where I left the mother wolf. The other black one that I fired the second shot at was never seen afterward, so I may have killed him too. On the hill where I killed them there must have been ten or twelve coyotes. They were running in all directions.

This band of three wolves must have killed several hundred head of cattle in the two winters before I killed them, as I found eighty-four head that they had killed within two miles of our ranch the winter before I got them.

At this time the country west from North Platte City and north of the North Platte River was all cattle ranches. No claims had been taken, and all the land belonged to the government and the Union Pacific Railroad Company. The cattle men had no rent to pay, the cattle lived the year around without hay or feed of any kind. In the summer ranchmen kept men enough to hold his cattle pretty nearly on the range that he claimed, but in the fall, after the beef was shipped and the calves branded, the cattle were turned loose for the winter; that is, they were allowed to go where they pleased, and often in the spring some of them would be found more than a hundred miles from the home range. There were no fences and the cattle of the different owners were all mixed up. Then in the spring we had a roundup to gather and separate them and drive them to the home range.

To give some idea of the number of cattle on the ranges north of the Platte, I will mention some of the big companies. On the Birdwood was the ranch of John Bratt & Co., who had fifteen thousand head. Next, west of him twenty-five miles, was the William Paxton Co., fifteen thousand; then came the Bosler Brothers, with thirty thousand, and, still farther west, were the Powers Bros.; then the Sheedy herd with thirty thousand, and these herds were all on the Platte River. North, on the Niobrara, there was the Newman herd of forty thousand, the Hunter & Evans herd of perhaps as many more, and a great many small herds of from one to ten thousand head.[6]

Every spring it was necessary to roundup all these. On the Platte roundup there were two hundred fifty men, and about twelve hundred and fifty cow ponies, and twenty-five or thirty wagons in which to haul the provisions and bedding. The roundup would start out at our ranch and work down to the mouth of the Birdwood, and then up the Platte River. While on our range Frank was captain; when on

6. The Bosler brothers, who began operations in 1873, owned extensive herds and held contracts to supply beef to the Red Cloud and Spotted Tail agencies. They listed their range with the Wyoming Stock Growers' Association as "North Platte [River] north of Ogallala." E. S. Newman listed his range as Running Water [Niobrara River], as did Hunter, Evans and Hunter (*Cattle Brands Owned by Members of the Wyoming Stock Growers' Association* [Chicago: 1882], as reproduced in Louis Pelzer, *The Cattlemen's Frontier* [Glendale: The Arthur H. Clark Co., 1936], Appendix; and Norbert Mahnken, "Ogallala—Nebraska's Cowboy Capital," *Nebraska History*, XXVII, 2 [April-June 1947], 89).

Bratt's range he was captain, and at each range we changed captains.

We used to drive in from the hills to the valley about ten thousand head of cattle, and these were divided into three herds and rounded up into as small a space as possible, and twenty or thirty men, or perhaps more, would hold them together. The captain of the roundup would choose two men from one of the companies, and send them into the bunch to cut out the cattle that had their brand. When they had them all out, two more from another ranch were sent in. This was kept up until all were out but the ones belonging on the range, when they were driven down the river and turned loose.

Those that had been cut out were taken care of by their respective owners, and driven along with the roundup, and herded nights until there was several hundred, or perhaps a thousand or more, when they were sent home. It was pretty strenuous work. We used to get out as soon as it was light in the morning, and work until dark, and then have a couple of hours of nightherding.

Some of the cow ponies showed great intelligence in cutting out cattle, and one horse in particular stood out above all others. He was a steel blue roan, and belonged to George Bosler. One spring while on the roundup Cody was with us. He had some liquor with him and he and George Bosler got somewhat hilarious. George said that Old Blue (the horse) knew his brands, and to prove it he rode into the bunch of cattle and pulled the bridle off him.

Old Blue walked around among the cattle until he came to a big wild steer with Bosler's brand, when he began to drive it out to the edge of the herd. The steer was very wild and didn't want to leave the bunch, and when at the edge turned back to fight. Old Blue sprang at him and threw his head across the steer's neck, and with shoulder against the steer pushed him out and over to the Bosler bunch. The whole roundup stopped to watch the performance, and everyone said they didn't believe there was another horse in the world could do it. A good cow horse was worth at that time about fifty dollars, but Dennis Sheedy offered Bosler one thousand for Old Blue.

It was on this roundup that I first saw the electric flames run up a horse's neck and the points of his ears. I was on nightherd; it was very warm and the air was full of moisture, and it was also very dark. I was sitting on my horse and he was standing still, when suddenly it seemed to get so dark that I could not see his head; then a little blue flame seemed to start up from his neck, and run up the mane to the top of his head, and then up his ears, where it blazed off the points like a candle. The horse stood perfectly still and hardly seemed to breathe; the cattle also were still as death, and little points of flame could be seen everywhere over their heads and backs. The flames blazed up and died down like northern lights, only on a very small scale. It lasted only for two or three minutes, when a little breeze sprang up, the cattle, my horse and myself took a long breath, the lightening flashed and the rain began to pour down, and that was all there was to it.

I expected a stampede, but the cattle turned their backs to the storm and stood still. The five years we were on the ranch I saw three of these black nights, and I never saw any one of them anywhere else, and only around a bunch of cattle on the bedground.

After getting back from our first roundup we branded our calves—five hundred of them—and Al Pratt and I did the range riding all that summer, and I found out many curious and interesting things about cattle. The coyotes were bad and would kill calves whenever they could find one alone. The cows seemed to understand that, and ten or fifteen of them would always feed together, and about noon when it was time for them to go for a drink, they would all get the calves to nurse, then get them to lie down close together, when all but one of them would go to the creek or lake for a drink, while the one stood guard. After they had drank they would come back, and the one that had been on guard would go to the water.

One day I came across a bunch of ten cows and calves, and one yearling steer, and when the cows went to drink they left the steer on guard. I was curious to know how long they would be gone, and waited until they returned. It was two hours, and the steer never laid down while they were gone. It was a very hot day, and he must have been thirsty, but he waited until they came back before he started for the lake, which was about two miles away. I followed him, and when he got his drink he came out of the water and layed down in a bunch of about a hundred steers, where he stayed for an hour, then got up, took another drink, and went back to the little valley where he had left the cows. They had gone, but he seemed to know where, and crossed a low ridge of sand hills into another valley, where he joined them.

One of our ranch houses was on the shore of a small lake west of the head of the South Dismal River. The lake was about a quarter mile in diameter, and at the upper end was a thick growth of canes or cattails. There were many muskrats in the lake, and they built their houses of these cattails. Some of them were three or four feet above the water, and the spring after we built our house there, a pair of trumpeter swans nested on top of one of the muskrat houses.

The nest was in a bayou, and on three sides was surrounded by the canes, with a narrow opening to the lake on the east. It was out of sight from the shore, but we had a skiff and by rowing out to the middle of the lake we could see the female swan on the nest. After she had been sitting for a week or so, I took some pieces of bread, and rowing to where I could see her, put the bread on the water and left it. The wind was in the east and it soon drifted up near the nest, and the mother bird came down from her nest and got it. I had rowed out of sight but was watching her.

I took out food of some kind every day, and left it for her, and in a week or ten days as soon as I came in sight she would come down off her nest and swim out to meet me. She hatched two of the four eggs that were in the nest, and she and the young ones got so tame they would follow me all around the lake every time I went in the boat, and would come so close I could touch them with the oars. The male bird never came quite so close, but would come within twenty feet of the boat.

In the fall when the young ones were almost big enough to fly, we were away from the ranch for a few days on the beef roundup, leaving one man at the ranch, and while we were gone a cowboy from the ranch of the Rankin Cattle Co. on the Middle Loup came to the ranch. He told our man that if they caught the young swan and took the end joint off their wing, so they couldn't fly, we could keep them all winter. They did that, and, of course, the young ones could not fly. The old mother bird tried to teach them and stayed on the lake long after the other wild fowl had gone south.

Then one evening, when it was snowing and blowing, we heard her after dark flying over the house on her way south. The next morning the young ones were gone. A few days after one of the men found where they had been torn to pieces by the coyotes about three miles south of the ranch. They had started to walk south and the coyotes had caught them.

Now comes the strangest part of the story. In December when the lake was frozen over solid, except a hole about twenty feet in diameter where there was a spring, the mother swan came back and stayed three days looking for her young. She would fly around and around the lake through the day, calling for them, and at night would come to the open water to sleep. I fed her every day. On the third day

it turned cold and she flew away. The same pair came back
the next spring and stayed for two or three weeks. They
inspected their old nest on the muskrathouse, and came to
me to be fed, but after a while they flew away to the north
and that was the last I ever saw of them.

When we built our ranch there was no other ranch house
between us and the Platte River, but the next spring the
Hinman Brothers built a house at the forks of the Birdwood,
thirty miles from our ranch, and the firm of Stearns and
Patterson located on the north fork of the Dismal River seven
miles from us. Ten miles to the west of us the John Bratt
Company had a winter camp, where they kept three men in
the winter, so we had some company.

In the summer of 1878 some cowboys that had driven
cattle from Texas to the Rosebud Agency, after delivering
the cattle stole a band of the Indians' horses and drove them
to North Platte, where they sold them. They passed our
ranch on the way to the Platte and stopped long enough to
get their dinner. They left the horses that they had stolen
about a half mile from the house, and we supposed they
were the horses they had used in driving the cattle to the
agency.

The second morning after they passed our ranch when I
went out to drive our horses I couldn't find them, but found
mocassin tracks on the trail that the cowboys had come
over. We had three or four horses at the ranch, so I went
back and told Frank that the Indians had our horses, and Al
Pratt and I started out to see if we could find any they
might have missed. We found twenty or more, but the rest,
thirty-two head, were gone. We drove in what we found
and Frank, Al and I started on the trail after the Indians.

They did not follow the cattle trail leading north, but cut
across the sand hills to the north fork of the Dismal, then
followed down to where the trail crossed. We couldn't follow very fast, and when we got to the crossing it was late

in the afternoon. We found a wagon camped there and three cowboys from the Rankin ranch on the Middle Loup.

They told us that a couple of hours before we got there the Indians came into their camp with our horses. There were seven of them. They asked for something to eat, and after getting it went on with the horses. The boys were only armed with six shooters, while the Indians had Winchester rifles, so they didn't try to get the horses.

After we had supper with them we started on after the Indians. It was dark by this time, but the moon was shining. Frank sent me on ahead to follow the trail, and we made pretty good time until the moon went down. We were then about three miles from the creek, and I lost the trail. Rankin's ranch was up the river a couple of miles, so we went up there and stayed the rest of the night.

Early the next morning we went down the river and two miles below the ranch we found where the Indians had camped. We had passed within a half mile of their camp. They were gone, and after following them for a few miles, we gave up trying to catch them. They had all of our best horses and the ones we were riding were about tired out.

A little later we sent Al Pratt from our ranch and Jim Lawson of Rankin Ranch to the Rosebud Agency to see the agent about it. He called in Chief Spotted Tail and told him what the boys were after.

Spotted Tail said that their horses had been stolen by cowboys and that they had trailed them to our ranch, where they found some horses and took them, and that they were going to keep them and they did. The agent, the boys said, seemed to be afraid of old Spotted Tail. Of course the Indians were not to blame, as they were being robbed continually by horsethieves and cattle rustlers.

In the fall of that year the Cheyennes, under Chiefs Little Wolf and Dull Knife, left their reservation in the Indian territory—now Oklahoma—and came north through Kansas and Nebraska.[7] They crossed the North Platte River near the mouth of White Tail Creek and, keeping on north into the sand hills, made a camp on a lake about fifteen miles northwest of our ranch. From this camp they raided the surrounding ranches for fifty miles, running off horses and killing the ranchmen when they got a chance. Frank Morehead of the firm of Morehead Brothers was killed by them, and three or four men near Court House Rock. Jack Southard was found dead in the sand hills, and he was probably killed by them. A couple of troops of cavalry was only about an hour behind them when they crossed the North Platte River, but they went into camp on the river while the Indians camped on Whitetail Creek, not more than seven or eight miles from them.

One of Paxton & Weavers cowboys saw the camp, and went to the soldiers camp and offered to guide them to the camp, but the commanding officer would not move until the next morning, and when they got there the Indians were gone.

At this time Frank and I were both in Chicago with our shipment of beef steers, and before we got back some Sioux Indians from the Rosebud Agency made a raid on the ranches on the Platte and took some horses. The North Platte Guards, of which Frank was Captain, with Lieutenant John Bratt in command, got out after them and recaptured the horses and chased the Indians out nearly to our ranch, when they went back to the Platte. Al Pratt and another man were at our ranch, and they heard the Indians trying to break into

<hr />

7. For detailed accounts of the Cheyenne revolt of 1878-1879, see Mari Sandoz, *Cheyenne Autumn* (New York: McGraw-Hill Book Co., 1953) and George Bird Grinnell, *The Fighting Cheyennes* (Norman: University of Oklahoma Press, 1956).

the stable that night, but they couldn't make it and we didn't lose any horses that time.

As soon as we saw by the papers that the Cheyennes were in the country, we came home and went out to the ranch. A couple of days after we got there, I started for Bratts Ranch, to see if the men there were all right, and at the same time to look for a few of our horses that had been missing for a few days. When within a mile of the ranch I saw off to the south a bunch of cattle and some horses with them. I looked at my watch and it was ten minutes of eleven.

I thought I could ride over to the bunch of cattle and then get to the ranch before noon, so I turned off the road. When I got to them I found it was our horses, and instead of going on to the Bratt Ranch I drove them back to our ranch.

That night about nine o'clock Bill Burke, one of Bratts cowboys, came to the ranch. He said that at eleven o'clock that morning the Indians made a dash on their ranch and ran off all their horses but two. They came out of a ravine about a quarter of a mile below the ranch, and had I gone on instead of turning off after the horses I would have ridden right into them. There was only one man at the ranch, the cook; Bill Burke, and John Hancock were out riding range. When they were coming in to dinner John Hancock saw the Indians and hurried to the ranch.

Burke was farther to the west, and the first he knew the Indians were shooting at him, and although he was within a hundred yards of where they were lying behind a ridge of sand hills, they missed him. He got off his horse and walked backward, leading his horse and shooting at every Indian that showed his head, until he got to a ravine out of sight, when he mounted his horse and ran for the ranch, which he reached in safety.

The ranch was partly a dugout in the side of a steep hill, and the Indians got on top of the hill and fired on the roof pretty nearly all the afternoon. The roof was made of split cedar poles covered with straw, and a layer of dirt about a foot deep, so only a few bullets came through. In the evening the Indians went away, and as soon as it got dark Bill Burke came to our ranch. He stayed with us that night.

The next morning Johnny Higgins and Bill Gibson, two cowboys from the Stearns & Patterson Ranch, came in. They were riding a pair of work horses. They said the Indians had run off all of their horses but these two. Before they got there, Frank, Al Pratt and myself had gone to the Bratt Ranch with Bill Burke. We found the two men there all right, and went on up about two miles further, where Bill had had the fight with them the day before.

When we got to where Bill had gotten off his horse, he found his glove that he had dropped the day before. He pointed to a sand hill about fifty yards away and said one of the Indians was there, and when he raised up to shoot a second time he got a good shot at him. That was all he said, but I knew he was the best shot I ever saw, so I felt sure that one of the Indians was accounted for.

When we got to the hill we saw where the Indian had fallen backwards, and there was a small pool of dried blood there, a pony track and several mocassin tracks, where his companions had put him on a horse. We turned back from there and went to the Bratt Ranch.

Frank told the men that if they were going to stay out there they had better all come down to our ranch and stay there, but John Hancock, who seemed to be in charge, thought they had better go over to the home ranch at the mouth of the Birdwood on the Platte, and they packed up what they could carry on the two horses and abandoned the ranch for the winter. They went with us to our ranch, where they stayed that night, and the next morning started for the Platte.

[ 258 ]

Johnny Higgins and Bill Gibson could hardly make up their minds what to do, but finally said they would go back to the ranch and stay until they could hear from their employer. Mr. Stearns was manager, and they thought that he would probably come out as soon as Bratts men got in. In the evening Frank and I rode over to their ranch with them, and then came back to our ranch.

The next morning early Higgins and Gibson came to our ranch on foot, and said the Indians had come back the night before and taken the two work horses, leaving them on foot. We still had about forty horses, and as we had put up a lot of hay that year we herded them pretty close to the ranch in the daytime, and at night tied them up to the fence just as near to the house as we could, and fed them hay. I had a thoroughbred bull terrier, and he was a splendid watch dog, and we felt pretty sure that no one could come around without his giving us warning.

When Higgins and Gibson came to the ranch, Higgins said that the night before they had put blankets over the windows when they lit their lamp, and they were both sitting at the table reading and had their rifles lying on the table in front of them. Johnny was sitting with his back to the door, which they thought was locked, when they heard a noise outside. They looked at each other and then listened, when without any warning the door opened and an Indian stepped in. He immediately jumped back out again and jerked the door shut again.

The boys blew the light out and got out of range of the door, Johnny on one side of the room and Bill on the other. They both kept very still at first, and then Bill whispered, "Johnny I can hear them putting something up against the house; they are going to burn us out."

Johnny said he knew what it was that Bill heard; it was his heels rattling against the house, but he didn't tell Bill that. After a while, as nothing happened, they began to breathe easier, but they didn't sleep any that night.

The day after they came to our ranch, Frank took a team and wagon and went to North Platte with them. He said he would try to have some soldiers sent out from Ft. Mc-Pherson. Al Pratt and I were to stay at the ranch and take care of the horses until he got back. He thought he would be gone about four days. We turned the horses out every day, but kept them in the valley near the ranch and saw nothing of the Indians.

After a week had passed and Frank didn't come, and no soldiers, I began to get pretty uneasy, and when another week had gone by, I made up my mind that something serious must have happened to Frank, and one evening I told Al Pratt that the next day he should go to North Platte and find out what was the reason of Frank's long stay, and that I would stay and look after things at the ranch.

The next morning we both started early, and when we were about fifteen miles from the ranch I said, "We will ride up on that hill off to the right, and from there we can see the road clear to the head of the Birdwood, and if everything looks well I'll go back to the ranch and you can go on alone."

When we got to the hill I took out my fieldglasses and, looking down the road, I saw about four miles away a team coming. We went on until we met it and found it was Frank, and we all went back to the ranch.

When he had reached North Platte with Higgins and Gibson, he found a telegram there from Columbus saying that his wife was very seriously ill, so he sent word to General Carr at Ft. McPherson, telling him about conditions in the sand hills country, and asking if he could send out some troops. He then wrote a note to me saying that probably the soldiers would be out soon, and that he would be back as soon as possible. He hired a man to take the note out to me,

[ 260 ]

and then went to Columbus. The man he hired got scared out before he had gone ten miles, and turned back.

When we got to the ranch we found everything in good condition, and the next day, in the evening, a squad of soldiers with a sergeant in command, and eight or ten cowboys with them, came to the ranch. The morning after they got there we all went northwest of the ranch about fifteen miles, and found where the Cheyennes had been camped, but they had moved a short time before. In the valley where they had camped we found the carcasses of more than seventy head of cattle that they had killed.

They moved on farther north, where they made another camp, but they took no more horses from the ranches as far south as the Dismal River. The two boys, Higgins and Gibson, with another cowhand, John Alexander, came out to the Stearns & Patterson Ranch with a few saddle horses, and stayed there, and occasionally some one would see one or more Indians, but all the damage they did was to kill cattle.

One day Johnny Higgins was riding range about ten miles from our ranch, and he saw two Indians. He was in a low place in the hills, and they hadn't seen him. He watched them until they rode up to the top of a pretty high hill and got off their horses. There was a long ravine that ran up to within about one hundred fifty yards of them, and Johnny said he thought he would take a shot at them, so went up it until he was as near as he could get and got off and picketed his horse, and crawled up to the top of the bank of the ravine.

He had a sharps rifle, and he took an extra cartridge from his belt and had it in his hand, so that after firing he could reload quickly. Just as he pushed his gun up through the grass over the bank, another Indian rode up from the opposite side of the hill and dismounted. Johnny said he hesitated a moment, and then concluded he would try to [get] the

[ 261 ]

three of them, but took two or three more cartridges out of his belt to have them handy. By this time two more Indians joined the three, and Johnny put his cartridges back in his belt, and just as he was going to back down the bank two more men showed up.

He said he slipped down the bank, climbed on his horse and rode for our ranch. When he got this far in his story I asked Johnny, "Did you run?"

He said, "Well old Brownie was feeling pretty good, and I let him come right along."

About the time we went into the cattle business there was a gang of horse thieves and cattle rustlers in that country, headed by a man called Doc. Middleton. I am not sure that they were as bad as they were pictured, but it was said that they stole cattle from the ranches and drove them to the Black Hills, where they were sold and butchered.

Doc. Middleton also had the reputation of taking horses from the ranches, whenever he happened to want them. He would go to a ranch and if he found a horse there that was better than the one he was riding, he would tell whoever happened to own him that he would trade horses with him. Then he would change his saddle from the horse he was riding, take the other horse, and ride off. He ranged the sand hills from Niobrara on the north to the Platte River on the south.

We often heard of him as crossing the South and Middle Loup east of us, and as having been seen at North Platte; but he never came to our ranch, and so far as I know, never took any of our horses or cattle. Finally, he was run down, and after a gun fight with the officers that went after him, in which he was shot through the hip, he was captured.

When they were taking him to Lincoln to serve his time,

they brought him through Columbus. He stayed in Columbus over night under guard, of course, and while at the hotel he sent word to my brother, J. E. North, requesting him to come to the Clother House to see him. My brother was very much surprised at the message, and not a little curious, and went to the hotel.

When he went into the room, Doc said, "I guess you don't know me."

My brother said, "No, he did not," and then Doc told him where he had seen him.

Three years before my brother had made a business trip to the Black Hills in the winter, and the weather was very cold. He went by stage coach from Sidney, Nebraska, and took a big buffalo robe for protection. When the stage coach reached the first station out from Sidney, a man got on to go to Ft. Robinson. The stage was full, and this man was obliged to ride with the driver on the outside. My brother saw that he was not very warmly clad, and had no overcoat, so he gave him the buffalo robe to wrap around him. He wore it until they got to Ft. Robinson, when he returned it to my brother. This man was Doc Middleton.

The night before the stage coach left Sidney, he had quarreled with some soldiers and had killed one of them. He had walked out to the station, where he got on the stage coach. He told my brother that the buffalo robe kept him from freezing to death, and that this was the reason he never bothered our ranch. This may have been true, but one of our men, Bax Taylor, knew Doc in Texas, and said that when he left there he stole one of his (Bax's) horses, and Bax swore that if Doc ever came to the ranch while he was there, he would kill him.

I do not know why this man was called Doc Middleton. Bax Taylor said his name was Jim Cherry, and that he knew him well in Texas. After serving out his time, Doc returned

[ 263 ]

to the northwest of Nebraska, and lived for some time in Chadron. He died a few years ago somewhere in Wyoming.[8]

In the spring of 1879, just after starting on the rounds, I was in my first stampede, and it came near being my last one too. We had gathered about three thousand head of cattle and were driving them toward the Platte River. It was late in the evening and we camped on the west fork of the Birdwood at its head. I was on herd, and at about ten o'clock it began to rain. The cattle had been lying down, but got up when it commenced to rain. They were standing quietly when, without the least warning, they were off.

There was a narrow valley a couple of miles long out from the head of Birdwood Creek, and they ran up that. I was on that side of the herd, and the only thing to do was to outrun them. It was very dark, and, of course, one couldn't see where they were going. When we had gone about a mile and the cattle were beginning to string out some, I came to a small sand hill up which my horse ran. There was a blowout on the top of it and he jumped into this and fell, throwing me over his head, and then got up and ran off, leaving me on foot.

I was up about as soon as he was and made a grab for bridle, but missed it in the dark. I think the sand hill saved my life, as the cattle seemed to split on each side of me. I was wearing my slicker and I jumped up and down, shaking it and yelling at the top of my voice. A steer would rush past on one side of me and I would jump to the other side and touch one over there with my hand. I suppose they were all past me in about five minutes, but to me it seemed a long time, and I thought there was a million of them.

8. See Chapter 6, footnote 14.

When all had passed I shouted, thinking that some of the other boys on night herd would hear me, but I got no answer. I went back to camp on foot, and there I found them. They had started after the cattle when they first ran, but soon found they could do nothing in the dark, because the valley was too narrow to turn them in.

The next morning we followed them and before we had gone more than five miles began to find some of them, and none of them ran more than ten or twelve miles. I found my horse with the first bunch of cattle. This was a mixed bunch of steers, cows and calves.

I was afterward in a stampede of beef steers one night. They got away from us, and when we followed them the next day we could see by their tracks that they had run for twenty miles, and they kept right on traveling after they stopped running. They were forty miles away when we overtook them. Joe Powers told me that on one drive from Texas these cattle stampeded and they lost forty steers. He followed back on the trail for one hundred miles, when he came to a camp of buffalo hunters, and they told him the cattle had passed their camp the night before, or about twenty-four hours after they stampeded. The hunters said they were still walking fast, and occasionally they would break into a trot. Joe gave them up and came back to the herd. He said he guessed they went back to Texas.

When on the 1879 roundup we had with us a man named Bob Lewis, who came from some ranch over to the north of ours and was sent over to go with us up the North Platte River, and if he found any cattle belonging in the Niobrara country, to put them in with ours and bring them to our ranch. He was a goodnatured loud talking fellow, and knew everybody on the roundup, and whenever a new outfit joined, Bob soon got to know them.

When we got up to Blue Creek, we were met by Tom Snow, who was manager of the Van Tassell Cattle Co., and the first day that Mr. Snow was with us he was sitting on his horse watching the men that were cutting out cattle, when Bob rode up to him and asked who he was and where he came from, and several other questions.

Finally Snow said, "What outfit are you with, and who do you represent?"

I was close to them and Bob waved his hand toward me and said, "Mr. North and I are in Cahoots in the cattle business. Mr. North has the cattle and I have the Cahoots."

Blue Creek was as far west as we ever went with the roundup, and the year before we had gone back down the river to the Birdwood,[9] and then north to our ranch. There was a strip of the sand hills from the head of the Blue to the head of the Middle Loup, about 60 or 70 miles, that was supposed to be dry, but Frank thought there might be water somewhere on the way, and we made up our minds to go back that way.

We went up to a lake at the head of the Blue, and filling everything we had that would hold water we started one morning just as soon as it was light. We had a couple of hundred head of cattle, but they were all steers and we knew they could stand a long drive. Frank had me go ahead to pick out a road for the wagons. The sand hills in this dry country were all alike, and it was very easy to get lost in them, but as long as the sun was shining there was not much danger of getting lost.

We traveled about twenty miles before we stopped, and while the teams and cattle were resting, I took a fresh horse and went on in the direction of the Middle Loup. After riding for about fifteen miles I rode up to the top of a big sand hill, and could see off to the east a long valley and a bunch of cattle.

I went back to camp, where they had just started to follow

9. Blue Creek flows southward through Gardner County, Nebraska, into the Platte River. Birdwood Creek is in Lincoln County.

in the direction I had gone, and that evening we got to the valley I had seen and found a good pond of water and cattle trails leading to it, that showed many cattle were in that vicinity. We made up our minds to camp there, and the next day to hunt cattle.

We started out early the next morning, leaving two men with the cattle we had, and in about an hour we had found over seven hundred head of cattle. They were wild as deer, and some of them that were three years old had never seen a man. About half of them were six or seven-year-old steers that belonged to the Rankin Ranch on the Middle Loup; one hundred twenty were mavericks, unbranded cattle, under three years old. We got them in with our bunch of steers and it took all of us to hold them.

After eating dinner we started on down the valley and traveled about twenty miles before stopping, then made a dry camp. It took the whole force to nightherd them, but fortunately the moon was shining brightly all night, and we had a big flat to hold them on. A couple of the three-year-old bulls broke out of the bunch and ran for the hills, but the boys overtook and roped and tied them down.

A couple of days later we got to the Rankin Ranch, where we branded the mavericks. A Mr. Stern was manager and a part owner of this ranch, and he was very much pleased to get this stock back. They had probably wandered out there in the winter time three years before, and finding the water hole had stayed near it all those years. The feed there was good, and there was nothing to disturb them. It was June when we found them, and although our cattle were still pretty thin at that time of the year, these cattle were fat enough to ship to market. I believe Mr. Stern did ship them about the first of July.

When we reached our ranch after this roundup we found Cody and a party of his friends camped there. Among them was Dave Perry. They had plenty of liquor with them, and every time that Dave would get a little too much, he would insist on showing the crowd what an expert rifle shot I was by putting a nickle in the end of a split stick and holding it in his hand while I shot it out. There was probably a dozen others that could have done the same thing, but Dave always chose me.

One day while the crowd were sitting in the shade trying to keep cool, I rode in from riding the range and Dave walked out about thirty yards and held up his nickle. The stick he had it stuck into was about six inches long, and he held it up between his thumb and finger. I banged away, and instead of hitting the nickle I cut the stick off about an inch from his fingers. He looked at it as if rather surprised, then threw it on the ground and came back to the crowd. He did not say a word, but for the remainder of the time that they stayed on the range he never again asked me to shoot nickles.

Dave was quite a character. He had a saloon in North Platte for a good many years, and was in several gun fights, and in one he was shot through the lung, but came through it all right. I think he was ordered out of the city when John Bratt was elected Mayor. About that time Mr. Grinnell and I were going to Wyoming, and when the train we were on stopped at Grand Island for dinner, I saw Dave at the station.

I said, "There is a friend of mine," and introduced Grinnell to Dave. Then I asked Dave how he happened to be there. He said the d--d stranglers got after him at North Platte and he had to leave. He was a rather likable fellow in many ways, and had courage of a high order.

I was in North Platte one morning when a soldier from a

camp near there came up the street carrying his rifle, and with the avowed intention of killing Dave the soldier stopped across the street from Dave's saloon, and fired a shot in the air, and then hid behind a big drygoods box and re-loading his rifle placed it over the box for a rest, and waited for Dave to come out of his saloon.

Dave came out and, looking around, saw the soldier behind the box. He walked straight across to him. When part way over the soldier stood up and aimed the gun at him.

Dave said, "Don't you shoot," and kept right on, and when he reached the soldier took his gun away from him.

I never saw him after seeing him that time at Grand Island, and don't know what became of him.

One spring while riding range I found a white tail fawn, and took it to the ranch, where we raised it, and not long after I caught a young sand hill crane, which we also raised. In the fall I sent the deer to my niece, Frank's daughter, and she kept him for a year, but he became so cross during the second year of his life, that they had to get rid of him.

The crane got very tame and one day one of the horses kicked him and broke his wing so badly that he could never fly. When the wild cranes came to the lake near the ranch he would go down and stay with them all day, but always came home in the evening. When it got cold in the winter I put him in the stable with the horses, but he liked to stay out unless it was very cold or stormy.

One night the dog seemed uneasy and kept running out to the stable and then back to the house. He growled and whined and acted as though he thought there was something we ought to look after. It was very dark and pretty cold.

We thought there might be Indians around, so I took my rifle and went out. The dog went ahead of me toward the stable, then he would come back and rub against me and whine. I didn't know what to make of it, as he had plenty of courage and was ready to tackle most anything.

Back of the stable there were two haystacks, and the dog went to them. When we had passed one and came to the end of the second, he would not go on except when I pushed him with my knee. I had the gun all ready, and as I stepped past the end of the stack, feeling sure it must be an Indian, up jumped the crane, and spreading his wing hissed at us.

I had my finger on the trigger, and I don't know why I didn't shoot, but somehow I did not. I spoke to the bird and he soon quieted down and crawled back into a hole he had dug in the hay, and the dog followed me back to the house.

Our house was infested with mice that winter, and in the evening we used to bring the crane into the kitchen where the mice had a runway along one side of the room from the door to the corner, where there was a hole. The distance was about eight feet. The crane would stand back about three feet from the wall, and when a mouse started to run from the hole to the door, he waited until it was about half way when he would strike. His long neck and bill would flash out quick as lightening and I never saw him miss, but after he had killed and eaten about three, he would stop. After a while I got to taking them away from him. At first he objected, but soon seemed to conclude that this was what he was catching them for, and gave them up without any objection.

He was very good natured with almost everyone, but there was one man we had there that he hated, and whenever he came within reaching distance he would peck or fly at him and strike him with his wings. It was no fun for the man, as he had black and blue spots wherever the crane hit him. The second summer after I caught him he took to wander-

ing long distances from the ranch, and one night he failed
to return and that was the last we ever saw of him.

In the autumn of 1879, Frank and I took our beef steers
to Chicago. While there we were stopping at the Old Sherman House. Frank was suffering with asthma; and one
morning we got up pretty early and when we came from
our room they were sweeping the lobby, and as the dust
made Frank cough we walked out the front door.

As we were standing on the steps a bootblack came past
us and said, "Shine, mister?"

Frank was coughing and instead of answering he made the
Indian sign for him to commence. The boy dropped his box
and began to talk to him in the deaf and dumb language.
Frank couldn't understand, but nodded his head and pointed
to his shoes.

The boy went to work on them, and just then another
boy came along and said, "Mister let me shine." The other
one, the first boy, said, "Oh go away, the old fellow is deaf
and dumb."

When he had finished Frank took some small change out
of his pocket and motioned for the boy to take what he
wanted. He took ten cents, and just as he turned to go away
a man who lived at North Platte came down the street and,
seeing Frank, said, "Hello Major, when did you get in?"

Frank replied, "Yesterday."

The bootblack turned around and looked for about a minute, then said, "Well I'll be d---d," and went off down the
street.

While we were in Chicago Cody was there with his
troupe. He was playing The Prairie Waif, I think, at any
rate he did some trick shooting on the stage, shooting an
apple off a girl's head when standing with his back toward

[ 271 ]

her. He placed the gun over his shoulder, and sighted through a mirror. A few weeks later, he was playing in Portland, Maine, and when he did the shooting act a man in the audience got up and challenged him to shoot a match at fifty yards off hand, ten shots string measure. The man was Yank Addams, and he claimed to be the Champion of Maine.

Cody accepted the challenge and the match came off some two or three weeks later. Among the spectators was Frank Wesson, and he brought with him a rifle that he offered as a prize to the winner of the match.[10] Cody won by the narrow margin of half an inch in the ten shots, and the rifle that he got he sent to me. This rifle I still have. It was the best gun that I ever had, and I won many matches with it.

After our return to the ranch I was one day riding range when I saw a couple of deer, and as they were grazing on a sidehill I kept out of sight, and presently they went out of sight behind the hill. I left my horse and started to walk across the valley toward them. When I had gone part way across a big buck deer that had been lying down got up near where the two had gone out of sight. I dropped down in the grass almost out of sight, and he started for me on a run.

I waited until he was within about one hundred fifty yards of me, when I raised up, thinking he would stop to look at me, and I would get a shot at him while standing still. The wind was blowing pretty hard and I didn't want to miss him. He kept coming as fast as he could run, and when he was about fifty yards away I fired. He never slackened his speed, and I thought I had missed him.

I tried to get a cartridge out of my belt, but my hands were so cold and numb that I was slow, and before I could

10. A member of the firm of Smith & Wesson, manufacturers of guns.

load he had gotten to me. I jumped to one side and he went past me striking me on the arm with his antler so hard that I thought he had broken it. He stopped as quickly as he could, and turned back toward me, but as he again started for me he stumbled and fell. I had hit him in the breast and the bullet had gone through him lengthwise, but he never slacked his speed at all.

A little later that fall a party of hunters from the Republican River came out to the Dismal River hunting. They were camped ten miles down the river below our ranch, and one night one of the party failed to show up. The next day the rest of the party started to hunt for him. They found where he had killed two deer within two miles of their camp, and they followed his tracks until they came to a place where a lot of cattle had gone over the same path, and they could no longer see the tracks. He was traveling away from their camp and they thought he must have been lost.

They moved their camp up to our ranch, and we hunted for the old man—he was sixty-three years old—for several days, but could not find him. Then they went home, and about ten days later his son and some of the men that were with the first party came out to look for him again. They stayed for several days and finally said the next day they were going home. One of the men said he was going out once more, and went over toward the North Dismal, and on returning when about three miles from our ranch he saw some fresh antelope tracks crossing the road. He followed them about thirty yards to the top of a sand hill, and just over on the other side lay the body of the old man. The signs showed that he had sat down just under the top of the hill, and that a buck deer had walked up the hill from the other side, and seeing him there had attacked him, and after knocking him down had jumped on him and trampled him to death.

There were only two empty shells in the man's belt, and

they would account for the two deer he had killed. The deer must have attacked him without being wounded. This case, and that of the deer that had charged half a mile to get to me, are the only instances I ever knew of where a wild deer attacked a man, unless it was wounded.

In the autumn of 1879, we built a sod ranch about fifteen miles northwest of our home ranch, and kept two men there through the winter to hold the cattle from straying out into the dry country. I used to go up and stay with the men for a day or two every two or three weeks. They had a dog, a bull terrier, at the ranch with them, and he slept in one of the windows. The walls of the house were three feet thick, and the windows were set in even with the inside wall, which left plenty of room for the dog to curl up in. He always slept in the window on the south side of the house, and there was a window on the west side also. One night when I was there we were all sitting by the table reading, when I happened to look up at the west winder and said, "Why the dog is sleeping in that window tonight!"

Al Pratt, who was near the other window looked around and said, "No, here he is in this window."

I looked closer and saw that what I had taken for the dog was a coyote. We blew out the light and went out the door, which was on the east side of the house, and got the dog and took him around and shoved him into the window with the coyote. They both came out together, and after fighting for a minute or two the coyote got loose and ran away with the dog after him.

It was a still clear night and we could hear them running for a long ways. Finally they went out of hearing, and I said, "Well, I guess the coyote got away."

We were just going into the house, when we heard them

coming back as hard as they could run. We waited, and pretty soon the coyote ran past us and jumped in the window where he had been before. The dog was quite a ways behind him, but when he got there he jumped in after him, and soon pulled him out and killed him.

Now what made the coyote come back? He could easily outrun the dog. He was a full grown male and was in good condition. I never could figure out why he did it, for they are the most intelligent and crafty animals that I know of.

The morning I left the boys for the home ranch there was about six inches of snow on the ground, and it was cold. When about half way home I shot a deer, and when he fell I started to walk over to him, leading my horse. When about half way to him, a prairie chicken flew up from a tuft of grass right under my horse's nose, and frightened her so she jumped and jerked away from me [and ran] for the ranch. I went after her, thinking she might stop, but she was soon out of sight.

I walked along toward the ranch thinking that when she got there one of the men there would catch her and come out to meet me, but no one came, and I walked until I was within sight of the ranch. As soon as they saw me one of the men there came out to meet me, leading my mare.

He said that just before my mare got home our man Cassell had ridden in from the north as fast as his horse could run, and said he had seen a band of Indians about three miles from the ranch. Then when my mare came galloping in, covered with sweat, they thought sure I had been killed, and they didn't know what to do.

When I got to the house and questioned Cassell about the Indians, he at last said that they were on top of a big sand hill and that all he could see was their heads. I told him to get on his horse and go with me and show where the Indians were. He didn't want to go, but I finally persuaded him to do so, and we started.

[ 275 ]

When we came in sight of the hill he pointed, and said, "I could see their heads sticking up on the edge of that blowout, and one of them had feathers tied on his hair. I could see them fluttering. He was off by himself; the others were farther over to the east."

The hill was about a half mile away, and as Cassell was pretty nervous I told him to stay where he was, and I would go over and take a look. I had a pretty good idea what I would find when I got there. I looked back but Cassell had disappeared, and when I got to the top I found a ridge of sand about one hundred yards long that the wind had blown up, leaving behind it a flat space a couple of feet wide. The sand ridge was nearly three feet high, and on the path behind it were the tracks of seven or eight deer. They were probably walking along there and when they saw Cassell, they stopped to look at him. All he could see was their heads, and he mistook them for Indians. Over at the place where he had seen the feathers a hawk had been sitting on the edge of the blowout.

When I got back to the Ranch I found Cassell there, and when I told him what I had found, he was quite crestfallen. Cassell was not a cowboy and hadn't been long in the west, and was not with us very long.

In the summer of 1880, we went to Ogallala, where we bought two thousand head of yearlings, and when we got to the ranch we started branding them before turning them loose on the range. At the ranch on the head of the river, we had a large corral, circular in shape and built of cedar logs about six or eight inches in diameter at the large end, and twenty four feet long. We set two posts every twelve feet, just far enough apart to lay the poles between them, and after building the fence eight feet, as high as we wanted it, we wired the posts together at the top.

We thought it was strong enough to hold any number of the largest steers, but the second night after we got home we had fifteen hundred of the yearlings in the corral—having branded the rest and turned them loose—when something scared them and they stampeded. It was about ten o'clock at night, and I was just returning from the ranch at the lake. I was a quarter of a mile away, and as soon as they jumped I started on a run for the corral, and when I got there those little yearlings were just beginning to come over the top of the fence, and then the fence gave way. The posts were broken off and a good many of the poles were broken.

Just as they came out Bax and Buck Taylor came up from the ranch. They were riding bareback, as we had no horses saddled, never having any idea that those yearlings could break the fence, even if they did stampede.

Between the corral to the sand hills was a big flat a mile wide, and we managed to turn them before they reached the hill, and soon had them running in a circle, and after a while stopped them. We rode around them singing to them, but they were still frightened, and about every half hour they would jump and run, and we would race with them. We kept this up all night, and when daylight came we still had them in sight of the corral, and they were so tired that they all lay down, and we could not get them to move.

About noon they began to get up to eat, and we got about two hundred of them down near the corral, where we roped and branded them; but until we finished our branding we never got them into the corral again; they could not be driven in. This made the branding a pretty big job, as every one of them had to be roped and thrown. There was seven dead ones where the fence gave way, and about a wagonload of horns that got knocked off, besides several with broken legs and other bad bruises. When we finally finished branding, we were about forty head short, and Buck Taylor and I went over toward the Platte River and found them. They must have escaped unnoticed the night they stampeded.

The winter of 1880-81 was a very cold and long one. The snow came in October and the ground was covered until the end of March. Many thousands of cattle died that winter, and a good many ranches were abandoned the next spring, as they had no cattle left. Bax Taylor and I went to North Platte in January, and Mr. John Bratt and other ranchmen gathered up a bunch of cowboys to try to move the cattle off the River Valley back into the sand hills, where the feed was better.

We were to meet at Bratt's Birdwood Ranch, and work west from there. There were about twenty-five of us, and on the valley above the ranch there was ten thousand head of cattle and not a thing for them to eat. We tried all day, but could not get them to move; the snow at the foot of the hills was two feet deep, and they would not go into it.

After working all day we gave it up, and left them where they were. A couple of days later the weather got warmer and they went into the hills without driving. Fortunately for us, most of our cattle stayed in the sand hills, and our loss was not so heavy and of the two thousand yearlings that we had bought, the summer before, we gathered seventeen hundred and forty in the spring roundup.

Soon after the roundup of 1881, while I was out riding one day I came across a trail that I took to be cow calf tracks, and followed to see whose they were, and when I came in sight of them, I almost fell off my horse with astonishment, to find it was a herd of buffalo. There were twenty-eight grown ones and five calves in the herd. That country had been ridden over for four years by cowboys and hunters by the hundred, and no one had ever dreamed of seeing any buffalo there. They were lying down when I first saw them, and I kept out of sight, and went back to the ranch.

Frank was at the ranch and his daughter, a girl of twelve, was there. Ed North, a son of my older brother, was also there, and the four of us went out again to where the buffalo were. Ed had never seen a wild buffalo before, and, of course, wanted to kill one. When we made a dash at them they ran off in two bunches, and Ed and I went after one bunch, and pretty soon he killed a three-year-old heifer. Frank and his daughter Stella ran after the other bunch and cut out a calf, which they chased around until it was so tired it could not run, but Frank had no rope and he didn't want to kill it, so let it go. I had a rope, but they were not in sight of me. This band of buffalo were afterward killed by some Indians from the Spotted Tail Agency, and I think they were the last buffalo ever seen on the north side of the Platte River in Nebraska.

At this time the country was becoming settled with homesteaders, and we made up our minds that the time of free range for [the] Platte was about over,* and in the summer of 1882 we sold our ranches and cattle to the John Bratt Co.[11]

That ended our living on the frontier, as we came back to our home in Columbus, where I have lived until the present time.*

11. Bratt paid $75,000 for the Cody-North holding (John Bratt, *Trails of Yesterday* [Lincoln: The University Publishing Co., 1921], 278).

## SUPPLEMENT

EXTERMINATION OF THE BUFFALO (page 238)

"The development of the range cattle industry on the Plains was coincident with the extermination of the bison. So long as these shaggy beasts occupied the Plains, there could be no room for cattle. Moreover, while the bison remained plentiful, the Indian had the wherewithal to maintain resistance against white encroachment. . . . The extermination of the bison occurred after the discovery in the early Seventies that their hides could be used in the manufacture of harness, belting, shoes, and other leather goods. To satisfy the demand thus created, commercial hunters went out on the Plains in gangs, armed with high-calibre, long-range rifles, and in a few short years they literally wiped the bison off the face of the earth. Conservative estimates place the kill on the Plains at more than ten million during the years 1870-1875. Moreover, this was simple, wanton destruction. Whereas the Indians had used virtually all of the animal, the commercial hunters took only the hide, leaving the carcass to rot where it fell" (Olson, *History of Nebraska*, 191-192).

TEXAS CATTLE (page 238)

"Any history of the cattle industry in the West must begin with Texas since that state was the original home of ranching on a large scale in the United States, and from its vast herds were drawn most of the cattle for the first stocking of the central and northern plains" (Edward Everett Dale, *The Range Cattle Industry* [Norman: University of Oklahoma Press, 1930], 21).

Ogallala superseded Schuyler and Kearney as the Nebraska shipping point for Texas cattle. The first longhorns had been brought into the region between the forks of the Platte in 1869, and small herds had successfully wintered there. Between 1870 and 1874 pioneer cattlemen began to occupy ranges in the Nebraska panhandle—along the North Platte, Pumpkin Creek, and Rush Creek. When the campaigns of General Crook and Colonel Miles put an end to the threat of Indian raids, a boom began which brought 75,000 to 125,000 Texas longhorns to Ogallala each season (Norbert R. Mahnken, "Ogallala—Nebraska's Cowboy Capital," *Nebraska History*, XXVII [April-June 1947], 85 ff.).

END OF THE CATTLE BOOM (page 279)

The Norths and Cody sold out at a strategic time—the end of the boom was in sight. "As the years passed, the herds from the south tended to pass more and more into the hands of a few purchasers. Consolidation and large-scale organization characterized the industry during the early eighties. Many of the wise old pioneers of the range, looking into the future, decided to sell their holdings during 1882 and 1883. So they disposed of their stock at inflated prices which brought $30 to $35 a head for mixed range stock, yearlings included, which as late as 1880 would have brought only $20 or less per head . . . . When the trail-driving business collapsed after 1884 its sudden end surprised everyone except these old-timers. The last great drives of Texas cattle over the Western Trail into Nebraska came in 1884. This was the last season of this colorful business. Western Nebraska was no longer the cattlemen's exclusive paradise . . . . As the despised 'nesters' became more numerous the drovers found it ever more difficult and more expensive to attempt to force their way through the settlements and on to Ogallala" (Mahnken, "Ogallala—Nebraska's Cowboy Capital," 105-106).

## THE NORTH BROTHERS IN POST-FRONTIER DAYS (page 279)

In the fall of 1882 Frank North was elected to the Nebraska legislature by a popular majority vote of Platte County. He served only one term. During 1883 his wife, the former Mary Louise Smith, died and his mother, Jane Townley North, came to make a home for him and his daughter Stella. (The Frank Norths' only child, Stella, had been born in 1869.) Frank then joined Cody's Wild West Show; he had charge of the Indian performers, including some of the Pawnee. During a performance in Hartford, Connecticut, in the summer of 1884, his saddle turned and he was seriously injured. Weakened by the injury and by illness, Frank died at his home in Columbus on March 14, 1885. At this time Luther North joined the household and looked after it until Stella's marriage in 1888.

In 1886, Luther, who previously had been occupied with farming and cattle-raising, became a Deputy Collector of Internal Revenue and until 1890 lived in the Black Hills country. He then moved to Omaha where he was employed as a storekeeper gauger. In 1898 he married Mrs. Elvira Sprague Coolidge. An anecdote about her recounted by North suggests that they had at least one talent in common.

In the spring of 1880, Cody and his family came up to the Cody & North ranch . . . where a roundup was about to take place. One of the diversions was target shooting at 50 yards with rifles. Mrs. Timothy Coolidge, who had been Miss Elvira Emma Sprague, shot three times offhand and made three bull's-eyes with one of Cody's Winchesters. None of the men (Cody himself, Jason Backus, a market hunter, and John Hancock, an ex buffalo hide hunter and cowboy) did as well. Anyone who could beat them was surely a crack shot. I was not at the ranch that day (Bruce, *The Fighting Norths*, 69).

Robert Bruce, in the same source, tells that Mrs. Luther North was the daughter of a Vermonter, James Kilby Sprague, who went to California in 1848, "afterward returned as far east as Nebraska, married and again set out for California, where Emma Elvira was born" (69). Her first husband, Timothy Coolidge, died four years before her marriage to Luther North.

In 1917 the Norths returned to Columbus and from then on Luther lived in semi-retirement. All during his long life he was actively concerned with the story of the Pawnee Scouts and was sought out by many interested in the doings of the Scouts and in the Plains Indians Wars. In 1925 he completed his recollections, which he had begun perhaps ten years before. In 1930 he received the Distinguished Service Medal of the Lincoln (Nebraska) Kiwanis Club. The last surviving Pawnee Scout officer, he "sometimes refers philosophically to the fact that his career and most of his years are behind—but adds, 'I have had a long life, and a bully good time!'" (Bruce, *The Fighting Norths*, 70). He died in Columbus on April 17, 1935. Mrs. Elvira North died in 1940. They had no children.

# MAPS

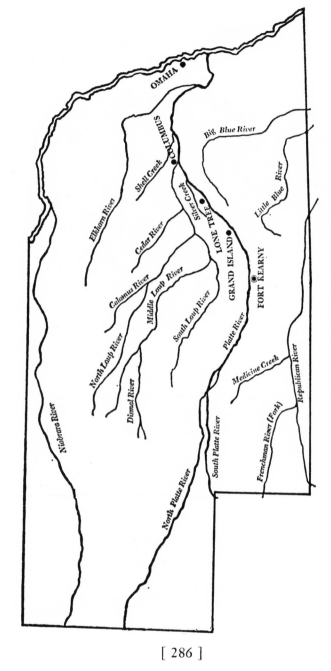

1. NEBRASKA RIVER SYSTEM

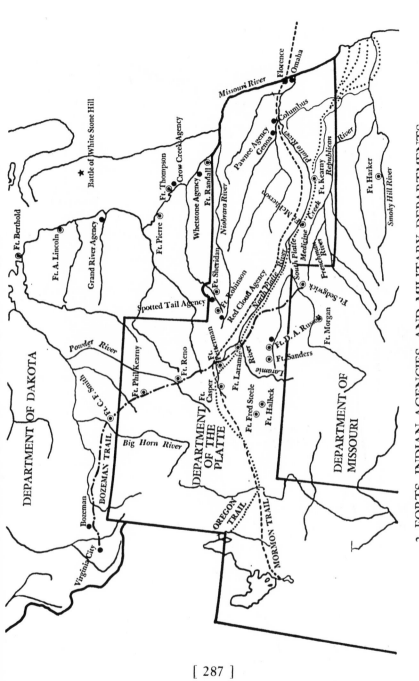

2. FORTS, INDIAN AGENCIES, AND MILITARY DEPARTMENTS

[ 287 ]

3. LOCATION OF GREAT PLAINS INDIAN TRIBES

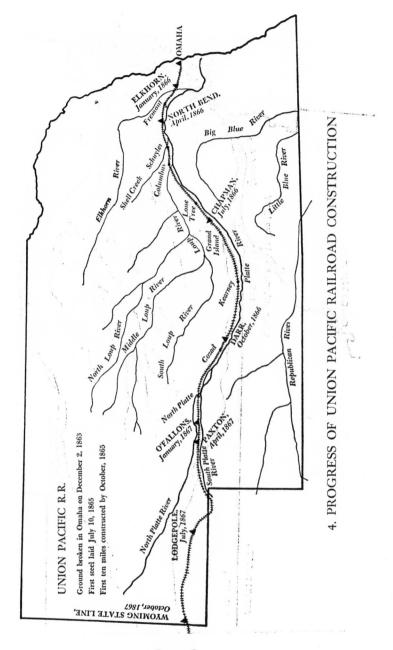

UNION PACIFIC R.R.

Ground broken in Omaha on December 2, 1863
First steel laid July 10, 1865
First ten miles constructed by October, 1865

4. PROGRESS OF UNION PACIFIC RAILROAD CONSTRUCTION

5. NORTH'S ROUTES IN PURSUIT OF SIOUX HORSE THIEVES

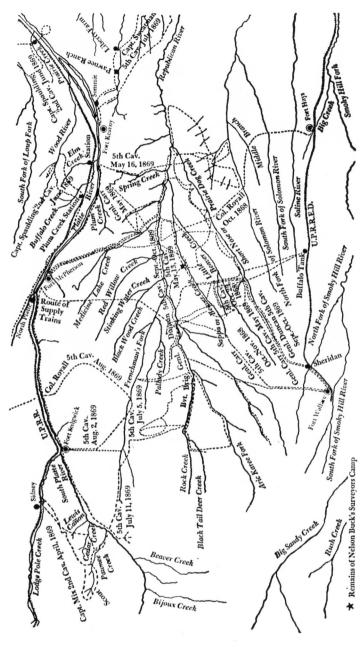

6. THE CAMPAIGNS OF 1869

(From an official map indicating lines of march of scouting parties, 1868–1869. Courtesy of the National Archives.)

[ 291 ]

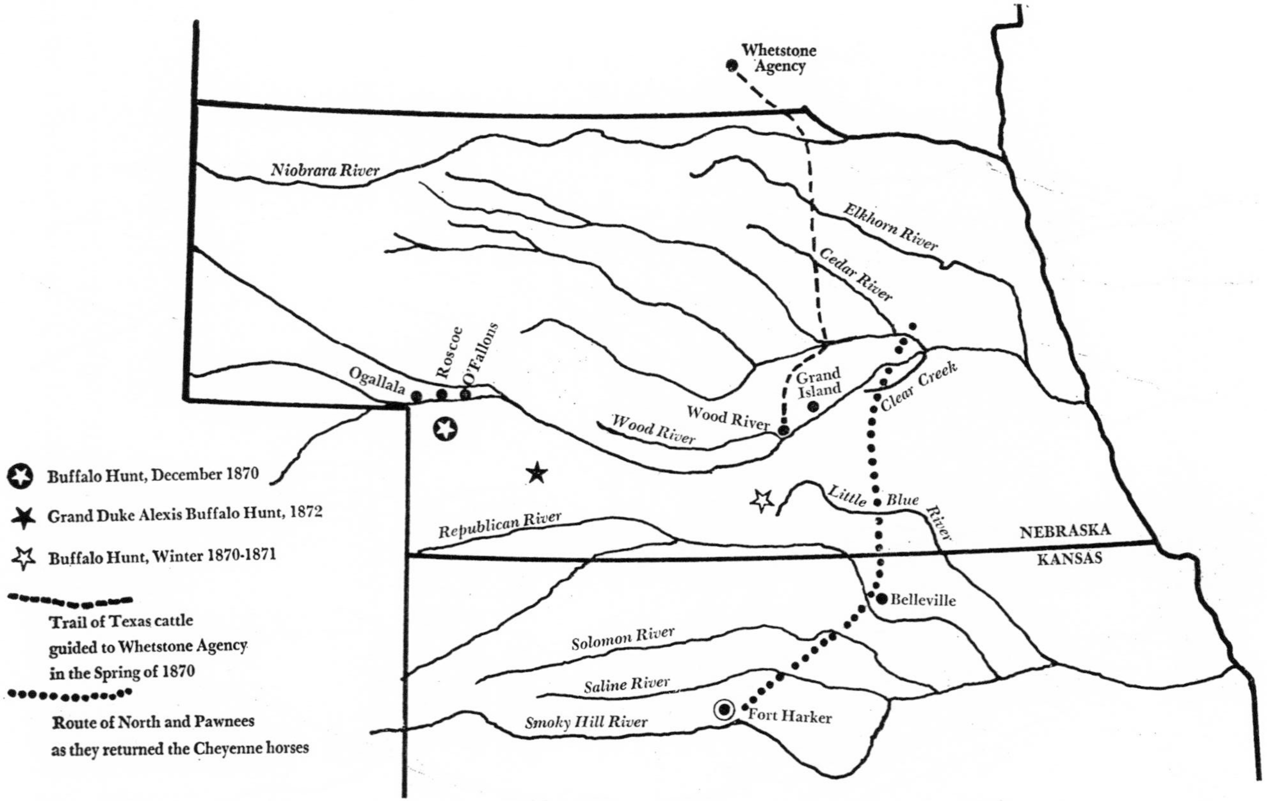

Rivers and places labeled on the map:

Whetstone Agency

Niobrara River

Elkhorn River

Cedar River

Clear Creek

Grand Island

Wood River

Little Blue River

Belleville

NEBRASKA

KANSAS

Fort Harker

Solomon River

Saline River

Smoky Hill River

Republican River

O'Fallons

Roscoe

Ogallala

⭑ Buffalo Hunt, December 1870

★ Grand Duke Alexis Buffalo Hunt, 1872

☆ Buffalo Hunt, Winter 1870–1871

▬▬ Trail of Texas cattle guided to Whetstone Agency in the Spring of 1870

••••• Route of North and Pawnees as they returned the Cheyenne horses

7. ACTIVITIES OF NORTH AS HUNTER AND GUIDE

[ 292 ]

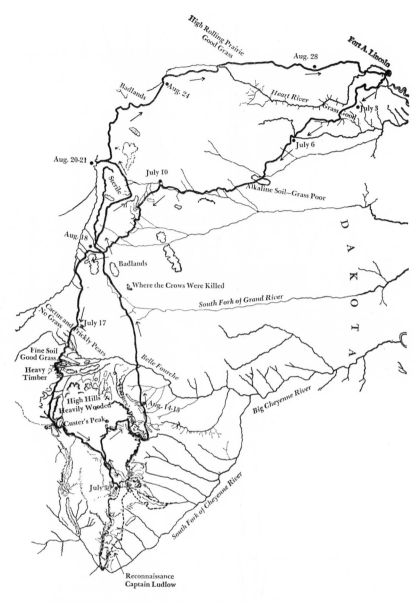

Fort A. Lincoln

High Rolling Prairie
Good Grass

Aug. 28

Heart River

Grass Good

July 3

Badlands

Aug. 24

July 6

Aug. 20-21

Sterile

July 10

Alkaline Soil—Grass Poor

D
A
K
O
T
A

Aug. 18

Badlands

Where the Crows Were Killed

South Fork of Grand River

Cactus and
No Grass

July 17

Prickly Pears

Fine Soil
Good Grass

Belle Fourche

Heavy
Timber

High Hills
Heavily Wooded

Big Cheyenne River

Custer's Peak

Aug. 14-15

July 30

South Fork of Cheyenne River

Reconnaissance
Captain Ludlow

## 8. THE BLACK HILLS EXPEDITION OF 1874
*(From official map of Custer's Reconnaissance of the Black Hills by Captain William Ludlow, Corps of Engineers)*

[ 293 ]

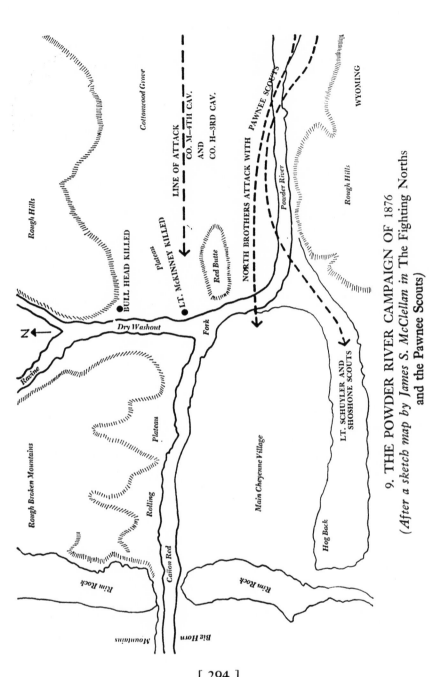

9. THE POWDER RIVER CAMPAIGN OF 1876

(*After a sketch map by James S. McClellan in* The Fighting Norths *and the Pawnee Scouts*)

# APPENDIXES

# APPENDIX A

*From the large collection of Luther North letters in the archives of the Nebraska State Historical Society, two groups have been selected as of unusual interest or of particular pertinence to the recollections. The first group includes three letters written in 1874-1875 by North to his uncle, John Calvin North. They concern events described in the text and it will be noted that they occasionally differ in detail from the recollections written so many years later.*

LETTERS OF LUTHER NORTH TO JOHN CALVIN NORTH

## I

*Columbus, Neb.*
*Nov. 25th, 1874*

DEAR UNCLE:

Your good letter was rec'd a few days ago and I will now try and answer and give you a short sketch of my doings since I left Michigan in the spring of 1867. I come home as you may remember in March and just stopped long enough to visit the folks here and then went on to Fort Kearny where Frank was camped with his Battalion of Pawnees he (Frank) gave the charge of one of the companies to me and in a few days we were ordered to Ft. McPherson where we staid only two days and were then sent to the end of the U.P.R.R. to act as guard for the track layers for two weeks before we got there the Indians had been coming down every morning to fight the track layers and Graders and the next morning after we got there they came again as usual and Frank started me out after them with twenty men there was

[ 297 ]

about fifteen of the Indians and of course they run for it I followed them about ten miles and had to give it up without catching any of them, the next morn they come down again and run off a lot of mules and Frank took twenty of our Scouts and after a running fight of fifteen miles succeeded in getting the mules back and killed one Indian and wounded several more the one that he killed proved to be a brother of the celebrated Chief Spotted Tail and that put a stop to further depredations in part of the country everything went on quietly then for about two weeks when Gen. Augur came up from Omaha and he detailed my company and one other to escort him to Fort Laramie, we traveled up the south Platte to the mouth of Crow Creek and then followed up that to near where Cheyenne City now stands and from there we crossed onto Lodge Pole Creek and followed up that to the mouth of Cheyenne Pass (if you will look on a map maybe you can understand me) the day we got to the Pass we ran across some Arapahoe Indians and after a lively little chase for four or five miles we killed two and got three ponies from them. We left Gen. Augur here and started south into the hills west of Cheyenne and camped with a party of Engineers where Granite Canon now is, we staid there for about a month when I was ordered to the end of the track again which was then where the town of Sidney now is on Lodge Pole Creek. I camped with end of the track from July 9th untill the first day of Oct. nothing of note took place during that time we had to move camp from one to two miles each day and the bal. of the time I put in hunting on the first day of Oct. I was again ordered to right forward fours right *march* and away we go for Fort Fetterman as escort for Col. Merrell we went by way of Cheyenne and after hard marching for ten days we reached Fetterman and was then relieved by a company of white soldiers and ordered back to Cheyenne. From there we were ordered to Fort Kearny and after laying in camp for about two weeks we were disbanded and sent home thus ended my first campaign as a Pawnee Scout.

I must tell you here of one of Franks exploits during the summer, he was camped with one company of forty six men at Plum Creek Station when one morning a man rode into his camp and reported a large body of Indians on the opposite side of the Platte River Frank did not have much faith in the report but thought he would go and see anyhow, when he got over there he found the report true and found himself facing one hundred and fifty splendidly mounted and well armed Sioux and Cheyenne warriors retreat was almost impossible for the Platte River with its treacherous quicksands was behind him and so that glorious old Brother of mine ordered a charge and before the astonished Sioux warriors knew what they were about forty six Pawnees with the invincible White Chief was riding them down like a whirlwind the charge was so sudden and irresistable that the Sioux made but little resistance and Frank chased them for fifteen miles killing seventeen and capturing 33 horses and one Squaw and one papoose do you wonder that I am proud of such a brother Franks loss was five horses killed and one man slightly wounded I will close again for that year and go on with my own story.

*Nov. 28th*

I was interrupted the other day and have been so busy ever since that this is the finest chance that I have had to go on with my little story, when we came home in the fall of 67, I hired to Jim to clerk in the trading post at the Pawnee Reserve I commenced work the first of Jan. 1868 and stayed with him for over one year I might tell you how the Sioux came down that summer and run off all of our horses and how we followed them and once caught them and there was such a large party that we were glad to get away without fighting them but it would not be very interesting so I will just say that every thing passed off quietly that year untill Christmas when Libbie and Phannie were married at that time Phannies husband had a beautiful little Bay horse and he and Phan gave him to me for a Christmas present you dont know how proud I was of that horse well I rode him home to the Pawnee Reserve and four days after the Sioux came down and broke open our stable and took him out. I was pretty sure what band of Indians it was that took him and immediately wrote to their Agent and in about three weeks got an answer that he had the horse so I started after him he was at Fort Randall on the Missouri River and when I got there the Commander of the Post said he could not give him up without I went on to the Whitstone Agency which was twenty five miles above there and get an order from the Agent, he let me have my horse and I started out and got to the Agency about dark that night came near being my last on earth I had gone into the Trading Post with a Frenchman that I was acquainted with, the store was full of Indians and some of them asked the Frenchman who I was he told them that I was a brother of the great White Chief of the Pawnees and in less time than it takes to write it there was about twenty five big Sioux Warriors flourishing butchers knives tomahawks and war clubs around my head I was sitting in one corner of the store behind the stove and knowing that perfect coolness was all that could save me I never got up off from the chair I didnt even look up the excitement lasted about one minute (it seemed to me one year) and then a chief named Walk-under-the-ground who had been smoking passed me his pipe I knew that meant safty but the Frenchman told me afterwards that if it had been any other Indian but the one that it was that smoking the pipe of peace wouldnt have saved me that night. The next morning I had to ride the distance back to Fort Randall by myself and as the road is a bad one runing through deep ravines and thick willow brush I did not breath very free till I got there but I did get there all right and from their home nothing of importance occured, after staying at home a couple of weeks Frank got orders to recruit a company of Pawnees and on the 10th of Feb. 1869 we started to Fort McPherson where we drew rations clothing horses and itams, and on the 13th I left the Fort for a ten days scout on the Republican River and Frank went home to enlist another company. I went on to the Republican and there met with two companies of White Cav. and on the 18th of Feb. we started back to Ft. McPherson it would be impossible for me to tell you of all the horrible suffering of that days march it was snowing and blowing a gale from the North West and we had to face the storm for twenty five miles and when we got into camp we didnt have a tent in the whole outfit my hands and face were badly frozen and I do believe I would have died that night if it hadnt been for my men as soon as we got to camp they tore the covers off the wagons and while some of them were making a Wigwam others were cleaning away the snow and cutting dry grass with their butcher knives while one of my sergeants as noble an Indian (of whom I will have more to say by and by) as ever lived was rubbing my hands and face with snow to take the frost out in half an hour we had a big fire in our Wigwam and was sitting there in our shirt sleeves as comfortable as could be not so the poor white soldiers they had gone on about a mile farther and they all laid out that night and it was bitter cold there was over fifty horses froze to death that night, none of the men died but about twenty of them had to have their feet taken off when we got to the Fort. I might tell you what a time we had the next morning crossing the white mans bank of the Republican R. and how I was the first man to cross but am afraid that you might think I was boasting so will only say we got to the Ft. all right after laying in camp at Mc-Pherson about four weeks I was ordered to Ogallala Station on the U. P. R. R. and staid until the first of June when I was recalled to join Gen. Carr's expedition to the Republican and we left McPherson on the 14th with seven companies of cavalry

and two companies of Scouts Frank had met me at the Fort
with one company when I came down from Ogallala but he was
ordered back home to enlist a third company and as I was capt.
of company A it left me in command of the two companies we
reached the Rep. in four days and then marched down the
River two days in the afternoon of the second day just as we
were sitting down to supper we heard a couple of shots fired
and immediately after the well known war hoop of the sioux
my men all sprang up and started for their horses and I did the
same catching the first horse that I came too. I shouted to the boys
to hurry up and away I went I felt confident that there were not
many of the sioux and that they had just dashed in to run off
our stock, they failed to get any but shot two men and killed two
mules by the time I had got across the River there was ten of my
men with me and about three quarters of a mile ahead was the
sioux they were not riding very fast for they know how long it
usually [took] Cavalry to get started but as soon as they saw us
coming and heard the Pawnee Warhoop they began to use their
whips and away we go up hills and deep ravines (that would make
your hair stand on end to ride down on a walk) we went tearing
along for fifteen miles but it was all in vain darkness was coming
on and the sioux were still a quarter of a mile ahead so we turned
slowly back tired and sore and hungry, we reached camp about
midnight and the next morning the Genl. sent for me I went up
to his tent and there before all of his Officers he reprimanded
me for leaving camp to pursue the Indians without orders from
him, I answered as civily as I could that the only way to fight
Indians was to go for them as fast as possible whenever they
were found, he said that he understood his business and that all
I had to do was obey orders. I told him that I expected to obey
orders but that when the Indians attacked a camp that I was in
I intended to go for them and that I shouldnt wait for orders
from him nor any other man having spoke my little piece I
touched my pony with the spurs and dashed away to the head
of my company I expected that I would be placed under arrest
but was not and every thing went off quietly, three days after
this Frank joined us on the Solomon River with another company of Scouts we now had one hundred and fifty Pawnees and
about four or five hundred White Cav. after scouting down the
Solomon about twenty miles we turned North West and in five
days we were back to the Republican where we struck the Trail
of a large band of Indians we laid in camp a few days to recruit
our tired horses and then started out on the trail this was on the
fourth of July we followed right up the River and on the morning of the 6th some of our men that were out scouting ran across

a small party of Indians and succeeded in killing three of them but it let the Indian Camp know that we were in the country and the next day we lost their trail they had scattered out all over the Prairie and it was almost impossible to follow them still we kept on up the River to its head and then turned around and took our back trail down the River the night we turned back the Sioux attacked our camp about midnight and attempted to run off the stock but failed. They shot one of my men however, we knew then that they had been watching us and guessed rightly that that was their farewell and so it proved, the next morning we left the River and started North towards the Platte and traveled forty miles before we found any water and when we did find it we found ourselves on the Indians trail again and with a better prospect of catching them than ever before for of course they had seen us turn back and thought we were going straight to Fort McPherson I want to tell you right here one of the Indians failings when he knows that an enemy is after him it is impossible to take him unawares but let him think himself safe and he is the most careless being on earth, the next day we followed them again and passed two of their camps and camped at their third and the day after we did the same and the place where we camped that night the Indians had just left that morning. The next morning we were on the trail before daybreak Frank had picked out thirty five of our best men and fastest horses and the Genl. sent us on ahead about two oclock in the afternoon one of my men who was a little ahead of us rode to the top of a hill off to our left and the moment he got high enough to look over he wheeled his horse short around and came back to us a flying and said that he could see the Sioux camp Frank who had been riding a mule and leading his Grey horse now changed and while he was getting ready he sent a man back with a dispatch to the Genl. and in a few minutes all was ready, we were about four miles from their camp but thought that we could not get any nearer without their seeing us so it was decided to charge from there. Frank made a short speech to his men and when all was ready we started at a long steady Gallop. There were four of us white with the Pawnees and Frank had said when we started that we must all stick together but somehow we got separated and after going about three miles I looked around for the other boys two of them was behind me but where is Frank he is no where to be seen about a dozen of our men are ahead of me and I let go of my mare and in a moment I am up to the leading man and about a quarter of a mile ahead Frank is just going up the side of a ravine all thought of danger to myself was gone in a moment their was my Brother rushing into a large Indian camp alone could I overtake him I knew the little Grey that he rode went (as the Indians say) like a bird but my mare had never been beaten on a long race and I slacked the reins and patted her on the neck she seemed to know what she had to do and streched out her neck and laid back her ears and almost flew over the ground Frank now looks back and I wave my hat at him and in a few moments more I am up to him and on we go when right before us up jumps a sioux warrior and leaping on to his horse dashes into the camp and Frank says now for some fun our men are close up now and Frank gives the warhoop and we are amongst them warriors rushed out of the tents to be shot down before they were half awake and in fifteen minutes the fight is all over and the Chief old Tall Bull and fifty two of his warriors have gone to the happy hunting ground and we have captured everything that he had in his camp and one hundred and twenty mules and over three hundred ponies and all that without losing a single man and out of the fifty two Indians killed our thirty five men had killed 38 of the sioux and that big Bro. of mine had killed the chief, my sergeant the one that I spoke of before killed four in this fight and was presented with a medal for his bravery. We then started for Fort Sedgwick on the Platte to rest and recruit our horses for in about thirty days we have marched over one thousand miles and our stock is teribly run down, on the way I had a few words with Genl. Carr and when we got to the Fort I resigned and come home the first of August, now for fear this wont be very interesting I will close for this time and if you want any more of it say so and if you dont want it say so. I am ever so much obliged to you for your good advice but you must remember that I am twenty eight years old in fact too old to be led much goodby and love to you all from

Your afft. Nephew

Lute

## II

*Columbus*
*Jan. 22nd, 1875*

DEAR UNCLE:

Yours came sometime ago but it was near the end of the year and I was very buisy and now my man has left me and I have to attend the stable myself so dont get much time to write but will get on as fast as possible, I left off in the fall of Sixty nine well

[ 303 ]

I staid at home that winter most of the time had one buffalo hunt that lasted about two weeks and that was all. In the spring of Seventy I hired to a man by the name of Cooper to Guide a drove of Texas cattle from Fort Kearny on the Platte River to Fort Randall on Missouri it was a bad Indian country all the way but we got through all right when we got to the Fort I found that we had to go on up to Spotted Tails Reserve I didnt like it much but went and about the first Indian that I saw was a boy some seven or eight years old that we had taken prisoner the fall before in our fight with Tall Bull and I tell you it didnt make me fell any easier but I said nothing and after we had got rid of the cattle we started out and went down the River about five miles and camped, the Boy watched me every minute till we went away and you may believe that I didnt sleep much that night however nothing happened and the next day we traveled fifty miles and got to the *Niobrara* River (Running Water) it was almost sun down when we got there and the River was Booming high. I cant tell you what kind of a Stream it is but it runs so swift that a man cant stand up in it where it is waist deep, it had been raining some through the day and I had put on my overcoat and without thinking I played my horse in and started across the balance of the crowd waited to see how I would come out, I got along all right untill within about fifty feet of the shore when I struck swimming water and the old Plug that I was riding wouldnt swim a lick but went to the Bottom like a stone. I stuck to him for a moment but found that wouldnt do and thought that I could make the bank so let go of him and struck out for shore, I had my Gun in one hand and one hundred and twenty cartridges in my belt and an army overcoat on so you may guess that I didnt make much head way I soon found that I would have to let go of my Gun and I did so about the time I dropped it I noticed a Willow tree that had been washed out by the Roots and the top had fallen out into the River and right there the channel ran out towards the middle of the stream I was getting terrible tired but knew that I must make that tree or drown and I tell you I put in some big links about that time and just managed to get hold of the top of the tree I had just strength enough to pull myself onto the bank and I lay there and gasped for about fifteen minutes before I could get up the boys were running up and down the bank on the other side and didnt know what to do, and although they were all good Swimmers not one of them would attempt to cross untill I took off my cloths and hunted a Ford for them, I tried to find my Gun for we were yet about one hundred and fifty miles from home but could not get it, we never saw a single Indian on the whole trip

[ 304 ]

home but I tell you I never was so nervous and scared in my life as I was after I lost my Gun if we would scare up a Deer or Wolf my heart would jump up into my mouth I never want to pass four more such days as those were. I got home all right however and found the folks all very anxious about me as I had been gone two weeks longer than I expected to be when we started, I staid at home about three weeks and then hired to the Pawnee Agent to go to Fort Harker in Kansas with some Ponies I took nine Indians and started, when we had got into Kansas about one hundred and fifty miles from here we camped one day on a small creek about a mile from a village and I laid down under a tree and went to sleep in about an hour one of the men woke me up and said there was a lot of white men around our camp and that they all had Guns I got up and found our camp was surrounded by at least one hundred men I knew that the Cheyennes were pretty bad in that part of the country and so started towards the nearest party to explain to them what we were there for after telling them one very pompous old fellow wanted to know if I had any written authority to go through that country and added that if I hadnt it would not be very healthy for me or the Indians I felt some angry at the way he talked but simply said that I had letters from the Pawnee Agent and also from Gen Augur that I would let them see if they would go down to the camp with me so fourteen of them went with me and I showed them my papers after reading them old pompous said young man this dont look right how am I to know but what you wrote those papers yourself in fact I think you did and I think the whole lot of you ought to be hung but we will let you go if you will go immediately if you dont we will kill every one of you that kind of talk didnt suit your mild tempered Nephew and I told the old Gent in language more forcible than polite that he was an old fool and that I would stay there just as long as I felt so disposed and if he didnt like it to commence the killing buisiness as soon as possible while I was talking I stepped around to where my Gun was and picked it up, the Indians saw that something was wrong and one of them a chief went up to the old Gent. and showed him his commission from Washington and that stopped further proceedings for old pompous was satisfied that that was Genuine he attempted to apologize to me but I told him to save his breath when the crowd that was standing around on the Hill saw that everything was quiet they all came down and shook hands with the Indians and some of them who had been reading Ned Buntlines Novels wanted to know if I had ever seen Buffalo Bill when I told them that I had been with him for a year they thought I was quite a hero and

[ 305 ]

wanted me to stop there all night but I was in a hurry and could not accomodate them, we reached Fort Harker on the seventh day all right and I turned over the Ponies to the Commander of the Post and started back the next day. I had taken my horse (the one that Fans husband gave me) Mazeppa along to ride back home on but the Indians were a foot we had two hundred and fifty miles to travel to get home through a very rough country and the hottest weather that I ever knew and we come home in five days we saw a few Indians on the Trip but kept out of sight of them one evening we camped on a small creek and about sundown we saw a party of White men watching us and I knew from their actions they intended to attack our camp in the night so as soon as it got dark we quietly picked up our traps and moved off about a mile from the creek and laid down and went to sleep of course they didnt find us, nothing else occurred to disturb us on the Trip, and we got home safe and sound but oh wasnt I tired how the Indians stood it was more than I could see the last day we traveled over seventy miles and the sun poured down blazing hot that was the only time that my Mazeppa ever acted tired while I had him, he was a splendid swimmer and whenever I crossed a stream I would put my knees on the saddle and he would take me over without getting wet but that day when we came to the Platte it was high and when he got into swimming water he dropped down till nothing but his head was out then I knew he was tired.

I now staid at home for a little over a month and on the first day of Sept. we were ordered out with the Scouts we were out four months but had no fights that fall and nothing exciting happened Uncle Howe came out to visit us and come to my camp at Plum creek Station on the U.P.R.R. and I went with him on a Buffalo hunt had lots of fun, through the balance of the winter we staid at home and the next summer I was at home most of the time went hunting a few times but nothing of importance happened, in the spring of 1872 I was employed by the Government to act as hunter Scout and Guide for two Companies of Soldiers that were camped on the Loup Fork about one hundred miles above here I staid there nearly two months we were out Scouting one day with a company of Cavalry and I was about four miles ahead of the company with five men when we found a camp of about seventy or Eighty Sioux Warriors they saw us about as soon as we did them and come for us a flying we were near a big Ravine with high banks and I told the boys we would get into that and we could fight them off till the command came up but one of the men (another of Buntlines heroes called Little Buckshot) told the boys they would kill us all in a minute and kicking the spurs into his horse away he went and the rest all followed him so of course I got onto my horse and run too after going about one mile Buckshots horse began to get tired and the boys all left him behind I was still behind him and the Indians were almost within Shooting distance of me so I slacked the reins on Mazeppa and went up to Buckshot when I got to him the hero of a hundred Battles (on paper) was Balling like a calf and begged of me not to run off and leave him of course I staid with him although he had done his best to leave me in the start I was expecting the Indians to fire every minute but they didnt and as soon as we came in sight of the command they stopped, now what do you suppose the old Whiskey Bloat that was in command of our party done he halted and dismounted his men and right there we staid for two hours and the Indians walked off thats about the way the Regular Army Officers fight Indians, about two weeks after that I came home and a few days after a young Gentleman from New York City and one from Kentucky came out for a Buffalo hunt and I went out with them we had a nice time and killed a good many Buffalo then I came home and staid till the next summer when the same man from New York came out and I took him out to have an Elk hunt we were only gone a week and managed to kill three Elk when we came back I went up the Road to Cheyenne and after staying with Frank for a week I went to work building Telegraph Line worked at that two months and come home and the next day I got a dispatch from Frank to come back up there right away, I started back that night and when I got there the next day I found that Prof. Marsh of Yale Colledge wanted me to go out with a party of men into the Bad Lands of Colorado to get Fossils for the Yale Colledge Museum there was five of us in the party and we had a small tent one team and three Saddle horses we started out the 28th of Oct. and got back on the 10th of Dec. had a nice trip and got lots of Fossils the night before we got back to the R.R. we laid out in ten inches of snow with no wood to build a fire and the Thermometer eighteen Degrees below zero. How would you like that kind of a life. I froze one of my feet a little but was all right otherwise, I staid at Franks a few days and then come home and bought into this Livery Buisiness in May of last spring Prof. Marsh wrote me that he wanted me to go with his Assistant on Genl. Custars Black Hills Expedition and I started for Fort Lincoln on the 3d day of June and met Mr. Grinnell (Prof. Marshs Asst.) at St. Paul Minesota and we went on together to Fort Lincoln, we left Lincoln on the 2nd of July and for twenty days we traveled over the most barren country that I ever saw, we could hardly find grass enough for our horses to live on and the watter was just awful the ground was covered with Prickley Pear and alive with Rattle Snakes, on the 22nd day of July we entered the Black Hills and I tell you it was nice. I cant begin to Describe the Hills to you sometimes we would be traveling through a Deep Canyon with that was just wide enough for the teams to pass through the walls of Rock on each side six or eight hundred feet high suddenly we would come to the End and would find our selves in a beautiful Park maybe half a mile square covered with pine trees say one foot through and about ten feet apart there would not be a sign of any underbrush and the Ground would be covered with a soft velvety grass, it was nice and we all felt sorry when we had to leave the Hills, which we did on the 16th of Aug. we had some miners along and they found some Gold but the Reports that you saw in the papers were very much exagarated we got back to Lincoln on the last day of Aug. and the next day I started for home and got here on the 3d of sept. having been gone just three months.

I have been doing all the work in the stable for the last two weeks and have had to stop writing every ten minutes and I know this is very imperfect there are a thousand and one things that I wanted to tell you about that I havent mentioned but you will have to wait till I come to see you next fall and then I will tell you all about it I think I could tell you somethings that would make you laugh and you dont know how bad I want to hear you laugh, please write soon again to your loving nephew.

Lute.

III

*Columbus*
*Feb. 1st, 1875*

**DEAR UNCLE:**

I send you today the balance of my little story I find in looking it over that I forgot to tell you what became of my pet horse I must tell you a little more about him I trained him for a hunting horse and he knew so much that if I was riding him ever so fast the moment that a deer would jump up and I would pick up my Gun from the saddle he would stop and stand like a Rock till I would shoot if I killed anything I would get off and turn him loose and he would eat around till I would get the meat ready to pack him when I would hold up a peice and he would trot up to be packed, his powers of endurance were wonderful I rode him one day twenty miles in one hour and twenty minutes at another time I rode him over a fearful rough country through a blinding snow storm fifty five miles in six hours and while Scouting up the Loup in one day and part of the night I rode him one hundred and forty miles he never got tired apparently and I never touched him with whip or spur in his life, two years ago this winter he was taken sick with the Eppizootic that was raging at that time and it finaly run into the Glanders so I took him out and shot him you dont know how I felt about it, it was like having a death in the family we all thought so much of him, when I was on his back I never felt afraid his long springy gallop I knew could carry me away from any Indians horse in the world Poor Mazeppa I shall never see his like again.

Lute

LETTERS OF LUTHER NORTH TO DR. RICHARD TANNER

*The Nebraska State Historical Society Collection also includes letters from North to George Bird Grinnell, Addison E. Sheldon, Robert Bruce, Clarence Reckmeyer, William Fowler, and Dr. Richard (Diamond Dick) Tanner. The group which follows consists of letters to Tanner: North wrote more freely to this colorful old friend—a medical doctor and showman—than to many of his other correspondents.*

*Several of these letters concern publications of which North did not think too highly. In Letters IV and XV he is apparently alluding to* Last of the Great Scouts: The Life Story of Colonel William F. Cody *as told to his sister Helen Cody Wetmore (Chicago and Duluth: The Duluth Press Publishing Co., 1899). Pawnee Bill, whose circular is referred to in Letter IV, was Major Gordon W. Lillie (1860-1942), a showman and trick shot, for a time in partnership with Cody—their "Two Bills Show" played at Madison Square Garden in 1908. In Letters XI, XII, and XIV the references probably are to a brochure,* Blake's Western Stories, *published by Herbert Cody Blake in 1929. It included a derogatory account of William F. Cody's frontier activities, "The Truth about Buffalo Bill." A number of the men North mentions—Frank Grouard, Baptiste "Big Bat" Pourier, "Little Bat" Garnier, and Charley White (Buffalo Chips)—are quoted or discussed in the Blake brochure. In Letter VIII the book called to North's attention by Robert Bruce was Captain George F. Price's* Across the Continent with the Fifth Cavalry *(New York: 1883). In Letter XII the article by Charles*

# MAN OF THE PLAINS

R. Nordin, "Dr. W. F. Carver: 'Evil Spirit of the Plains,'"
appeared in Nebraska History, X (October-December 1928),
344-351.

## IV

*Columbus Nebr*
*Oct 6th 1927*

MY DEAR DR

. . . I will enclose you a circular of Pawnee Bills a friend of
mine sent it to me with a very indignant letter saying where
does he get that last of the Scouts Stuff. I wrote him that Bill or
the author was advertising the Book and as far as I was concerned I didnt care whether he was the last Scout or not. it
dont pay to get into an argument with those fellows. I wrote
one Very inocent letter telling of a Shooting Match (at Target)
between My Brother Frank Wild Bill Hickok and John Talbot
in which Frank won Talbot was second and Bill a rather poor
third. I got jumped on plenty for that. it was absolutely true
and I dont mind telling you that both Frank and Talbot beat
him many times and in the three years that he (Bill) lived at
Cheyenne Frank said he never Saw him try to shoot with his left
hand and the day I saw him shoot he was very deliberate and
took careful aim closing his left eye. if he could shoot from
the hip he never did it there. he always got his man and he was
a mighty good fellow and in all the three years that Frank knew
him he never had a Gun fight though he did beat up a Mule
Skinner in a fist fight—I am afraid this isnt Very interesting to
you. hope you are all right again and that you will get down to
see me before long . . .

Sincerely your Friend

L H North

## V

*Columbus Nebr*
*Dec 4th 1927*

MY DEAR DR

I just ran across a clipping that you sent me sometime ago by
W.H. Pryor and I dont believe I ever answered your questions. I
dont know who this man is and maybe he can cut a can into
starting at fifty feet but Id rather see it than hear him tell it. as

to using two Guns I never saw any one do it but that is no reason that it cant be done. the story of the two bad men killing each other and one being hit four times and the other five I can beat. in the Spring of 1877 at Sidney a Gambler and a Bull-whacker had a Gun fight in Jack Williams Saloon. one fired five and the other six Shots across a Billiard table. the Whacker didnt have a Scratch and the Gambler was just ticked on the lower end of his ear. the crowd [of] about fifty men made a dash for the Door with me with them but there was so many beat me to it that I couldnt get out so I turned around and watched the fight. they didnt shoot Very fast but neither of them was still a second they were jumping and dodging all the time. now both of these men were said to be lightning fast on the draw and were supposed to be dead Shots. can you account for it they were both cold sober too. an outsider got shot through the leg just above the ankle. Ill bet a n[i]ckle you can make Mr. Prior look like a two spot at trick Shooting. how do you stand the cold weather I dont like it but get out a little every day. where is Two Gun Nan she was here last summer but I wasnt at home

Sincerely

L H North

VI

*Columbus Nebr*
*Jan 17 - 1928*

MY DEAR DR

. . . why dont you come down to see me some time. I cant write but we could talk all night. I just had a letter from Clarence Reckmeyer he is in Wyoming and had just gone over the Battle field on Tongue River where General Connor fought the arapahoes in 1865. Frank with 100 Pawnee was with him. it was Frank with five of the scouts that discovered the village. he couldnt tell how big it was so waited until night and sent one of his men on foot to find out this Pawnee went down the creek so near the camp that a Squaw coming after water was so close to him that he said when she stooped down to dip the water he could have put his hand on her head. Frank sent two of his scouts back to Connors Camp 40 miles with a note to him and he (Frank) hid in a Canyon two or three miles and watched the Indians. when the scouts reached the spot where they had left Connor he had moved camp and they had to follow him twenty

[ 311 ]

five or thirty miles before overtaking him. Frank had expected he would come in about 24 hours from the time he sent the message to him and it was almost 48 hours before he got there. the Indians however didnt discover them and were taken by surprise. about fifty were killed and several Squaws and children taken prisoners. 250 Lodges and all their camp Equipage & provisions and Eleven hundred horses were captured. the Lodges and all of the camp stuff including hundreds of Tons of Dried Meat was piled up and burned

whenever I get started on something that Frank and the scouts were in I dont know where to stop . . .

Sincerely L H North

Lesharoo-Kit-ti but,

Little Chief

VII

*Columbus Nebr*
*Feb 16th 1928*

MY DEAR DR

. . . did I tell you what old White Eagle Said to me when I was down to Pawnee five years ago. he was telling me something that happened in 1830 and I said my child you are growing old you are losing your mind. soon after that he was asking me about the people up here that he used to know. they were all dead and finally I told him they were all dead but me he pondered this for awhile and then Said and where is the Star. I tried to remember who they called the Star but gave it up and said dont remember the Star. he laughed and said oh my father you are growing old you are losing your mind you dont remember your Brothers child. he knew Franks Daughter Stella as the Star and I had forgotten it. wasnt that pretty good for a man over a hundred years old. he died about three years ago and he must have been at least 105 years old. he said he was big enough to ride a horse and follow the Warriors the day they took the Medicine arrows from the Cheyennes and that was in 1830.

L H North

[ 312 ]

## VIII

MY DEAR DR

it certainly does mak a fellow feel good to get the kind of letters from a friend that you write me and I thank you for the faith you have in my truthfulness. and now I want to tell you a little story. in 1884 the Wild West Show had Pawnee Indians and Frank had charge of them while showing at Hartford Conn. in the charge on the Stage Coach Franks Saddle turned and a lot of horses ran over him he was teribly hurt. Seven of his Ribs were broken five of them in two places his neck was badly hurt and he was bruised and trampled from head to foot. he couldnt lye down and they had him braced up in a chair in his room at the Hotel. the Pawnees were told that he was dying and when the show was ready to leave there they refused to go until they had seen him. the Dr finally said that one or two might come to the Door and talk to him. when they come one of them asked him if he was badly hurt he said yes but that he would get well. he told them to go on with the show and he would be with them in 30 days. they went back and told the others what he had said and then said our father (Frank) never told us a lye he will get well. the next day I got to Hartford and stayed with him until he was able to be moved. on the 29th day he told the Dr he must go. he (Dr. Pelletie) tried to Dissuade him and so did I but he said I told my boys Id be with them tomorrow and Im going. the next day the Show was to be in Albany, N.Y. we got there in the night and the next morning I got a carriage and we drove out to the Grounds. Frank was still on crutches. Bill hadnt expected him but the Indians told him that Frank would be there. I wish you could have been there to see that meeting. of course Frank was not well enough to take part in the show and the next day I brought him home. this shows you how they trusted him and why.

I am going to enclose a letter in this that I got from [Robert] Bruce day before yesterday. he had asked me if Volkmar at one time had saved Franks life and if I had read across the continent with the 5th Cavalry. I told him I hadnt read the Book. That I knew both Volkmar and Price that I was not with the expedition in Sept 1869 and that I had never heard Frank say anything about Volkmar saving his life. then he sent me this

[ 313 ]

letter and I hunted up an old Diary of Franks here is what he says

Sunday Sept 26 1869 today we marched 24 miles and I and Cody came ahead to the Creek and 6 Indians got after us and gave us a lively chase I got my men out and they killed an Indian and got two Ponies a Mule and a lot of trash. this doesnt look as though he was in much danger does it. I sent this to Bruce. I was on detached service so know nothing of what happened except what I got from Frank. as I remember it he said the 6 Indians took after them they ran to draw them on and soon came in sight of the Pawnees. Frank Signaled them to come and then got off his horse to wait for them. the Indians saw the scouts and turned back. Frank and his men Chased them and overtook and killed one and that was all there was to it. the Indians were so far away while chasing them that they never fired a shot at them. what do people want to write that kind of stuff for

Bill in one of his books tells of this incident and speaks of the Bullets raining around them he says there were 50 Indians and I believe he says something about Volkmar but I dont know what it was.

again thanking you I am

ever your Friend

Lute

## IX

*Columbus Nebr*
*Dec 7th 1928*

MY DEAR DR

. . . we still have an Oldtimer here J.H. Galley who went through here for Salt Lake in 1853 came back and Settled here in 1859 the same year we came here. he and I enlisted in the Second Nebraska Cavalry together in 1862. he is 5 years older than I and is blind. he lives in this block and I get over to See him as often as I can. he can walk well yet and we both belong to the G.A.R. there are 6 members and we meet every two weeks. I Pilot Jim to the meetings. I told him the other day it was the Blind leading the Blind. well I guess Ill have to close for this time

Sincerely

L H North

[ 314 ]

# X

*Columbus Nebr*
*Febr 17 - 1929*

MY DEAR DR

I Sat down yesterday to write you then concluded to wait for the afternoon mail and your letter came in it. I was afraid you was not well but hope you are all right now. I am glad that Deadwood Dick is in town we old ducks need some one to look after us. fifty or Sixty years [ago] it was different. I lived in a Sod house in the Sandhills for six weeks one winter and didnt see a human being white or Red in that time and two or three days after Frank and the boys got back my horse sliped and fell with me spraining my ankle and fracturing the bone so I didnt walk for two months. I must tell you about that. I was about ten miles from the Ranche and it was after sundown with the Thermometer showing 25 below zero. when the horse got up I got up to but my ankle gave way and I fell against him. he jumped jerking the Reins out of my hand and started off. I said who[a] and he stoped. now Dr. Believe it or not a few days before that this horse had left me a couple of miles from the Ranche and I had to walk in but when I said who[a] he stoped and looked back. I got up and using my Gun for a crutch started towards him. he was a nervous horse and when I got near him he would flinch every time Id hop but he stood still until I managed to climb on. Say Dr I couldnt put that foot in the stirrup and when it hung down I thought it would drop off. well I got to the Ranc[h]e with frosted face and fingers but what if he had left me. I think that was about as narrow an escape as I ever had. I know I was scared D---n near to death. well I guess this will be enough of an Infliction for this time

Your Friend

Lute

# XI

*Columbus Nebr*
*Febr 23d - 29*

MY DEAR DR

I also got one of the Blake Books and what I am writing to you is not for publication. Blake hated Cody I dont know why but he couldnt be fair to him and in quoting me he has left out many things I said and made what I did say sound worse than it should. of course Cody lied about the killing of Tall Bull and when I told the straight of it in camp where there was more than fifty men Bill acknowledged that he wasnt in the fight but said that Ned Buntline wrote it into one of his stories and of course he couldnt deny it. Frank was there and when someone asked him why he hadnt told that he killed Tall Bull he said I am not in the show business and anyway I didnt know it was Tall Bull until three days afterward and what difference does it make who killed him. Blake leaves the impression that Cody was a coward but I never saw him show any cowardice. it is quite true that I never saw him kill an Indian. in the two years 1869-1870 that we were on expeditions together I never saw him in a fight with Indians but that was not his fault as he was always with some party that didnt find the Indians. you see he was scout for the 5th cavalry and had nothing to do with the Pawnee Scouts though his Biographers (and Bill himself) give the Impression that as Chief of Scouts he had charge of the Pawnees. Blake discredits his shooting so does Carver. now when he & Carver were partners Cody did *all* the shooting on horseback and Carver and Bogardus gave exihibitions with Shotguns while standing on the ground. the reason Cody used shot in his shells was because of the danger of using Bullets. he could break glass Balls from the back of a running horse with Bullets and Ive seen him do it and told Blake so and more than that he could beat any man I ever saw Shooting a Rifle from the Back of a Running horse. he was a great Lyer a great Show man and hell of a good Fellow. there was no Vote as to his Killing Injuns. Carver said he never killed one and nobody disputed him. I said nothing because *I never saw him kill one.* this letter is for you Dear Dr. not for the public

Yours

Lute

## XII

*Columbus Nebr*
*March 3 - 1929*

MY DEAR DR

I got your letter yesterday but should have written you today anyway. Grinnell sent me one of the Books I shall not comment on it but if I ever get to see you again we can talk it over. the more I think about Blakes Book the more I dont like it—he wrote me once asking if my wife rode on horseback and I said she did and that she rode pitching horses and that she was a good Rifle Shot and had beaten Cody shooting at Target. this was a personel letter and I never thought of his publishing it. he added to it [that] it was Ducksoup for her to kill Buffalo. She never killed a Buffalo in her life and I never wrote him that she did. in quoting my letters he cuts out parts of them and uses just what suits him but what the hell can I do. I dont intend to do anything but it has made me might[y] leary about what I write to most people but with you it is different and I write you anything I happen to think about and here is something that may amuse you it is a rather long story but as you already know something about it Ill give you the rest

among the invited guests at the Banquet given by the State historical Society and the Sons and Daughters of Nebr. was a Mr. Howe. he was on the Programme for an address. a good many years ago he wrote articles for some of the Sporting Magazines Ive forgotten which one. in one of the articles he tells of his killing of the Sioux Chief Whistler and his two companions Fat Badger and Handsmeller. later Doc Carver wrote the story of how he killed these Indians but Doc was warned that the story had already been written So he didnt have his published and I guess it wasnt published until after Doc['s] death when Norden got it in the Historical Magazine last Summer. now here is the funny part these Indians were killed in the fall of 1872 *before this man Howe was born.* here is the true story of the killing. there was quite a few Sioux Indians camped on the Medicine and other streams at that time and with them were several Squaw men old John Nelson the two Cliffords Hank & Monty and perhaps Al Gay. Newton Moreland and a man named Logan were camped on the Medicine somewhere near the head. I guess the three Indians Whistler Fat Badger and Handsmeller were going to Fort Mc Pherson and they stoped at Morelands camp for supper—and Moreland and Logan killed them. Morelands story was that while the Indians were eating he heard Whistler tell the other two that when they got through eating they kill the white men (Newt couldnt talk Sioux). Newt told Logan what they said and pulled his Revolver Logan did likewise. they were behind the Indians. Newt Shot Whistler in the back and Logan shot one of the other two. the third one Ran for his Gun which was leaning against a tree but Newt killed him before he got to it.

the next day a party of settlers from the Medicine on there way to McPherson found these Indians and buried them. in the party was one of the Squaw men I dont know which one. he told the others that when he got back to camp he would have his Squaw tell the rest of the Indians that the Pawnees killed them for if they knew it was white men they would raise hell with the Settlers. this was done and the settlers on the Medicine Many of them thot the killing of the Pawnees next year 1873 at Massacre Canyon was to revenge the death of Whistler and his friends. I saw Newt Moreland at Kearny in 1873 I think it was it was said there that he had a Spotted horse that he got from Whistler. Newt lived here and at the Pawnee Reserve when he was a boy and I [knew] him well.

a little more about the man Howe. I am told he is a fine fellow and that when he wrote his story about killing these Indians he did it as a joke at any rate he was one of the Speakers at the Banquet in Lincoln. My wife & I were Invited as Guests but as you [know] we were both sick I would have liked to have Met Mr Howe.

Sincerely

Lute

## XIII

*Columbus Neb*
*Jan 14 - 1930*

MY DEAR DR

I dont wonder you havent time to write. I hardly see how you get through with your work. as to Shrinking from cold I am with you I cant go out of the house without freezing and we used to camp out without even a tent when it was 35 and 40 below zero. I rode from Crazy Woman Creek one night with five of my Scouts to the clear fork of Tongue River 30 miles with the Thermometer showing 25 below. there was no snow on the Crazy woman Creek but before I got to Clear Creek it was Belly deep to the horses. Genl. Crook had sent me to find out if the Cheyennes had come out of the Big Horn Mountains there. I was all night getting there and found nothing as the snow covered the Trail (if there was one) and it took me all day to get back 24 hours on foot and horseback. then Frank went up to Crooks tent to report to him. he said Genl. my Brother just got back, and before he could say more Crook said where has he been. Im Dammed if he hadnt forgotton about Sending me. what do you know about that

[ 318 ]

as the feller was supposed to say such was life in the far west.
I guess Id better quit

Your Friend

Lute

I wish youd tell me what Idaho Bill does for a living and who
he is

Lute

XIV

*Columbus Nebr*
*March 7th 1931*

MY DEAR DR

Your letter just Recd. and I am mighty glad to hear you are
better and hope you will continue to improve. I had a Birthday
yesterday though I dont think that is anything to Brag about.
I had 84 of them before this one and I dont See that any of them
done me much good. about Frank Grouard I dont know much
about him. I suppose you know that he said he was a Sandwitch
Islander. now I dont know what they should look like but Frank
looked Very Much like a Negro. he was Genl. Crooks favorite
Scout and it was Said Crook would take his judgement in
preference to any of his officers. Frank knew the Mountain
Country and as he lived with the Indians for several years he
should have been (and I guess was) a good Guide as I say I
knew but little of him. I never cared much for the colored
Brethren and didnt have but little conversation with him but it
seems as though he must have been good or he wouldnt have
held the position he had as chief Scout. by the way Dr. I think
Chief of Scouts is a mistake Frank Grouard was Crooks Chief
Scout but he had no authority over the other scouts. Bill Hamil-
ton Big Bat Little Bat Charley white (Buffalo Chips) and others
they all took orders from Genl. Crook or any other campaign
Commander. Cody (Buffalo Bill) was Chief Scout for the 5th
Cavalry but California Joe John Nelson the Cliffords Hank and
Monty never took orders from him. My Brother Frank was
Chief Scout at Fort Russell but the other Scouts there were not
under his Orders. even I your friend was Chief Scout for Major
Sweetzer but Wentworth (Little Buckshot) although he was
with the Same expedition didnt take orders from Me. So much
for the Chief Scouts. when we had the Pawnee Scouts out and
Frank was Major and I was capt if any Officer of the Pawnee

[ 319 ]

Scouts was Sent with a squad of Pawnees on a Scouting Party if Cody wanted to go along he would have to get permission from the commanding Officer and would be under the order of the Officer in command (Myself, perhaps) as long as he was with us. I have never told this to anyone for the Very Simple reason that it would give the Thorpes and others like them a chance to get some advertising by denying it. one time when Bill was with me My Men discovered a Trail. we was about 20 miles from where we knew the command would camp that night. I wrote a note to Genl. Carr telling him of the Trail and gave it to one of my men to take to him. Cody said he would take it for me but I declined. I knew what a spectacular arrival he would make at camp and maybe bring the whole command over there so I told the Genl. it was just a small party and I would follow and find out what they were and would let him know if he would stay in that camp for one day. it was a small party they had about 20 stolen horses. we charged their camp captured the horses killed three of the Cheyennes but the rest 6 or 7 got away. we turned back and got back to the command the next day without galloping a whole Regiment 25 or 30 miles. but did the Pawnee Scouts get all the credit. Not so you could Notice it. in the Report Col. Royall with a troop of Cavalry and some Pawnee Scouts found a war party and affter a runing fight killed three or four and captured the horses etc. etc. oh h-ll

Yours allways

Lute

## XV

*Columbus Nebr*
*Oct 29th 1931*

MY DEAR DR & WIFE

thank you so much for the picture and we are both delighted to know that you are coming down to see us before long tell Mrs Tanner I am sure she will land you here safe and sound. did you ever know Dave Perry of North Platte he had a saloon there he and Cody became great cronies. after this fight. the horse known as Buckskin Joe that Cody Speaks of in his Book was a Govt. horse and belonged to the Pawnee Scout Battallion and was Ridden by Capt Cushing in 1869 (this *isnt* the story that Cody tells). when we were mustered out that fall the horses were turned in to the q.m. at Fort Mc Pherson and Cody got Joe.

he used him as his hunting horse for a couple of years and in
1872 when the Grand Duke Alexus came over and Genl. Sheriden
and Custer took him on a Buffalo Hunt he Rode Buckskin Joe.
soon after that Cody went on the Stage. the horse was kept at
Fort Mc Pherson and sometime later he was condemmed and
Sold. Dave Perrey bought him and gave him to Cody he (Cody)
kept him at his Ranche or rather his home in North Platte. in
1877 when we went in the cattle Business with Cody Buckskin
Joe was Totally Blind. the next year Cody was coming out to
our Ranche on the Dismal River and he hitched Joe with another
horse to a spring wagon to drive out. they camped on the Birdwood the first night and in the morning Joe was gone. he was not
seen again for three months when we ran onto him on the head
of the Birdwood. I took him to the Ranche where we kept him
until we sold out in 1882 when I took him to Codys Ranche at
North Platte where I guess he died. this isnt Very interesting to
you I guess. thank you ever so much for the picture, and I want
to see that coat and Gun. my wife is asleep but we both send
love to both of you and dont be to long in coming

your friend

Lute

# APPENDIX B

The Pawnee were the most numerous and powerful of the tribes belonging to the Caddoan language group and one of the most important of the Great Plains region. Since the earliest definite historic mention of the Pawnee (1673), they had lived in Nebraska and the extreme northern portion of Kansas, particularly on the Loup, Platte, and Republican rivers.

Among themselves the Pawnee people are called *Chahiksichahiks:* men of men. They originally migrated from the south, and according to tradition established themselves in the Plains region by right of conquest. The territory claimed by the Pawnee was bounded on the north by the Niobrara River, on the south by the Arkansas or possibly the Canadian, and on the east by the Missouri; on the west it extended rather indefinitely toward the Rockies. However, the actual area over which the Pawnee hunted and exercised chief control was far more limited. It comprised a strip beginning with the Niobrara (between its mouth and Plum Creek) and extending southward to include the Platte between Shell Creek and the present city of North Platte, thence into Kansas to include the Smoky Hill drainage between the Republican River and the ninety-ninth meridian, with the western periphery swinging westward by south toward the upper reaches of Arkansas, and the eastern limit running toward the southwestern corner of present Kansas. The permanent villages of the tribe were located in the valleys of the lower Loup and Platte rivers, and on the Republican and the Blue; the region to the south served solely as hunting and wintering grounds.

Their villages were far enough removed from the region contested by the Spaniards and the French in the seventeenth and

[ 323 ]

eighteenth centuries so that for a time the Pawnee escaped the influences which proved disastrous to other tribes. After the Louisiana Purchase of 1803 they came in increasing contact with the whites, and were in close touch with the principal trading center, St. Louis. At this time the adjacent tribes were the Cheyenne and Arapaho on the west, the Teton Sioux to the north, and on the east the Omahas and Ponca north of the Platte and the Otoe south of it.

A confederation of four bands made up the Grand Pawnee Nation. These were the *Chaui* or Grand, the *Kitkehaki* or Republican, the *Pitahauerat* or Tappage (sometimes called Noisy), and the *Skidi* or Wolf Pawnee. Ordinarily each functioned as an independent unit, retaining charge of its own administrative and other affairs through a hereditary, but often purely nominal, chief, who was assisted in matters of importance by secondary chiefs and a council of leading men. The Grands were generally recognized as the leading band, and where situations arose involving relationships between the several bands, or affecting the tribe as a whole, the principal chief of the Grands acted as spokesman and adviser for the entire tribe.

Each of the four bands consisted of several sub-bands or villages. Each village had its own name; its medicine bundle of sacred objects and priests who had charge of the rituals and ceremonies associated with these objects; and its own council composed of hereditary chiefs and leading men. The tribe was held together by long-established ceremonies in which each village had a place, and by the tribal council composed of village chiefs. Similarly, the confederation was united by the grand council whose members came from the councils of the respective tribes.

Pawnee religious beliefs were associated with the cosmic forces and heavenly bodies. The dominating power was Tirawa, generally spoken of as "father." Tirawa's messengers were the heavenly bodies, the winds, thunder, lightning, and rain. Among the Skidi, the morning and evening stars represented masculine and feminine principles for the perpetuation of living forms upon the earth. Ceremonies related to reproduction and increase of life began with the first thunder in the spring, reached their climax in human sacrifice at the summer solstice, and closed after the maize was harvested. At each stage of the series of rituals, certain shrines or medicine bundles became the center of the ceremony. The bundles were in the care of hereditary keepers, but the rituals and ceremonies were conducted by a priesthood open to all proper aspirants. In each tribe there were secret societies, which had grown out of a belief in supernatural animals.

[ 324 ]

Their functions were to call game, heal disease, and to confer occult powers; their rites were elaborate and the ceremonies dramatic. Religious rites accompanied corn planting (maize was known as "mother"), hoeing, and harvesting, and religious ceremonies also attended the building of the Pawnee earth lodges.

On the tribal buffalo hunts, officers were appointed to maintain order and to see that each family got its share of the game. War parties were always initiated by an individual and were made up of volunteers. When a village was attacked, the warriors fought under their chief or some other recognized leader. Warriors shaved their heads except for a narrow strip of hair from the forehead to the scalp-lock, which stood up somewhat like a horn. Breechcloths and moccasins were the essential parts of their clothing; in cold weather and on special occasions they wore robes and leggings. Face painting was general, and heraldic designs frequently were painted on tent-covers and on the robes and shields of the men.*

Women wore their hair in two braids at the back, and painted their faces as well as their hair partings red. Moccasins, leggings, and robes were the ancient dress for women; skirts and tunics came later. After marriage a man went to live with his wife's family, and descent was traced through the mother. Polygamy was not uncommon.

The Pawnee never joined other Indians in war against the United States. However, increasing contact with the white race brought new diseases, reduction in population, and loss of tribal power. In the early nineteenth century, the Pawnee may have numbered 10,000. An 1850 missionary report (the first actual

---

* "Referring to the time and care taken by Indian warriors in preparation for a fight when time and opportunity allow, it should be remembered that with the aborigines of the Plains a battle is somewhat in the nature of a grand ceremonial. It is the ultimate goal and supreme test . . . wherein [the Indian's] standing among his people and reputation as a warrior are finally determined. Thus, the more spectacular the better, as evidenced by the war bonnet. . . . On their old Nebraska reservation in 1861-62, I saw some of the great Pawnee warriors paint their horses, particularly if they were white or had white spots on them, which would make them better marks for the guns or bows and arrows of their enemies. They would also braid the tails of their horses, and fasten colored feathers in the tails and manes. I have known them to take at least two hours to paint their faces, tie colored feathers in their scalp locks and prepare themselves and their horses for a fight. That was in the tribal battles between the Sioux and Pawnees . . ." (Luther North, quoted in Bruce, *The Fighting Norths*, 71).

[ 325 ]

count) gave the total as 6,244. More than 1,200 died when the tribe was stricken by cholera in 1849, and in 1862 their number was reported by the agent as 3,414. By 1879, after their first five years in Indian Territory, the number had dwindled to 1,440; by 1905 it was reduced to 646. Since that time there has been a slow but steady population increase.

PAWNEE TREATIES AND LAND CESSIONS

1818 A treaty of peace and friendship with the United States signed at St. Louis by a chief from each of the four bands.

1825 Treaty of Fort Atkinson (near present-day Fort Calhoun, Nebraska). The Pawnee agree not to molest U.S. citizens on their way to and from Santa Fe; the U.S. agrees to give the Pawnees "such benefits and acts of kindness as may be convenient or seem just and proper to the President."

1833 Treaty signed on October 9 at the Grand Pawnee village ceding to the U.S. all Pawnee territory south of the Platte in return for $1,600 in goods and the promise of $4,600 in goods each year for twelve years.

1848 Sale to the U.S. of an eighty-mile strip on the Platte, which included the Grand Island.

1857 Treaty of Table Creek (near present-day Nebraska City). The last of the Pawnee lands ceded to the U.S. The Pawnee agree to accept as their reservation a tract on the Loup fork thirty miles from east to west and fifteen miles from south to north, including lands on both banks of the river. The tribe was to receive $40,000 a year for five years, and thereafter $30,000 a year in perpetuity. The government agreed to build an agency, and to protect the tribe from the Sioux.

1875 Cession of the Pawnee Reserve and removal of the tribe to Indian Territory (Oklahoma).

Sources: Waldo Rudolph Wedel, *An Introduction to Pawnee Archeology*, Bureau of American Ethnology Bulletin 112 (Washington: U.S. Government Printing Office, 1936); George Hyde, *Pawnee Indians* (Denver: University of Denver Press, 1951); "Pawnee," *Handbook of American Indians*, Vol. II, Bureau of American Ethnology (Washington: U.S. Government Printing Office, 1910).

[ 326 ]

# APPENDIX C

Thomas Jefferson North was born near Ludlowville, New York—a few miles from Ithaca on the eastern shore of Cayuga Lake—on April 5, 1813. He was the son of Joshua North, a farmer. Thomas married Jane Elvira Townley, a resident of the same area, in January, 1837. The Townleys, like the Norths, were of British descent; they had come from England about 1745. Jane was born on February 7, 1820, in Tompkins County, New York. Left an orphan at seven, she grew up on the farm of an uncle, Nelson Townley, near Ludlowville.

Directly after their marriage the Norths moved to Richland County, Ohio. They lived mostly in the village of Rome, eight miles east of Plymouth and midway between Mansfield and Huron. Thomas and Jane had five children: James E. North (1838-1913), Frank Joshua North (1840-1885), Luther Hedden North (1846-1935), Sarah Elizabeth North (1848-19??), and Alphonsene North (1850-19??). All the children were born in Ohio except Frank; he was born in New York State where Mrs. North spent part of 1839 and 1840.

In 1855 James, aged 17, went west to Des Moines, Iowa, and was joined by his father early in the winter 1855-1856. The rest of the family soon came after them. The following transcription of a letter written by Mrs. Jane Townley North to an unidentified kinsman summarizes their experiences.

*Columbus Neb March 1885*

My Dear Cousin

I am now going to try to tell you something of my life in Nebraska, we'll commence with our leaveing Ohio, my Hus-

[ 327 ]

band and eldest Son came to Omaha in May of /56, went out
on a Survey for three months, where they encountered many
hardships, came near being scalped by the Indians, and had one
or two very narrow escapes from drowning, I followed them
(with our other four children, aged respectively 16, 10, 8 & 5
the two youngest being girls,) in July, we came by water &
Rail to Iowa City (then the capitol of Iowa) from there by
Stage, I could only procure three seats for five of us, so you see
I carried one in my arms about three hundred miles while the
rest had to do the best they could, when the weather was fine
some of the gentleman would ride outside, then we were more
comfortable, when we arrived at Des Moines one of the girls
were sick, & I was obliged to lay over twenty four hours, the
night after leaveing there we were lost on the Prairie in a fearful Thunderstorm, finally when daylight came, we found the
road and continued our journey to Council Bluffs without
further mishap, met my Husband & Son & remained there
untill the first of Oct, when we moved across the Missouri
River to Omaha my Husband & two Sons got to work, as soon
as we were settled, I took boarders for we were very poor
(my husband haveing lost all in Ohio) Omaha had at that time
a population of 300 or 400, now it is a city of 50,000, the winter of 56 & 7, was the most severe we have ever experienced,
however we pulled through tolerable comfortable, until March
when the dreadful blow fell upon us, my Husband left home
the morning of the 12th in company with three other gentleman to hunt land, they drove out ten miles, put up the team
& started on foot over the snow to find the corners of sections,
it being where Mr North had Surveyed he was well acquainted
with the country, they walked all day, became very much exhausted & when night came on they were several miles from
any house, the men seperated, it was very dark, & the sup-
position was that Mr North got bewildred and was obliged to
lie down, he was not found till the next day, when he who left
me so full of life & hope was brought back to me a corpse,
the days following that sad event are allmost a blank to me, as
I told you, we were very poor, & I feel now that it was a
blessing that we were, if I had not been obliged to work, to
help my dear Boys, take care of the three that could do nothing for themselves, I think I should have lost my reason, we
staid in Omaha a year after their Fathers death, then I went
to Ohio & New York with the three youngest, & the two
oldest James & Frank came out here and took up land that was
the Spring of /58, that Summer I saw your dear Father &
Mother in Ludlowville, it was the last time I ever saw them,

the Spring of /59 I came back, and settled here near Columbus, We kept what was then called a Ranche, it was a stopping place for travellers and freighters, as there was no RR here then, and everything had to be freighted with mules or Oxen That fall the Pawnee Indians moved onto their Reservation twenty miles above or west of us, the first two or three years we were very much troubled with them, they were continually around begging & thieveing, & where they could find a woman alone would frighten her into cooking every thing she had in the house for them, they are great Coffee drinkers, The Summer of /62 I moved on the Reservation, went as housekeeper on the government farm Frank had learned to talk the Pawnee Language and he hired as clerk in the trading Post, Lute worked on the farm, & my Daughters were with me, James was married and lived on the Ranche & we staid there one year, before we left there Lute, only 17 years old enlisted in the 2' Nebraska Cavalry, for home protection, for in the mean time the Indians had broke out and went to war with the whites, all but the Pawnees, they were allways frendly, but Lute was not left in Nebraska, one Batallion were ordered up into Minnesota where the Indians were murdering the whites, he was away nine months & suffered allmost every, thing for four weeks only had two hard crackers pr day, and many a day divided those with his Horse, as there was no feed for them, & those were dreary days & sleepless nights for me, the year we were on the farm at the Reservation, I saw two or three battles between the Sioux & Pawnee, saw a Sioux warriour scalp a Pawnee Squaw that happened only a few rods from the Farm house, at another time the Pawnees killed a Sioux Chief, cut him to pieces, and rode by our house carrying a leg or an arm, we had a company of Soldiers near us, they with the Pawnees were good protection, but it was a hard way to live, the fall of /63 Frank recd a Capt Commision from the gov ordering him to enlist 100 Pawnees for service, that fall we had a great many Indian scares, hardly knew when we went to sleep at night if we should be murdered before morning or not, Frank left Columbus with the 100 Pawnee Soldiers in Feb of /65 marched west in Company with white Soldiers under Gen Conner, they were all through the Big Horn Mts the Yellow Stone Country, had several fights with Indians, at one time when Frank was out with his company on a scout, he came on a party of thirty Cheyennes, had a severe fight killed all the Cheyennes but did not lose one of his men, & I think there were none wounded, the Pawnees say that the great Spirit protects Frank, they call him their Father or White

[ 329 ]

Chief, while Frank was away Lute came home, so we had him
& James to stay with us, Frank was away about a year at that
time then in /66 he received a Majors Commission and got up
a Batallion of Pawnees, Lute went with him then, as Capt
James had the Tradeing post on the Reservation, the girls &
I were in the Pawnee School on the Reservation where we
remained a year & a half, I as Matron one of the girls as
teacher the other as seamstress, James remained several years,
Frank & Lute were out with the Indians most of the time till
1870, had a great many hard fights & times. the girls Husbands
have been out with Frank, as Capts so you see my family have
had a good deal of Soldiering and I a great deal of anxiety &
care, but I am very happily situated now with my family all
settled near me and all comfortably situated . . .

From 1868 until her death in 1908 Jane Townley North lived
with various members of her family. Her daughters, Mrs. Cushing and Mrs. Morse, and their families moved to Wenatchee,
Washington, in 1901-1902.

James E. North traded with the Pawnees and later was in the
real estate business in Columbus. A substantial and respected
business man, he served as sheriff of Platte County, mayor of
Columbus, and state senator. In 1886 he ran for governor on the
Democratic ticket, but was defeated by John M. Thayer (q.v.).
In January 1859 he married Nellie Arnold and they had six
children: Edward W., Lorena Rose, Mrs. Carol Evans, Sr.,
Frank J., Mary A., and Nellie A.

The respective careers of Frank and Luther North after 1882
are summarized on pages 282-283. Frank North's daughter Stella
married Edwin Hull Chambers on January 4, 1888. Their only
child, Helen Marguerite, died at the age of six in 1894. Stella
North Chambers died in 1960, and there are now no direct living
descendants of "the fighting Norths."

The events related by Luther North were a part of the history of the northern portion of the Great Plains. The huge, semi-arid, level, and treeless grassland lying roughly between the ninety-eighth meridian and the Rocky Mountains was the home of the buffalo and the nomadic tribes which hunted them. It was the land of fur traders, emigrants, railroad builders, hide hunters, cattlemen, and homesteaders as well as the Indians and the army. The region's unfolding history has been highlighted by uncertainties, conflicts, and accomplishments. Following is a chronology of some of the significant events of Great Plains history.

1803    The Louisiana Purchase places the northern Great Plains under the United States flag.

1804–1806 Meriwether Lewis and William Clark follow the Missouri River through the area. The expedition provides information concerning the vast new territory.

1806    The Zebulon Pike expedition makes the first official United States contact with the Pawnee. The American flag is raised over their village south of the Republican River in present-day Webster County, Nebraska.

1807    Manuel Lisa ascends the Missouri with a keelboat of trade goods.

1819–1820 Fort Atkinson, the first United States military post west of the Missouri River, is established at Council Bluffs on the Nebraska side of the river. The site is

[ 331 ]

near the present town of Fort Calhoun, Washington County, Nebraska.

1820     The Stephen H. Long expedition pushes west along the Platte from Fort Atkinson to the Rocky Mountains, visiting Pawnee villages on the Loup Fork. Long's report, like that of Pike, supports the theory that the Plains are a "Great American Desert."

1830     Fur traders Jedediah Smith, David Jackson, and William Sublette drive the first loaded wagons along the Great Plains portion of the Oregon Trail.

1832     Captain B. L. E. Bonneville's expedition crosses the Oregon Trail to the Pacific Northwest.

1840     The concept of a permanent "Indian Country," closed to white settlement, is adopted as government policy. The Great Plains comprise much of the region.

1842     Lieutenant John C. Frémont (The Pathfinder) crosses the continent and popularizes the Oregon Trail with his report.

1846–1847 The Mormons establish a new overland trail north of the Platte River in their exodus to Salt Lake.

1849     The California gold fields draw thousands of 49'ers across the Plains.

Fort Laramie is made a military post on the Oregon Trail.

1854     The Kansas-Nebraska Act marks the end of the Indian Country concept and the beginning of large-scale white agricultural settlement in the area.

Lieutenant John Grattan and his men are killed by Brûlé Sioux near Fort Laramie: the so-called "Mormon Cow Incident."

1855     General William Harney defeats the Brûlé at the Battle of Ash Hollow.

1857     Russell, Majors and Waddell overland freighting firm is formed.

1859     Ben Holladay stage lines begin operation.

1860–1861 The Pony Express provides mail service across the Plains.

1861     Telegraph lines completed across the continent.

1862     Uprising of the Santee Sioux in Minnesota.

1863     The first free homestead in the United States is filed on in Gage County, Nebraska.

Council Bluffs, Iowa is chosen as the eastern terminus of the Union Pacific Railroad by President Lincoln.

1864–1865 Sioux and Cheyenne strike at stations and traffic along the overland trails.

1865 The Powder River Campaign under General Connor in central Wyoming.

1866 Fort C. F. Smith, Fort Reno and Fort Phil Kearny established along the Bozeman Trail.
Longhorn cattle trailed north from Texas.
Lieutenant W. J. Fetterman and men wiped out by Sioux.

1867 The Wagon Box fight: the Sioux under Red Cloud attack a wood-cutting detail near Fort Phil Kearny and are beaten off.

1868 Treaty of Fort Laramie assigns the Black Hills to the Sioux and closes the Bozeman Trail.

1869 The Republican River Expedition culminating in the Battle of Summit Springs. The Union Pacific Railroad is completed.

1872 The Red Cloud Agency established on the White River.

1873 Brûlé Sioux fall upon the buffalo-hunting Pawnee in Massacre Canyon, near Trenton, Nebraska.

1874 Following Custer's Black Hills expedition word spreads that gold has been discovered in the Hills.

1875–1877 Pawnee and Ponca moved to Oklahoma.

1876 General Crook's forces turned back by the Sioux at the Rosebud and Custer's command annihilated on the Little Big Horn. MacKenzie defeats the Dull Knife Cheyenne at Crazy Woman Creek.

1877 Crazy Horse surrenders and is killed at Fort Robinson. The Sioux agencies moved out of Nebraska to the Missouri.

1890 The Battle of Wounded Knee marks the last major bloodshed of the Indian Wars.

The original manuscript of Luther North's recollections is typewritten and runs 208 pages. It bears two sets of emendations. One set, in ink, almost certainly was made by George Bird Grinnell. This may be established by a comparison of the manuscript with the passages from it quoted in *Two Great Scouts and Their Pawnee Battalion*. The emended spellings of Indian names in the manuscript correspond to those in the Grinnell book, as do editorial changes in the interest of a more polished style—ungainly sentences rephrased, word order altered, syntax corrected. A misspelled name "Furniss" for "Furnas" is uncorrected in the manuscript, and the same error appears in the same passage in the Grinnell book. The second set of emendations, in pencil, obviously was made after the manuscript was received by the Nebraska State Historical Society in 1938. The corrections appear to have been made by a person extracting material for an article: there is no attempt to preserve the original wording, phrasing is drastically altered, first person is changed to third, and there are pencilled notes to the typist about sections to be omitted.

The text of MAN OF THE PLAINS follows the unedited typescript—North's work as it stood originally, without any of the corrections and editorial changes made by Grinnell. With the following exceptions, the text is an exact transcription:

The manuscript has been re-paragraphed and divided into chapters.

[ 335 ]

Obvious typing errors have been corrected (e.g., *Spotted Trail* for *Spotted Tail; be* for *me; rurning* for *turning; scaled* for *scalped; brush-loading* for *breech-loading; Mad Bean* for *Mad Bear; hog cabin* for *log cabin; Whirland* for *Whirlwind; grizzle* for *grizzly; Dry Folk* for *Dry Fork;* and so on).

Errors in syntax have been allowed to stand, and the spelling, punctuation, and capitalization, although inconsistent and sometimes incorrect, have been followed exactly except for the addition of opening or closing quotation marks when one or the other was omitted. Also, the placement of a concluding comma or period in a quoted speech has been made consistent throughout. (In the original, the comma or period was sometimes placed inside the close quotation mark, sometimes outside it.)

Any words or letters supplied by the editor are enclosed in brackets, except for the dates in italic type on the margins of some pages. In Chapters Five and Nine these dates have been supplied from Frank North's Diary, as noted; elsewhere they have been inserted in a few places where the chronology is not clear from the text.

One footnote appears in the original manuscript. It is given in Footnote 15 of Chapter Three (page 60). All other footnotes and the chapter supplements were added by the editor.

In only one section, Chapter Two, pages 32-34, are there any signs of confusion. Here, as noted in the text, the author has transposed to the summer of 1865 events which actually occurred the preceding summer. On page 33 it was necessary to delete three words, indicated in the text by an ellipsis, to make the sense of the sentence clear. The passage originally read (deleted words in italics): ". . . and in one expedition under Colonel Cole, which passed through Columbus on the way to Powder River, Wyoming Territory, to meet the command under General P. E. Connor that was starting from Fort Laramie *in Cole's command*, there were sixteen hundred men and several pieces of artillery." Two other lapses occur in these pages: the name *Oklahoma* is given when *Columbus* clearly is intended, and a *what* occurs instead of a *when*.

The Luther North letters in Appendix A and the Jane

Townley North letter in Appendix C are transcriptions of the longhand originals at the Nebraska State Historical Society. No attempt has been made to paragraph them and they appear virtually unedited. Words or letters added by the editor are enclosed in brackets. In a few places periods have been inserted as an aid to the reader. Omissions are indicated by ellipses.

Not all the persons mentioned in the recollections could be identified, and in a number of instances no note is carried because the information available merely confirms or repeats what is stated in the text. Notes giving only geographical locations are omitted when the place or physical feature is shown on one of the maps. Notes identifying persons, places, or events do not always appear at first mention, but are given where they seem to be most pertinent or most useful to the reader. Since complete bibliographical data on sources consulted are given on the first citation of a work, no separate bibliography is carried.

# INDEX

[ 339 ]

Index

Chaui (Chaw-we), (Grand) Pawnee, 45, 49, 92, 169
Cheyenne: attack Pawnee in 1860, 9; derail U.P. train, 58; prisoners captured at Plum Creek, 59; raid Republican River Expedition, 107; night raid on Pawnee Scout camp, 111; village at Summit Springs attacked, 113ff.; prisoners sent to Spotted Tail Agency, 120; fighting qualities of, 188; scouts, 210; village attacked, 211; outbreak (1878), 256, 256n; kill cattle, 261; medicine arrows captured, 312
Cheyenne, Northern, 73
Cheyenne Pass, Wyo., battle near, 72
Cheyenne, Southern, 73
Cheyenne, Wyo., 61, 73, 151, 182
Cherry, Jim, alias Doc Middleton, 263
Chicago and Northwestern R.R., 49
Chief of Scouts, 319
Chimney Rock, 226, 236
Chivington, Colonel J. M., 41
Circular lodge, 168, 169
Clapper's hunting dog, 106
Clarks Bridge, 201
Clark, Major, 206, 208
Clear Creek, Nebr., 139
Clifford, Hank, 317, 319
Clifford, Monty, 317, 319
Cody-North ranch, 229; headquarters in Hooker County, 237; horses stolen by Brûlé, 239; house near Sandhill lake, 252; corral described, 276; sold to John Bratt, 279
Cody, William F. (Buffalo Bill), xvi, 102, 106, 108, 113, 118, 121, 131, 147, 148, 250, 268, 316, 319, 320; grocery wagon, 103; goes with Luther North to Fort McPherson, 103, 104; loses way, 104; claim to having killed Tall Bull, 128; Luther North on Cody's marksmanship, 150; ex-

hibition of shooting buffalo, 150; accident while riding, 159, 176; in cattle business with North brothers, 228, 237; Wild West Show, 239, 271
Coe, Isaac, 245n
Coffeeville, Kans. 196, 197
Cole, Col. Nelson, 33, 33n
Columbus, Nebr., 5, 22, 29, 49, 90, 96, 136
Colts revolvers, 50, 57, 79
Comanche, 74
Connor, Gen. P. E., 33
Cook, L. M., 11
Cooper, ——, 133
Corral described, 276
Co-rux-ah-kah-wah-dee, Traveling Bear, 97, 119
Co-rux-ta-puk, Fighting Bear, 139
Co-rux-te-cha-dish, Mad Bear, 111, 120, 127
Co-rux-to-chod-ish. See Co-rux-te-cha-dish
Cottonwood Springs, 10, 20
Council Bluffs, Iowa, 49, 69
Court House Rock, 99, 99n, 226ff., 236
Coyotes, 251, 274
Cozad, Nebr., 45n
Cranes, 269
Crazy Horse, 188
Crazy Woman Creek, battle of (1876), 211ff.
Crittenden, Major, 128
Crook, Gen. George, 194, 194n, 205, 209, 211, 219
Crooked Hand, 47, 158
Crow Creek, 55
Crow Creek Indian Agency, 16, 83
Curly Chief, 233
Curtis, Gen. Samuel Ryan, 29, 29n
Curtis-Mitchell expedition, 41
Cushing, Sylvanus E., 107f., 108n, 113, 115, 121, 149, 158, 159, 201, 223, 224
Custer, Boston, 185n
Custer City, So. Dak., 186

[ 341 ]

## ACKNOWLEDGMENTS

The editor gratefully acknowledges the assistance he has received in the preparation of this work. Mari Sandoz, distinguished author and authority on the American West, recognized the value of the North reminiscences and encouraged their publication. Others whose contributions of time, effort, and specialized knowledge have been most helpful are: Mr. Robert W. Richmond, Archivist of the Kansas State Historical Society; Dr. Gene Weltfish, New York City; Mr. Frank Gibson, Omaha Public Library; and Mr. Marvin Kivett, Mr. Roger Grange, Miss Myrtle Berry, Mrs. Phyllis Winkelman, and Miss Martha Ewarts of the Nebraska State Historical Society. Finally, the editor wishes to thank the University of Nebraska Press for suggesting the plan of this book, developed from the Press's experience with previous volumes of the Pioneer Heritage Series.